# WHOLE FOODS DIET COOKBOOK

# FOODS
# ET
# BOOK

## 200 RECIPES FOR OPTIMAL HEALTH
### IVY LARSON & ANDREW LARSON, MD

GIBBS SMITH
TO ENRICH AND INSPIRE HUMANKIND
Salt Lake City | Charleston | Santa Fe | Santa Barbara

To Ivy's mom, Gail Ingram, who has always given us both more than she takes and who has motivated, encouraged, and helped Ivy every step of the way through all of the stages in her life. We love you!

First Edition
13 12 11 10 09   5 4 3 2 1

Text © 2009 Ivy Larson and Andrew Larson

Published by
Gibbs Smith, Publisher
P.O. Box 667
Layton, Utah 84041

1-800.835.4993 orders
www.gibbs-smith.com

Designed and produced by Debra McQuiston
Printed and bound in Canada
Gibbs Smith books are printed on either recycled, 100% post-consumer waste, FSC-certified papers or on paper produced from a 100% certified sustainable forest/controlled wood source.

Library of Congress Cataloging-in-Publication Data

Larson, Ivy Ingram, 1973-
  Whole foods diet cookbook : 200 recipes for optimal health / Ivy Larson and Andrew Larson. — 1st ed.
     p. cm.
  Includes bibliographical references and index.
  ISBN-13: 978-1-4236-0492-1
  ISBN-10: 1-4236-0492-X
  1.  Cookery (Natural foods) 2.  Nutrition. 3.  Reducing diets—Recipes.
I.  Larson, Andrew, 1973- II. Title.
  TX741.L37 2009
  641.5´636—dc22
                                    2008043065

# contents

# preface

We'll be honest; we weren't born whole foods enthusiasts. We actually stumbled onto learning about the far-reaching health and weight-loss benefits of a nutrient-rich, anti-inflammatory whole foods diet early in our twenties after Ivy was diagnosed with multiple sclerosis; her neurologist at the University of Miami suggested she could improve her symptoms and her quality of life with dietary modification. It was 1998, and Andy was still in medical school at the University of Pennsylvania, and, frankly, he was highly suspicious of how a diet could help with MS. But Ivy's neurologist, William Sheremata, M.D., was a full professor at the University of Miami and had published over sixty high-quality, peer-reviewed research articles, and his academic credentials were just way too impressive for Andy to ignore. Andy hopped on a plane and flew down to Miami to personally meet with Dr. Sheremata and learn more about the diet he was suggesting. After the meeting and after doing a lot of research on his own, Andy was convinced a healthy diet could indeed help Ivy improve her quality of life.

At that point in our lives, we both had a *tremendous* amount to learn about what constituted a healthy diet, but we poured ourselves into the medical dietary research and soon began to understand the sweeping benefits of nutrition for a plethora of conditions way beyond MS. With mounds of research to back up our dietary recommendations, we began putting other people on our program and collecting real-life testimonials. In 2005 we published our first book, *The Gold Coast Cure*. It was a huge success as an Amazon.com #1 bestselling diet book. We followed up with our second book, *The Gold Coast Cures' Fitter, Firmer, Faster Program* in 2006. Andy then wrote a third book titled *Chicken Soup for the Healthy Living Soul: Weight Loss*.

Long story short, we've been walking the talk, eating, cooking, and writing about whole foods for over a decade now. When our son was born in 2001, we started him on the whole foods diet as soon as he could eat puréed food. He has reaped the benefits of good nutrition from birth; he is fit, strong, and *unbelievably* active.

Although we'd like to say we'd have eventually adopted our whole foods way of eating regardless of whether Ivy had been diagnosed with MS, we can't say with absolute confidence this would have ever happened. For one, we can't imagine why we would have ever taken the time to research and sort through the ever-shifting, conflicting, and completely contradictory dietary advice that has filtered its way into the media over the past ten to twenty years. Would we have happened to stumble upon an appealing, science-based natural-foods diet book? Maybe. But, probably not. To be honest, we're not sure the natural-foods stuff would have been attractive to us anyway. Back then the natural-foods world seemed too "fringe element" to be appealing.

Luckily, times are slowly changing. In fact, over the past decade we've noticed an increasing number of people going out of their way to buy "all natural" foods. The reality is that we are now just on the brink of a whole foods revolution as more and more people flock to natural foods stores and begin to stock up on items such as sushi-grade tuna, gourmet blends of wild rice, flaxseed, artichokes, edamame beans, and "designer" greens. Gone are the days when a twenty-ounce porterhouse steak is considered the ultimate in dining luxury. Today, an increasing number of people are demanding healthful, better-balanced, whole foods meals. They are also seeking an exotic adventurous style of cuisine offering international flavors, all with the added stipulation it will help them stay fit and trim. The whole foods revolution is just beginning to get into full swing. And it's about time.

# acknowledgments

A most heartfelt thank you to Ivy's mom, Gail Ingram, who pulled us through an extremely stressful time in order to meet our book deadline. On top of that, she generously and regularly donates her time, turns her own kitchen into a test kitchen, helps create and retest the recipes for all of Ivy's books and cooking classes, and does the food styling for the photos! Gail's got endless talent and energy bundled with unlimited generosity. To say Ivy owes her mom thanks would be a tremendous understatement. Ivy's dad, Norman Ingram, has continuously given support and enthusiasm for our books. And certainly no father could proselytize our work more than he. Thank you, Dad! Andy's parents, Ken and Elaine Larson, have always stood like a rock to lean on. We will never forget how much they helped us during those most difficult early years when Andy was in surgical residency and Blake was just a baby. We both truly have amazing parents, and we will forever be indebted to them for all they have done and all they continue to do for us.

We are particularly thankful to our agent, Linda Konner, whose wisdom and experience steered us in the right direction, aligning us with a wonderful publisher. Linda's enduring advice coupled with her continuous support and enthusiasm for our work are greatly appreciated. She has become more than a collaborator and colleague; she is also a trusted friend. A very special thank you to our publisher, Gibbs Smith, for believing in us and giving us a chance to come on board. To the most patient editor ever, Leslie Stitt, for her incredible dedication, attention to detail, and fabulously creative ideas; and a wholehearted thank you to Linda Nimori, who stepped in at the last minute to continue the project. Many thanks to publicist, Kelly Keiter, who enthusiastically listened to Ivy's never-ending input, all the while working so diligently to make the book a success. And, of course, we extend sincere gratitude to the sales and marketing team, art department, and all of the wonderful people at Gibbs Smith who have worked so hard to help us bring our vision to the public. It was a joy to work with each one of them.

A very special thank you to our photographer, Debby Gans, not only for her beautiful and artistic photos, her creativity and ingenuity, but also for making work fun! It's a bonus to have also found a good friend. Sincere gratitude to talented Whole Foods Market chef Joe Colavito, for generously donating his time, expertise, and culinary knowledge, and to all of our friends at Whole Foods Market, especially Brenna Bertram, for her continued support. And, of course, to all of our previous Gold Coast Cure readers, "Lifestyle Makeover" participants, and the people who eagerly attend Ivy's cooking classes—your enthusiasm keeps us moving forward!

To our culinary cheerleaders, Ilonka Pinello, Becky Grose, and Tara Pinello at In the Kitchen and especially owner Lenore Pinello, for opening up her shop, supporting our books, and graciously helping with the photo shoots and classes. Thank you, Lenore!

To our old friends, Peter Vegso, Kim Weiss, and Allison Janse, thank you for believing in us from day one. And last, but not least, to the "official" taste tester, our bright and energetic little boy, Blake, who makes living every day a sheer delight! XOXOXOX

Contact us at www.wholefoodsdietcoobook.com.

# introduction

**Viewed as a whole,** our national menu is rather atrocious from a health standpoint. Nevertheless, we can all agree that diet, nutrition, and healthy eating are hot topics right now. Ironically, in no period of history have we been so preoccupied with the subject of nutrition, yet in no period of history have we been so overweight and suffering from such an alarming number of early-onset degenerative and inflammatory diseases. And, of course, the obesity epidemic is so rampant, it's now infiltrating down to the next generation. When we both grew up in the early 1970s, it was rare to see an overweight child—now it's *almost* accepted. We are a nation obsessed with diet, nutrition, and healthy eating trends, but we don't have much to show for it.

It's time to wake up nutritionally. As primitive as it may sound, the personal adoption of an anti-inflammatory whole foods diet is as close to a "cure all" as modern scientific research can lead us in the treatment, prevention, or reversal of a wide variety of common ailments including obesity, type 2 diabetes, heart disease, and numerous inflammatory conditions. This means it's time to dethrone the dizzying array of empty-calorie fast foods, fake foods, and highly refined, nutrient-poor foods that are crowding out the *real* "whole" foods in our supermarkets, expanding our waistlines, and destroying our health. It's also time to trash the fad diets. In this book you'll learn that the secret to good health and effortless weight management is adopting an all-natural way of eating based on nutrient-rich and anti-inflammatory "whole foods." We emphasize a relaxed approach to developing a healthy dietary pattern rather than encouraging unnecessary preoccupation with fats, carbs, calories, and points. We'll show you how to stop judging your food based on whether it's high carb, high fat, or high calorie and learn instead how to rate your food based on its *nutritional content*. We'll provide you with a lifelong strategy and sustainable way of eating that is entirely compatible with modern lifestyles while simultaneously addressing both your need to be nourished *and* your need to enjoy delicious foods. And, yes, we place heavy emphasis on taste and the pleasure principles associated with good food.

But we won't just *tell* you how to eat; we'll take you into the kitchen and *show* you how to eat too. As part of a full-fledged cookbook, we've paired our nutrition guidelines with get-real recipes, meals, and menus emphasizing flavor-forward "real" food. You'll learn how to put a fresh and modern spin on naturally nutritious foods, and you'll be introduced to plenty of cooking techniques designed to eliminate the granola aspect so commonly associated with health food. Every recipe in *The Whole Foods Diet Cookbook* was created with an emphasis on maximizing nutrition and taste. Not only have we strived to increase the overall nutritional content of our recipes, including as many antioxidants, phytochemicals, essential fats, and fiber as possible, but we've also made each recipe low in saturated fat and very low in sugar (even the desserts), and we've used zero refined grains, flours, or processed oils.

People always ask us if we really do adhere to our whole foods way of eating *all of the time*. The truth is, we do. Regardless of what occasion it may be, whether it's a holiday, birthday, or bridal shower, we always stick to our whole foods lifestyle. In fact, one of the goals in writing this book was to prove that healthy eating can be an everyday occurrence, regardless of the situation. For instance, when we entertain people at our house, we don't even think of sacrificing our healthy eating habits. We don't feel tempted to make exceptions, because the foods we eat *truly* do taste delicious, and they aren't any more difficult or time-consuming to prepare than unhealthy foods. Again, this book is designed to provide a doable and delicious strategy for making a whole foods lifestyle work in real life.

To help you live a whole foods lifestyle everyday of the year, we've put together a compilation of stylishly contemporary recipes ranging from elaborate to simple, which include a mix of upscale comfort foods, ethnic cuisine, and gourmet meals for just about any occasion and any time of day—so there's no excuse not to eat well. In creating and compiling the recipe collection for this book, we really did our best to strike a balance between offering plenty of recognizable familiar favorites, such as Mac-n-Cheese (but with a "whole foods" twist of puréed butternut squash and white soybeans) or Reese-Swirl brownies (substituting all-natural peanut butter for saturated-fat-rich butter), as well as plenty of authentic and innovative recipes, including Seared Tofu Pockets with Artichoke-Ricotta Stuffing Topped with Red Pepper Purée, Volcano Ahi Tuna Salad Stacks, Children's Yogurt Cake with Cashew–Cream Cheese Frosting, or Emergency Decadent Chocolate Dessert. We've got the bases covered and something to suit the tastes of just about everyone.

Whether you cook out of enjoyment or out of domestic duty, if you are going to make the extra effort and time it takes to prepare a meal (and since you purchased this book, we're presuming you plan on doing a little cooking), then we believe you should make every effort to prepare high-quality, nutrient-rich wholesome meals. Why buy a cookbook that shows you step-by-step how to make an unhealthy meal when you can make a nutritionally superior meal that requires absolutely no more effort and tastes just as good, if not better? Plenty of opportunity exists to eat less-than-nutritionally stellar food from a restaurant, can, or frozen entrée box, but if you have the free time to cook, then think of the free time as a luxury and indulge yourself and your family with a meal that satisfies their need for good taste *and* good nutrition.

While some of the recipes in this book may seem more elaborate and more sophisticated than others, we assure you every recipe is easy enough for any home cook to tackle. Little to zero experience in the kitchen is required, and only a few basic kitchen tools, cookware, and small appliances are necessary. Ivy has created all of the recipes in the book, and she's admittedly a nonprofessional self-taught cook. She taught herself to cook by watching her mom, cooking shows (thank you, Food Network!), reading cookbooks, and experimenting for hours upon hours in the kitchen. (Andy and our son, Blake, have always served as the "official" taste testers.) She's utilized her nutritional knowledge combined with her enthusiasm for good food to create mouthwatering recipes that anyone can make. Since Ivy is often short on patience, nothing too fussy has made its way into this book. And because she realizes planning a meal can sometimes be every bit as difficult as preparing one, she has organized the book to help you orchestrate nutritionally complete meals based on complementary foods and flavors, so you won't have to read through hundreds of solo recipes and try to figure out what type of vegetable will go well with the chicken recipe or what type of grain to serve with the tofu or fish—she's already done the work for you.

Since we're big on the concept of eating "balanced" meals, our menu collection reflects this philosophy too. You'll find delicious, healthful, complete balanced meals for breakfast and brunch, everyday dinners, entertaining, holidays, and parties. We also include a section on decadent yet salubrious desserts. We'll show you how easy, fun, and delicious it is to make healthful and whole food living as much a part of your life as it is ours.

## Beyond "All Natural," "Organic," and "Vegan"

The "whole foods" title of our book surely conjures up images of an all-natural eating style, which it certainly is. And while the spirit of the New Age somewhat-elitist natural-foods movement is a big step in the right direction, not everyone fully understands there can be an *enormous* difference between eating natural foods and eating healthful, nutrient-rich "whole foods." In other words, the word "natural" is not synonymous with healthful. Neither is organic or vegan. Just because a food is 100 percent all-natural, 100 percent organic, or even vegan doesn't necessarily mean it's a healthy food.

Some natural foods (think white flour and bacon) should be relegated to the trashcan while others (think spinach and nuts) should make up the foundation of our diets. We can't emphasize enough that natural is not tantamount to healthy; again, neither is vegan or organic. Even hardcore vegans would be hard pressed to come up with any redeeming qualities for organic french fries. The notorious little grease sticks offer practically nothing in the nutrition department. The truth is, foods labeled organic or vegan are often completely overrated. Moreover, the word "natural" is one of the most abused terms in modern food marketing— probably because health-conscious consumers will pay an absurdly substantial amount more for a food marketed as "natural," even though that food might be nutritionally inadequate. (We saw this purchasing trend back in the fat-free nutritional era of the 1990s.) In the nutrition chapters of this book, we'll help you sort through the marketing gimmicks and show you how to easily identify truly healthy whole foods, because optimal nutrition goes beyond, *way* beyond, foods labeled 100 percent organic, vegan, and all-natural.

# Whole Foods Defined

There are six chapters in this book dedicated to explaining everything you need to know about how to adopt a whole foods diet, but the simplest definition is that whole foods are unadulterated, all-natural, and *nutrient-rich* foods packaged the way nature intended—they come straight from the plant or animal (preferably an animal that hasn't been treated with growth hormones and antibiotics, and one that has been raised on food nature intended the animal to eat). Whole foods should be free from stabilizers, preservatives, and artificial flavorings. And, while whole foods can be packaged as convenience items, they should be minimally processed, thus keeping the complete nutrition of the food intact; for example, hummus made with chickpeas, extra virgin olive oil, lemon juice, and salt; or flaxseed pressed into flax oil; or whole grains sprouted and made into whole-grain bread. You get the picture.

A true whole food is nutrient rich and brimming with antiaging, anti-inflammatory substances. What's more, the anti-inflammatory nature of whole foods packaged with their array of nutrients, essential fats, antioxidants, and phytochemicals makes for nature's ultimate fat-fighters: they curb your appetite, control food cravings, and support a healthy metabolism that favors fat-burning as opposed to fat-storing. This means whole foods are also super slimming, naturally.

While whole foods aren't necessarily vegan or vegetarian, if you make the extra effort to add more *nutrient-rich* unrefined plant-based foods to your daily diet, you'll maximize the nutritional bang for your food buck and reap the greatest health and weight-loss benefits of a whole foods diet—on a "flexitarian" part-time vegetarian basis. We'll introduce the concept of a flexitarian-style diet in more detail later in the book, but rest assured that if you adopt a flexitarian whole foods diet, you can still enjoy non-vegan whole foods like meat, fish, eggs, chicken, and dairy everyday; you'll simply try to increase the amount of plant-based foods you choose on a regular basis.

In a nutshell, this book reflects the latest trends in nutrition, flavor-forward gastronomy, convenience cuisine, and weight management. We won't ask you to join the wheatgrass fringe element at any point. The foods you'll eat and cook from the *Whole Foods Diet Cookbook* are becoming more and more mainstream and are widely available nationwide. Moreover, these foods will nourish your entire family, including your little ones. Our natural approach to good health, vitality, and energy benefits people of all ages. In addition, we even show you how to safely indulge and enjoy vices like coffee, wine, and sweets without tipping the scale or harming your health. Our goal is to show you how to have a delicious and healthy life with effortless ease—without gaining an ounce. Bon Appétit!

# whole foods breakthrough

**As the saying goes,** everything old is new again. It's ironic that after countless fad diets and innumerable misguided dietary recommendations, the latest interdisciplinary research among food science, nutrition, and health points back in time to the good old days when people ate real unprocessed food with unadulterated nutrients. Part 1 of this book is intended to give you a taste of the future by putting a fresh spin on understanding the basics of a very traditional way of eating. But, of course, even the experts agree that the food absolutely *must* taste good. Worry not. Eating healthy, eating well, and eating tasty foods—all starts here.

# the whole foods edge

achieving ideal health and the body that goes with it

**It's no secret** many people struggle to achieve an "ideal body" with health improvement as a mere afterthought. We certainly don't want you to give up on the idea of having a trim physique, but we do want you to flip-flop your goals and adjust your mindset. If you focus first and foremost on achieving ideal health, the inevitable side benefit will be a slimmer waistline. By forgoing the destructive cycle of self-denial and emphasizing something positive—in this case, your health and well-being—you can learn to eat in a way that is naturally satisfying, while simultaneously achieving or maintaining a healthful weight.

While we realize it's become practically cliché to adopt the "no diet" approach to weight loss, in our book, "diet" *truly* is a four-letter word. We don't "diet," we eat. Furthermore, the foods we eat aren't low fat, low carb or even low calorie. We won't encourage you to count points or weigh your food. Instead, we'll encourage you to adopt a healthy dietary pattern by choosing from a broad range of *nutrient-rich* "whole foods." If you happen to be among the discontented alums of high-profile, low-fat, low-carb, or low-calorie diets, you'll quickly see how a whole foods lifestyle offers a truly liberating solution to your past and current dieting dilemma. You'll never again need to ask what the diet du jour is if you follow our dietary recommendations. Even better, a whole foods eating style will also help you fight disease because it combats inflammation, malnutrition, and oxidative stress.

As we mentioned in the introduction, we've written three previous books proselytizing the far-reaching benefits of diet in combination with exercise and nutritional supplements. And, as we recommend in our previous books, we continue to exercise religiously and routinely take an array of vitamins, minerals, antioxidants, and essential fat supplements. However, as important as exercise and supplements are to good health and a good body, they can't hold a candle to the benefits of eating the proper diet. The truth is, absolutely nothing else you can do will improve your body more than adopting a well-balanced whole foods diet. Such a diet is rich in antioxidants and phytochemicals that work hard to prevent oxidation and protect the integrity of your cells; it's highly anti-inflammatory, thereby offering protection from a wide array of inflammation-driven diseases; and it's loaded with a wide spectrum of nutrients necessary to fuel a healthy metabolism and to maintain optimal health.

While the diet we recommend is primarily based on common sense, its basic tenets have eluded the general public, thanks in part to the ever-shifting dietary advice reported and, in many ways, endorsed by the media. We've been bombarded with so many conflicting messages regarding food and health, and we've all watched countless cosmopolitan diet trends come and go in such rapid succession, that we now stand as one completely nutritionally confused nation. In fact, Andy recently gave a speech at an American Heart Association's Go Red for Women fundraiser where someone in the audience asked him how in the world the average person should interpret all of the contradictory, dizzying dietary advice reported by the media and recommended by the nation's leading "official" nutritionists. This was an excellent question. Unfortunately, the answer is neither simple nor straightforward. While this book is certainly not about food politics, we can't help but touch upon the fact that government subsidiaries and clever (pricey too!) marketing campaigns by the food industry giants have a profound impact on many of the dietary choices the average person makes. Thus, many people are understandably baffled about what a healthy diet *really* is.

We want to help you make sense of the confusion and bring back a common-sense—and enjoyable—approach to healthful eating. We believe eating should not only be intuitive but also pleasurable. Yet, thanks again to a lot of the popular dietary advice recommended by mainstream nutrition experts in the last few decades, many of us have completely dismissed the fact that the food we eat should actually taste good. Our goal in this book is to prove how "delicious" can truly be synonymous with "nutritious." We also want to show you how to trust your own appetite and embrace a more holistic and natural approach to weight management. This means learning to reclaim your enjoyment of good food and stop stressing about calories, carbs, fat grams, and points.

But, of course, here in the land of plenty, calories, carbs, fat grams, and points are ubiquitous, and one can't deny that excessive intake of any of those will lead to weight gain and poor health. Yet, the oversupply of food in our diet is primarily derived from calorie-containing, foodlike substances, not necessarily *real* whole foods. One of the biggest problems with the modern diet is that it provides a surplus of calories with a deficit of nutrients. Diet fads add fuel to the fire as they encourage people to count calories, carbs, fat, grams, and points. Instead of "counting your food," learn to make your food count based on its *nutritional content*. The typical supermarket is a virtual wilderness of untamed empty calories, many lurking suspiciously inside packages specifically advertised as healthy. Yet such an oversupply has not produced excessive nutrition. Quite the contrary. The majority of people eating the S.A.D. (Standard American Diet) are overfed and actually *undernourished*. Malnutrition refers to inadequate nutrient intake—not inadequate calorie intake. Putting this concept in perspective, this means it is entirely possible to consume 3,000 calories a day and be fifty or more pounds overweight yet *still* be undernourished. It's also possible to be rather slim and consume a mere 1,600 or 1,800 calories a day and be very well nourished. In *Whole Foods Diet Cookbook*, we want to show you how easy it is to maximize nutrition without overdoing calories—naturally. Our way of eating allows you to leave the table feeling nurtured, nourished, and well fed without having overconsumed calories.

## Whole Body Health

An overwhelming number of studies prove an all-natural, nutrient-rich, whole foods diet made up largely from unrefined vegetarian sources is the optimal diet for preventing disease and maintaining good health. Foods that promote good health and offer protection from a vast array of diseases—ranging from cancer to heart disease—are nutrient rich and brimming with substances such as antioxidants, phytochemicals (also known as phytonutrients), vitamins, minerals, fiber, and essential fats. Processed foodlike "foods" don't have all of these important substances in their naturally occurring state (although some processed foods do have *man-made* versions of some of these substances, which are not easily recognized by your body); thus, processed foods don't promote good health. Processed foods do supply energy in the form of calories, but they don't provide optimal nutrition. Processed foods actually cheat you out of protective nutrients and cheat you out of achieving optimal health.

Processed foods also lack the nutrients we need to stay slim. The truth is, it's almost impossible to be truly healthy and simultaneously be fat. We don't really buy into the whole "fit and fat" concept. If you are overweight, you really are not in optimal health. Carrying around too much fat is toxic and taxing to your system and therefore does not create the ideal environment for promoting health. However, we don't advocate "dieting" as a way to lose weight. Instead, we encourage people to shift their mindset away from deprivation dieting and more toward getting the nourishment their body needs and craves. Once you start to get the nutrients your body needs from unrefined whole foods, weight loss becomes inevitable as your metabolism improves, food cravings cease, and appetite naturally regulates.

## The Whole Foods Edge

Too bad you can't just pop a pill to get the nutrients your body needs. The truth is, the best sources of nutrients do not come from isolated sources such as a vitamin or a specific antioxidant supplement. The best sources are from whole foods. Unadulterated whole foods harbor a whole array of compounds that have never been seen inside a vitamin bottle for the simple reason that scientists have not, until very recently, even known they existed, much less managed to infuse them, intact, into pills. For example, we now know traditional antioxidants such as vitamins A and C are not the only antiaging, disease-fighting substances found in whole foods; many phytochemicals found in plant foods are now being recognized for their amazing antioxidant, anti-inflammatory, and disease-fighting capabilities. These phytochemicals are believed to work synergistically to improve health and to support a healthy metabolism. Examples include lignans found in flaxseeds, polyphenols in cocoa, resveratrol in red wine, and isoflavones in soy. When foods are processed, many of their important phytochemical properties are stripped from them, and we miss getting the health-promoting edge these substances provide. Put another way, regardless of how many vitamins, minerals, and antioxidants a processed food has been artificially pumped with, the processed food will simply never be as nutritious as the whole food.

There is no such thing as a magic bullet food or nutrient. While it's certainly tempting to zero in on just one food as the miraculous elixir of life, the reality is that *dietary patterns* matter much more than individual foods. For example, when fruits and vegetables rich in beta-carotene showed up in multiple studies years ago, nutrition researchers began a mad rush to test isolated beta-carotene as the "ultimate cure-all"—experiments that infamously failed to show special benefits and even posed some dangers.[1] It's important to remember that foods are designed to be eaten in combination with other foods, not only for maximum enjoyment and taste but for maximum nutrition too. The bottom line is we need to eat a wide spectrum of nutrients from a wide variety of food sources everyday for optimal health.

## Ditching Your Calorie Counter

Don't accentuate the negative. Don't hone in and obsess about all of the "bad" foods you can't eat; rather, emphasize the positive. Learn to become pro-food. Focus on trying to increase your intake of the numerous nutritious whole foods your body needs. Your ultimate dietary goal should be to get the most nutritional bang for your food buck at every meal. This means you need to stop making food the enemy. Stop looking for ways to trick yourself into eating as few calories as possible and instead intentionally look for ways to increase your nutritional quotient for the day at every meal and every snack. Again, don't count your food calories; make them count nutritionally!

Weighing your food and counting calories sets the stage for failure. In the calorie-counter's mind, a 150-calorie sugary soda is the nutritional equivalent of 150 calories worth of all-natural nuts. Ridiculous. Yet, for whatever reason, many people resort to calorie counting and low-calorie diets in order to lose weight. Here's the deal: all calories are not created equal. We realize this flies in the face of what many nutritionists would have you believe, but hear us out.

It is true that when calories are burned in a laboratory, they are all "equal" from the standpoint of releasing energy. In a laboratory, it doesn't matter whether the 150 calories come from the "liquid candy" soda or from nutrient-dense nuts. However, the chemical processes that break down and metabolize food inside our body do not react to all calories equally. The foods you eat have varying amounts of substances (sugars, fiber, fats, etc.) that affect how quickly they are metabolized and what hormones they "turn on" or "turn off" once eaten. For example, sugary foods (like the soda), refined carbohydrates, saturated-fat-rich foods, and foods that contain trans fats all "turn on" pro-inflammatory hormones in your body that ultimately slow your metabolism and thwart fat-burning. Other foods that contain essential fats actually "turn on" anti-inflammatory hormones that speed your metabolism and facilitate weight loss. In the process of trying to digest highly refined carbohydrates (white rice and foods made with sugar and refined flour), your body produces insulin, a fat-storing hormone that also makes you hungry. On the other hand, fiber-rich foods actually "lose" calories during the digestion process, which means you don't fully absorb all of the calories in fiber-rich foods such as nuts, whole grains, beans, fruits, and vegetables.

The point is, you simply can't rely on counting calories as an accurate way of controlling your weight. All calories are not created equal; they are not created equal from a weight-management standpoint or from a health standpoint. Whether or not they have the same number of calories, soda and nuts are simply not nutritional equals. But didn't you know that deep down anyway?

In one particular study reported in the *Journal of the American Medical Association* in 2004, researchers placed two groups of people on a 1,500-calorie-a-day diet; one group followed a diet low in fat but rich in refined/processed carbohydrates while the other group followed a diet that was not low in carbohydrates but was low in refined/processed carbohydrates. Both groups did lose weight (most people would if they ate just 1,500 calories a day!), but the surprising thing was that the group who ate the diet rich in refined/processed carbohydrates had higher triglycerides, insulin, and blood sugar, higher blood pressure, and higher levels of inflammation. Phew! But, that's not all. Those on the highly refined carbohydrate diet had slower resting metabolisms and reported feeling hungrier than those on the unrefined carbohydrate diet.[2] Again, not all calories are created equal.

You need to focus on eating unprocessed whole foods that contain a wide spectrum of essential nutrients your body needs for good health and a healthy metabolism. Forget about trying to tally up calories in an effort to control your weight. Low-calorie diets actually slow your metabolism and make weight loss more difficult. Besides, it's next to impossible to get all of the many metabolism-supporting and disease-fighting nutrients your body needs on a low-calorie diet anyway. Furthermore, when you eat nutrient-poor, highly processed "diet" foods, you feel hungry, overeat, and suffer from relentless food cravings. One reason empty-calorie processed foods leave you feeling unsatisfied is because they lack nutrients (this is why they are called "empty-calorie" foods), and you need nutrients to curb food cravings!

You also need nutrients such as essential fats, B vitamins, chromium, calcium, and vitamin C to support a healthy metabolism and help your body burn fat for energy.

Adopting the whole foods way of eating gives you an unbelievable edge in preventing disease and literally "cures" the deprivation-dieting merry-go-round. It's the answer to providing your body with key metabolism-supporting and health-promoting nutrients in their most easily assimilated, most bio-available, and most natural form. Adopting a whole foods diet is also the "cure" for bland and boring meals—it's a win-win way of eating that provides maximum nutrition and maximum enjoyment. Who can argue with that (other than the manufacturers of processed foods, of course)?

# nutritional
# nuts and bolts

· · · · · · · · · · · · · · · · · · · · · · · · · · · · · · · · · · · · · · · · · · · · · · · · · · · · · · · · ·

## making your
## food count

**The body needs** an adequate and balanced intake of macro-nutrients in the form of carbs, fats, and proteins, but there is far more to eating for maximum nutritional bang than focusing solely on macronutrient consumption. To help you get the nutrition your body needs to fight hunger, fat, and disease, we've identified eight key dietary elements to incorporate in your daily diet. If you make a conscious effort to "make your food count" by trying to obtain the eight dietary elements presented in this chapter, you will be well on your way to eating for maximum nutrition and optimal health.

## Omega-3 Essential Fats

Essential fats are called "essential" because your body can't make them; you must obtain them from food or supplements. There are three types of omega-3 essential fats to be concerned about: ALA (alpha-linolenic acid), EPA (eicosapentaenoic acid), and DHA (docosahexaenoic acid). While ALA can be converted into EPA and DHA in limited amounts, it is best to eat a diet containing all three omega-3 essential fats. Many factors can hinder the conversion of ALA into EPA and DHA, including stress, vitamin deficiencies, too much sugar and trans fats in the diet, and viral infections, among others. While it is best to get all three omega-3 fats from food, supplements (especially with pharmaceutical-grade fish oil) are also very helpful and highly recommended.

ALA is found in vegetarian foods, including walnuts, hemp seeds, and canola oil, but the richest vegetarian source by far is from flax—both ground flaxseed and flax oil. EPA and DHA are found primarily in fish—the fattier the fish the better. Some of the new "designer" eggs contain DHA and a smidgen of EPA in their yolks, but fatty fish is by far the best readily available source.

Obtaining optimal amounts of omega-3 essential fats is absolutely vital to achieving your best body, inside and out. Omega-3 essential fats are widely recognized for their heart-protective and triglyceride-lowering effects. They are also famous for their ability to cushion the body's inflammatory response. In fact, omega-3 essential fats are the most powerful anti-inflammatory substances available without a prescription (and without negative side effects too!) and are therefore beneficial to people suffering from seemingly unrelated conditions that all have inflammation as the common denominator, including asthma, arthritis, psoriasis, and multiple sclerosis. Omega-3 essential fats support the health of your immune system, reproductive system, cardiovascular system, and central nervous system. That, in itself, is a good enough reason to be sure to obtain these fats in your diet.

Moreover, these fats are now beginning to be recognized for their slimming properties too. EPA binds to certain receptors in your cells that can improve your body's ability to burn fat while also making your cells more sensitive to insulin. Insulin is a key hormone that allows glucose (blood sugar) to be transferred from your bloodstream into your cells for energy use. It's an important hormone for sure, but it's also a fat-storing hormone; without insulin you wouldn't be able to properly convert food into energy. If you didn't produce insulin, you'd lose a lot of weight (which is what often happens to diabetics before they are diagnosed and before they are given insulin medication). If you want to keep your weight under control, then you want to be insulin-sensitive so your body only produces a little bit of insulin at a time; the omega-3 fats from fish oil help your body become more insulin-sensitive. When omega-3 fats are missing from the diet, your body is less effective at using insulin, and weight loss becomes considerably more difficult.

The anti-inflammatory properties of omega-3 fats also play a role in weight management. While a certain amount of inflammation is necessary for the body's natural defense system to function properly, chronic inflammation is *not* healthy. The latest obesity research recognizes inflammation as a primary offender leading to weight gain. Dietary habits play the biggest role in determining whether your body is in a state of systemic inflammation or not. This is because some foods are pro-inflammatory (such as trans fats, sugars, saturated fats, and refined carbohydrates) while other foods actively help decrease inflammation— *especially* foods rich in omega-3 essential fats. Anything that creates systemic inflammation is going to make you gain weight, and the weight you gain is going to increase inflammation further, creating a vicious cycle. The more overweight you get, the worse the cycle becomes because fat cells actually produce inflammatory hormones, and the inflammatory hormones make your body less sensitive to insulin, which makes weight loss even more challenging. To add insult to injury, fat cells also produce hormones that increase appetite. Yikes! However, by eliminating pro-inflammatory foods and eating more anti-inflammatory foods (especially omega-3 essential fats), you can reduce inflammation and improve your sensitivity to insulin, thus creating a metabolic environment that favors fat burning rather than fat storage.

The easiest way to get the omega-3 essential fat your body needs is to eat either one tablespoon of flax oil a day or three tablespoons of *ground* flaxseed a day *plus* 3 or 4 servings of fish a week. (Ideally you would also take a high-quality fish oil supplement every day.) Note: flax oil is very heat sensitive and must not be used for cooking; use flax oil only in cold recipes such as a salad dressing or drizzled on top of whole grains *after* they are cooked. It's important the flaxseed be *ground* or you won't be able to absorb the beneficial omega-3 fats. Ground flaxseed has a few advantages over flax oil. For one, ground flaxseed can be used in recipes requiring heat, which means you can add it to baked goods. Flaxseed also has the benefit of containing fiber; so, from a weight-loss standpoint, you'll benefit more from flaxseed than from flax oil. In addition, flaxseed contains nature's richest source of lignans—potent antioxidants that fight free-radical damage and help protect against hormone-sensitive cancers. (Flaxseed has at least seventy-five times more lignans than any other food!) "Designer" omega-3 eggs, the relatively new chicks on the block, are now widely available in supermarkets across the country and are also a good source of omega-3 fat (try to purchase organic cage-free eggs only).

## Omega-6 Essential Fats

Omega-6 essential fats are the other type of essential fats your body needs. These fats are broadly available in oil-rich seeds and the vegetable oils extracted from them. They also build up in the fat of grain-fed (but not grass-fed) animals we eat. For our bodies and metabolisms to function optimally, we actually need slightly more omega-6 fat than omega-3 fat (ideally in a ratio of about 2:1 or 4:1). However, because we eat such an overabundance of refined vegetable oils and so much grain-fed meat and so little omega-3-rich fish and flax, the average American consumes a very unhealthy, totally out-of-whack omega-6 to omega-3 fat ratio of about 14:1 to 20:1.

Most fast food is rich in omega-6 fat (from vegetable oil) and devoid of omega-3 fat. Frozen foods and baked goods all contain vegetable oils. And now that consumers are becoming savvy about the dangers of trans fats, food manufacturers are replacing trans fats with omega-6-rich processed vegetable oils. This is a big problem because eating an unbalanced ratio of omega-6 fat relative to omega-3 fat actually increases inflammation, which we now know thwarts fat loss and decreases insulin sensitivity. Ominously, studies have also linked diets rich in omega-6 fat to cancer and heart disease.

You might be questioning why omega-6 fat is even included in the list of eight "key dietary elements" that should be obtained everyday. The reason is, you still need omega-6 fat and you actually need *slightly* more of it than omega-3 fat. The form of omega-6 fat you get from food is called LA (linoleic acid), and it is converted into GLA (gamma linolenic acid), an omega-6 fat you can get from supplements such as evening primrose oil, black currant seed oil, or borage oil. GLA is a special fatty acid that stimulates the mitochondria to burn energy faster, which increases your metabolism and helps you burn fat. GLA also has anti-inflammatory properties that are beneficial to overall good health and even contribute to good skin. In addition, GLA has been shown to improve cell sensitivity to insulin and thus reduce the chances of developing heart disease, diabetes, and obesity.

Unfortunately, average Americans get most of their omega-6 fat from highly refined empty-calorie vegetable oils such as corn oil, "pure" vegetable oil, peanut oil, soybean oil, sunflower oil, safflower oil, and cottonseed oil. Despite their healthy-enough sounding names, most vegetable oils can be anything but healthy. Conventional, modern-day processing techniques used to refine grains and seeds into vegetable oils damage the omega-6 fat within the oil and make the LA (linoleic acid) incapable of converting to the beneficial GLA (gamma linolenic acid) our bodies really need. The modern-day processing techniques also strip the original "whole food" (corn, soybeans, sunflowers, and peanuts) of its other nutrients and antioxidants, thus rendering an empty-calorie, highly processed food. Furthermore, the vast majority of omega-6-rich vegetable oils have been heated to very high temperatures during processing, even though the omega-6 fats within these oils are very fragile and cannot withstand high-heat temperatures. Vegetable oils that are not cold pressed, or at the very least, expeller pressed, should be thought of as empty-calorie, highly refined foods—foods to be avoided.

The easiest way to avoid getting too much empty-calorie omega-6 fat is to eliminate processed vegetable oils (corn, "pure" vegetable oil, peanut oil, soybean oil, safflower oil, sunflower oil, and cottonseed oil) from your diet and avoid eating processed foods containing these oils. Instead, use healthier oils containing more omega-3 fats and more monounsaturated fats. (Healthy oil alternatives are presented later in this chapter.) You should also make every effort to purchase meat from grass-fed animals rather than grain-fed, since grass-fed animals have a more optimal omega-6 to omega-3 ratio. Finally, in order to be certain you are obtaining the omega-6 fats your body needs in their freshest, most nutritious form, eat "whole foods" sources of unrefined omega-6-rich foods daily, such as whole soybeans, corn, nuts, all-natural nut butters, seeds, all-natural seed butters, wheat germ, tofu, tempeh, whole grains, and soymilk.

## Monounsaturated Fat

We often think of monounsaturated fat as the "Mediterranean fat," probably because olive oil is among the most familiar monounsaturated fats associated with that region. However, plenty of other healthful sources of monounsaturated fat exist, including avocados, many nuts and nut butters, whole olives, many seeds and seed butters. (Remember, many nuts, nut butters, seeds, and seed butters also contain a good amount of omega-6 fat.) Three relatively new oils on the market—"high-oleic" versions of sunflower oil, safflower oil, and canola oil—are also classified as monounsaturated fats. Through hybridization, high-oleic oils have been transformed into oils that are high in monounsaturated fat and low in omega-6 fats. While the oleic acid in these hybrid oils is found in the cell membranes of olive trees, high-oleic oils are not considered by many as nutritious as extra virgin olive oil. However, these hybrid oils are lighter in taste and good for high-heat cooking in recipes where you don't want the strong or overwhelming flavor of extra virgin olive oil.

From a health standpoint, extra virgin olive oil is head and shoulders above other olive oils—including pure, virgin, or light olive oils—because it is not treated with heat or chemicals, and it is richest in antioxidants and nutrients.

Monounsaturated fats are particularly celebrated for being heart-healthy. They have the ability to increase good HDL cholesterol, which is the cholesterol that actually helps clean your arteries as it sweeps through. Unlike other fats, monounsaturated fats are naturally high in antioxidants; thus, they are less prone to oxidation than the fats found in omega-3- and omega-6-rich oils. It is only when LDL cholesterol oxidizes that it encourages the formation of plaque deposits in our arterial lining, causing our blood vessels to clog, which of course paves the path to coronary heart disease. Monounsaturated fats can help prevent this ugly process. Studies have also shown that replacing omega-6-rich vegetable oils with monounsaturated fat-rich oils such as extra virgin olive oil can decrease blood pressure. So, yes, it's true, monounsaturated fats can most definitely help keep your heart healthy for a number of reasons. And, as a rule of thumb, any food that is "heart-friendly" is also "waist-friendly."

While all fats help slow digestion and create a feeling of satisfaction after being eaten, not all fats are healthy or waist-watcher friendly. Monounsaturated fats have the unique ability to boost your body's capability of utilizing the "super-slimming" omega-3 essential fats; thus, they indirectly help your body burn fat for energy and improve your cell's sensitivity to insulin. In addition, monounsaturated fats are considered anti-inflammatory.

Adding monounsaturated fats to your diet is a matter of replacing one fat with another. Use predominantly extra virgin olive oil and small amounts of high-oleic versions of canola oil, sunflower oil, and safflower oil for recipes requiring heat. For no-heat recipes, try omega-3-rich flax oil. Monounsaturated fats are by far the healthiest choice for cooking as they can withstand high-heat temperatures and are very low in saturated fat. (Butter is also very heat stable, but it is rich in saturated fat, which is neither heart- nor waist-friendly.) Finally, try to eat at least one serving of nuts, all-natural nut butter, seeds, all-natural seed butter, avocados, or olives everyday to be sure to get a healthy dose of monounsaturated fats and antioxidants.

## Fiber

Dietary fiber is the indigestible component found solely in carbohydrate-containing, plant-based foods; fiber is not found in foods derived from animals. This means dietary fiber comes from carbohydrate-containing vegetarian foods such as fruits, vegetables, beans, legumes, peas, flax, nuts, seeds, soybeans, whole grains, and potatoes (with the skins). The optimal diet for good health and disease prevention contains *at least* 30 to 35 grams of fiber a day, possibly as much as 40 grams. The average person eating the SAD (Standard American Diet) consumes a pitiful 12 to 15 grams a day. Low-carb dieters rarely consume optimal amounts of fiber unless they also take a fiber supplement, which we don't recommend.

A fiber-rich diet will contribute greatly to a healthier-looking, healthier-functioning body. First, fiber is nature's detoxifier. By promoting regular bowel movements, it helps remove toxins from your body before they can be absorbed, and a detoxified body has a healthy glow with clear, beautiful skin. Second, research shows high-fiber diets help lower cholesterol and reduce risk of heart disease. In fact, one study showed a 10-gram increase in dietary fiber can reduce your risk of heart disease by a very impressive 29 percent.[1] Third, studies show that eating more fiber can lower inflammation and C-reactive protein levels. (C-reactive protein is found in the blood, and research shows high levels of this protein correlate closely with heart disease.[2]) Fourth, fiber helps protect against diseases of the digestive system, including colon cancer, and also helps thwart type 2 diabetes by regulating blood sugar levels. Of course, almost any substance that is heart-healthy, offers protection against type 2 diabetes, *and* reduces inflammation is also going to have slimming properties too. Not surprisingly, fiber is just such a super-slimmer.

We like to think of fiber as a sponge because of its remarkable ability to soak up fat and sugar in your stomach, thus actually preventing some calories from being fully absorbed. But, fiber also forces your body to work harder during digestion. This increases thermogenesis (which makes you burn more calories) · and slows the digestion process down. The slower your meals are digested, the less fat-storing insulin will be released, the more stabilized your blood sugar level will be, and the more satiated you will feel after meals.

Feeling full and satisfied is absolutely essential to maintaining a healthy weight. As part of his surgical practice, Andy often performs bariatric (weight-loss) surgery, and one of his patients' most frequent complaints before undergoing weight-loss surgery is excessive hunger. One of the primary reasons weight-loss surgery works so well, enabling severely overweight men and women to lose one hundred or more pounds, is because the functional part of the patient's stomach is made much smaller, thus altering the complex hormonal actions that stimulate "head hunger." However, even average-weight or slightly overweight people who are not genetically predisposed to obesity still have a difficult time maintaining an "ideal" body weight if they can't obtain complete satisfaction or satiety from their meals. The majority of these people have the genetic makeup to be trim *if* they eat the right foods.

We once attended a seminar taught by world-renowned weight-loss sur-geon Dr. George Fielding. One of his high-profile patients, Muhammad Ali's daughter, Khaliah, candidly and bravely discussed her battle with obesity. Khaliah explained that hunger drove her to eat excessive quantities of food and prevented her from losing weight without surgery. Weight-loss surgery "cured" her insatiable hunger and enabled her to finally lose weight.

Weight-loss surgery brings us back to fiber. Fiber certainly does not have the drastic weight-loss-inducing capabilities of bariatric surgery, but it comes as close as any natural-food-containing substance can to help you maintain a healthy weight without feeling hungry. Fiber-rich foods take up a lot of bulk and space in your stomach, and they work mechanically to help you feel full and stay satiated for hours after eating.

Unfortunately, but not surprisingly, fiber is not found in the majority of the packaged processed foods people typically eat. There is a simple rule of thumb when reading food labels. Read the Nutrition Facts and check the fiber content relative to the total carbohydrate content to follow. Choose foods containing at least 3 grams of fiber per 25 grams of total carbohydrate. This rule of thumb usually works pretty well, except for the foods that have been artificially pumped with fiber. Keep in mind you will always be better off eating a whole food rather than a processed food "made from whole food." In other words, choose oatmeal rather than a processed cereal that is "made from oats." And, of course, realize that adding extra fiber to a processed food doesn't make the food nutritionally stellar. This brings us to the subject of fiber supplements.

If fiber is so great, why not just chew a fiber pill and be done with it? Here's the deal: fiber is very important for weight loss, but the foods that *naturally* contain fiber are also very nutritious "whole" foods rich in a multitude of sub-stances such as phytochemicals, antioxidants, vitamins, and minerals that all work synergistically to promote good health *and* a healthy metabolism. Fiber supplements don't work for the same reason you can't substitute a multivita-min for a balanced whole foods diet. Your body knows the difference.

The easiest way to effortlessly consume 30 to 35 grams of fiber a day is to be sure to eat at least one fruit with breakfast and one *large* serving of vegetables with lunch or dinner. This will automatically provide you with approximately 10 grams of fiber. You also want to be sure to eat only *whole* grains (brown rice, millet, corn, oats, barley, quinoa, and sprouted whole grain or whole-grain bread) as opposed to processed grains, including white rice and those made with refined or enriched flour. Choose sprouted whole-grain breads and pastas over breads and pastas made with just whole-wheat flour. If you eat just two servings of *whole* grains a day, you'll get another 8 grams of fiber. Eating just two one-half servings of beans (including soybeans) or legumes will provide you with an additional 7 or 8 grams of fiber a day. Eat one serving of nuts or seeds and you'll have another 4 grams or so. Finally, if you eat your flax serving in seed form, you'll add 5 more grams of fiber to your diet.

## Antioxidants and Phytochemicals

Nutritionists have been recommending we eat more fruits and vegetables for years. More recently, they've been touting the benefits of other plant-based foods such as beans, nuts, seeds, soy, and whole grains, as diets rich in these foods also appear to reduce the risk of a number of diseases, including cancer, heart disease, and high blood pressure, especially when compared with meat-heavy diets. What else makes them so healthy? Research shows that the many different types of antioxidants and phytochemicals found in these foods act as powerful ammunition in the war against age-related diseases, and, excitingly, their anti-inflammatory benefits offer tantalizing insight into the role they can play in weight management.

Antioxidants and phytochemicals are micronutrients that work synergistically to keep your body in tip-top form, internally and externally. Without going heavily into the scientific data, antioxidants are substances that protect your cells from the damage caused by unstable molecules known as free radicals. Free radicals allowed to run amok can wreck havoc on your body and your appearance. Antioxidants come to the rescue by interacting with and stabilizing free radicals and by preventing some of the damage the free radicals otherwise might cause. Simply put, antioxidants work to prevent oxidative stress. While oxidative stress can activate the immune system, which may be helpful in the short term, the cascading inflammatory process that results from immune-system activation can cause a lot of harm too. When inflammation is allowed to run unchecked, it can lead to disease, which may help explain why certain chronic conditions such as Alzheimer's and arthritis increase as we get older.

Examples of antioxidants include beta-carotene, lycopene, and vitamins A, C, and E. While some animal foods contain antioxidants, plant-based foods are by far the richest and most abundant sources.

Phytochemicals such as plant sterols and flavonoids are similar to antioxidants but are *only* found in plant-based foods. Scientific evidence proves phytochemicals help prevent and treat at least four leading causes of premature death, including cancer, diabetes, hypertension, and cardiovascular disease.[3]

Phytochemicals from plant foods also behave like antioxidants to reduce oxidative stress. Examples of phytochemicals include isoflavones in soy, cocoa in chocolate, lignans in flaxseed, and resveratrol in red wine.

By ramping up your nutrient intake and providing your body with a flood of many different antioxidants and phytochemicals throughout the day, you can take control over the amount of oxidation that damages the cells inside and outside your body. If you reduce oxidized molecules in your body, you will make yourself healthier, improve your body's ability to burn fat, and even improve the appearance of your skin.

Because there are so many different types and because antioxidants and phytochemicals work synergistically and in tandem with many other naturally occurring chemicals, it is impossible to isolate any one particular antioxidant or phytochemical as the absolute best one. In fact, some studies even show harmful effects from taking isolated antioxidant or phytochemicals in supplement form. The best and safest way to get the full spectrum of these important micronutrients is to eat a variety-rich, whole foods diet everyday. Remember, processed foods do not contain antioxidants or phytochemicals, at least not in their naturally occurring form.

In addition to eating phytochemical- and antioxidant-rich plant-based foods such as nuts, seeds, whole grains, beans, fruits, and soy, it's essential to try and eat as many vegetables as possible everyday.

Why all the fuss over vegetables? Vegetables are notably calorie poor, fiber rich, and loaded with nutrients, an ideal combination for the perfect weight-management tool. All these features help you control your weight effectively and effortlessly. Being low in calories, vegetables enable you to eat lots of volume without consuming excess energy. And the high-fiber content helps fill your stomach faster and limits the total amount of food consumed while simultaneously slowing digestion, thus helping you feel full and satiated for hours on end. The presence of many nutrients plus other phytochemicals and antioxidants in vegetables supplies your body with the substances necessary to boost energy production within your muscle cells, reduce inflammation, and reduce oxidative stress. This gives you a natural feeling of vitality and the energy to become more active, helping to burn more energy throughout the day.

You want to eat a wide variety too. Think kaleidoscope colors. By eating a rainbow of vegetables, you'll obtain a unique set of antioxidants and phytochemicals from each vegetable. The more variety the better!

As long as vegetables are properly prepared, most grown-up palates are pleasantly surprised at how delicious they truly are. By preparing vegetables and salads with a little bit of healthy fat (think nuts, olives, extra virgin olive oil, seeds, flax oil, walnut oil, and such), you'll greatly enhance the flavor, increase your satiety, and even boost the absorption of many nutrients. Keep in mind that fat is one of the best natural substances known to convey the flavor of food most effectively, which is one reason why diet-style steamed asparagus tastes so bland compared to asparagus that is roasted with just a little bit of extra virgin olive oil. Besides, the assimilation of fat-soluble vitamins such as A, D, E, and K, as well as certain phytochemicals such as lycopene, actually requires the presence of a little bit of dietary fat. A fascinating study published by the *American Journal of Clinical Nutrition* showed people who consumed salads with fat-free salad dressing absorbed far less of the helpful phytochemicals and vitamins from spinach, lettuce, tomatoes, and carrots than those who consumed their salads with a salad dressing containing fat.[4] This is certainly good news for your taste buds! On top of this, dietary fat actually activates a satiety hormone called CCK (cholecystokinin) that acts like an appetite suppressant, sending the message to your brain that you are full. Bottom line, eat your vegetables, but be sure to eat them with a little bit of healthy fat for optimal taste *and* health.

What about fruit? We can certainly appreciate the nutritional benefits of fruit, but fruits pack more sugar, less fiber, and less total nutrients per calorie than vegetables. While you can pretty much eat vegetables with abandon, this isn't necessarily the case with fruit. In fact, since fruits are less satisfying than vegetables, you often need to eat twice or even three times the amount of fruit calories to get the same level of satiety you get from vegetables. And since many people eat fruit alone (for snacks) without any additional dietary fat, you don't get the same level of satisfaction or even nutrient absorption as you get from eating vegetables prepared with a little bit of fat. It's good to eat one or two servings of fruit a day, but you don't need more unless you are physically active, in which case fruit is an ideal way to boost your calorie and energy consumption while ensuring optimal nutrient and antioxidant intake.

To cover your antioxidant and phytochemical bases, aim to eat at least one large serving of vegetables with lunch and dinner; you can even try to incorporate vegetables into your breakfast or snack. Try to eat at least one fruit a day too. If you are exceptionally active, you might want to eat two or three fruits a day. You also want to eat a variety of other plant-based foods, including all varieties of whole grains, nuts, all-natural nut butters, seeds, beans, legumes, and soy (such as edamame beans, soy milk, and tofu). Wine, green tea, coffee, and dark chocolate also contain antioxidant benefits.

## Heart-Healthy Animal Protein

While carbs and fats have come under much dietary scrutiny, protein has, for unclear reasons, managed to remain unscathed. This is unfortunate because the average American routinely consumes excess quantities of protein, especially in the form of saturated-fat-rich animal foods. (At the center of most American dinner plates still squats, to be blunt, a hunk of meat.) What most pro-protein diet books don't tell you is that you can get the same benefit from other foods that you get from animal protein but without the negative effects. The bottom line is that eating excessive quantities of protein serves no health benefit, yet it can take the place of other nutrient-rich whole foods that *could* benefit your health. You can eat only so much in one day. If you routinely consume excess amounts of protein-rich animal foods, then those foods are, in essence, pushing other healthful, plant-based whole foods such as vegetables, beans, whole grains, and nuts right off your plate.

You really only need about ½ gram of protein per pound of body weight each day. This means a woman who weighs 120 pounds only needs about 60 grams of protein a day. In comparison to vegetarian foods, animal-derived foods are jam-packed with protein. It takes only a very small amount of these foods to meet your protein quota. For example, if a woman eats one cup of yogurt (11 grams protein), 6 ounces of chicken, fish, or lean beef (40 grams of protein), and 1½ ounces of cheese (10 grams protein), she's already eaten 60 grams of protein. Most women get far more than this amount eating the contemporary American diet.

The average person eating the average modern-day diet is most likely consuming extra protein from animal foods such as beef, dairy, and chicken, which contain very few antioxidants, zero phytochemicals, zero fiber, and only a smidgen of essential fats (with the exception of fish, which is loaded with omega-3 fats). But really, the main "beef" we have with animal protein is that many sources contain lots of artery-clogging saturated fat. Diets rich in saturated fat are proven to increase your risk of heart disease. Any food that is bad for your heart health is also bad for your waistline.

The reason we titled this section "Heart-Healthy Animal Protein" is because any animal foods you eat should be low in saturated fat, which means choosing the leanest cuts of meat, avoiding marbled meats, meticulously trimming all visible fat from meats, avoiding the skin on poultry, and eating low-fat dairy or limited amounts of full-fat dairy. (Full-fat dairy foods do pack a powerful flavor punch, so don't avoid them altogether.)

As for eggs, yolks and all, especially organic omega-3 eggs, they are very low in saturated fat and can certainly be included in a heart-healthy diet. Don't worry about the cholesterol in eggs either, since the three main dietary factors that contribute most to elevated blood cholesterol are trans fats, saturated fat, and refined carbohydrates; one egg only contains 1.5 grams of saturated fat with zero trans fats and zero refined carbs. You'll notice we use plenty of eggs in the recipe section of the book, and we don't recommend egg whites or egg substitutes. If it ain't yolk, don't fix it!

In becoming protein savvy, it's also important to know some dietary proteins are "complete," meaning they contain nine of the essential amino acids for the dietary needs of humans, and others are "incomplete," meaning they lack one or more of the nine essential amino acids. Animal foods such as meat, poultry, fish, eggs, and dairy are considered complete sources of protein. With the exception of soy, vegetable proteins are incomplete sources. However, even the strictest vegetarians, vegans, can still get the essential amino acids their bodies need if they are careful to consume the right balance of plant-based foods (more on this later). In defense of meat, it does contain significant amounts of iron, zinc, and vitamins B6 and B12, which happen to be essential nutrients strict vegetarians may have to supplement their diets with. To sum things up, heart-healthy animal proteins that are low in saturated fat can certainly be part of a healthy diet, but there is no need to overdo it. We suggest you mix things up a bit by getting protein from animal and plant-based sources every day.

For optimal health and a trimmer waistline, it is best to eat animal protein in moderation (ideally no more than two servings a day) and choose only heart-healthy sources that are low in saturated fat. Heart-healthy animal sources of protein include low-fat dairy products, omega-3 eggs (which are actually very low in saturated fat), skinless poultry, and the leanest cuts of beef, lamb, and pork. You might also try ostrich, bison, venison, or elk as super-lean, heart-healthy, and surprisingly delectable alternatives to saturated-fat-rich beef. Also, use butter, cream, sour cream, and full-fat dairy in small amounts. Finally, choose grass-fed and organic animal sources since they have less toxins and less saturated fat than conventionally raised animals.

## Plant-Based Protein

You don't have to be a vegetarian to reap the numerous overlapping benefits of vegetarian foods. Nor do you need to nosh on rubbery tasting "not" dogs and "fakin" bacon. You can eat real whole foods that are plant-based, nutritious, good sources of protein, and, yes, even delicious. Common protein-rich plant foods include nuts and nut butters, seeds and seed butters, beans, legumes, tofu, soybeans, edamame beans, tempeh, and soy milk. But, since protein is an essential part of plant cells, at least some amount of protein is found in *all* plant foods, including vegetables.

The primary reason you should look for ways to incorporate plant-based sources of protein into your diet is because all plant-based sources of protein are anti-inflammatory, all are very low in artery-clogging saturated fat, and all are rich in an array of antioxidants, phytochemicals, and even fiber. Furthermore, many plant-based proteins contain calcium that the majority of animal proteins lack. (Dairy is one exception.)

As mentioned earlier, incomplete plant-based proteins can be easily combined so that they supply adequate amounts of all the amino acids. For example, although beans and brown rice are both quite rich in protein, each lacks one or more of the essential amino acids. Yet when you combine beans and brown rice with each other, you form a complete protein that is a good substitute for meat.

This brings us to the joy of soy. Healthful soy foods include soybeans, edamame beans, soy milk, tofu, and tempeh. (Note: *Soybean oil* is NOT a healthy food since it has been heavily refined, and most of the nutrients have been burned out during exposure to high-heat temperatures used during the refinement process.) Soy contains all of the essential amino acids, making it the only plant protein that approaches or equals animal foods in providing a complete source of protein. And unlike most animal protein foods, soy is low in artery-clogging saturated fat. In human studies, soy has been proven to lower bad LDL cholesterol, decrease overall cholesterol absorption, and lower triglycerides— all contributing to improved heart health.[5] Soy even contains both omega-3 and omega-6 essential fats in their natural, unrefined form and in the perfect ratio.

Even more, soy contains anti-inflammatory fats that help fight disease, plus phytoestrogens that work to partially inhibit your body's own excess estrogen hormones and thereby reduce your risk of developing hormone-sensitive cancers such as breast and prostate cancers. In fact, no other dietary factor is more protective in preventing prostate cancer than soy. (This means "real" men should eat tofu!) The isoflavones in soy help women because they actually bind to estrogen receptors in cells and act like natural selective estrogen receptor modulators (SERMs); they take up parking space in your estrogen receptors, preventing excess inappropriate estrogen activity that increases the risk of breast cancer. Because soy isoflavones possess some "good" estrogenic properties, they can help ease maddening menopausal symptoms while at the same time reduce the risk of certain hormone-sensitive cancers.

Soy's waist-whittling properties are numerous. For one, soy comes in a nutrient-packed, low-calorie package containing ultra-slimming fiber. You'll simply feel more satisfied after eating soy compared to eating meat. And because soy is slowly digested, you will have fewer food cravings and feel full and satisfied longer after meals. Another reason soy helps with weight loss is because it contains less essential amino acids than animal protein and very few carbohydrates, so it causes a smaller insulin response. In addition, soy stimulates the release of glucagon to a greater extent than animal protein. (Glucagon mobilizes stored carbohydrates from your liver to keep your brain fueled with a constant supply of energy, thereby eliminating hunger and fatigue.) Soy really is one of the best little-known secrets to losing weight without hunger.

Aim to mix up your proteins by adding more protein-rich plant-based foods to your diet. Protein-rich plant foods include nuts and nut butters, seeds and seed butters, beans, whole grains, legumes, tofu, soybeans, edamame beans, tempeh, and soy milk. Try to consume soy protein several times a week. Avoid highly processed soy-based fake meats, soy protein isolate, and textured vegetable protein.

## "Whole" Carbs

Carbohydrates are the macronutrient responsible for supplying most of our energy; they are our bodies' first choice when it needs refueling. The reason we innately crave carbs is because we crave nutrition, and, in nature, whole carbs are one of our best sources of nutrition. Whole carbs provide vitamins to support a healthy immune system, minerals to assist with proper cell function, antioxidants and phytochemicals to fend off disease and inflammation, and fiber to naturally regulate hunger and appetite. Our bodies instinctively know whole carbs are healthy, which is one reason why food cravings can become unbearable on a low-carb diet. However, carbs can be either slimming or fattening, depending on which ones you choose to eat and how much you eat.

Slimming carbs found in their natural, unrefined "whole" form are loaded with essential nutrients, fiber, antioxidants, and phytochemicals that stoke your metabolism and support a healthy body in general. They are also slowly digested, thus they help keep blood sugar levels stable and hunger suppressed for hours. Whole carbs are difficult to overeat because they stimulate the digestive system's distention nerves, which then send nerve impulses to your brain via your vagus nerve to calm your appetite—so you simply feel too full to overeat! Need proof? An Australian study showed that 240 calories of plain boiled potatoes (which are whole carbs and rather bulky) satisfied test subjects an astounding *seven times* as much as a very nonbulky 240-calorie croissant serving. The boiled potato/

croissant study clearly demonstrates one reason why food bulk is so important in weight management—the more space a food takes up in your stomach, the more full you feel and the fewer calories you eat.[6]

Fattening carbs, on the other hand, are highly refined and stripped of all the good stuff we need to support a speedy metabolism and stay healthy. For example, to make enriched wheat flour, whole-wheat kernels are first stripped of their nutrient and antioxidant-rich germ, and then their fiber-rich bran is removed, leaving behind nutrient-poor, fiber-free, calorie-rich starch that is then "enriched" with synthetic nutrients your body can't utilize in the same manner as the naturally occurring nutrients found within the whole-wheat kernel. Even worse, digestion of empty refined carbohydrates calls on your body's own store of vitamins, minerals, and enzymes for proper metabolism. For example, B vitamins are absent in most refined carbohydrates, yet the breakdown and metabolism of carbohydrates cannot take place without B vitamins!

If all this isn't bad enough, fattening carbs enter our bloodstreams very quickly, igniting a nasty flood of insulin that stimulates hunger and promotes fat storage. It's no wonder carbs have gotten such a bad rap, since the major- ity of the ones most of us eat are from refined fattening sources that include white rice, white pasta, high fructose corn syrup, sugar, and baked goods made with enriched or bleached flour such as bagels, breads, crackers, snack foods, and muffins. The solution is not to eliminate carbs from our diets but to simply change the type we are eating!

Choosing slimming whole carbs is super easy. Select carbohydrate foods as close to their natural state as possible. All fruits and vegetables are whole carbs. Potatoes, yams, and sweet potatoes are whole carbs. Beans, lentils, legumes, and hummus are whole carbs (they are also good sources of vegetarian protein). Whole grains such as whole wheat, amaranth, barley, brown rice, corn, quinoa, rye, oatmeal, wheat germ, wild rice, bulgar, kamut, and millet are all whole carbs. Baked goods made with whole-grain flour are also considered whole carbs. Whole-grain pastas are whole carbs. Breads and pastas made with sprouted whole grains are whole carbs and are even better choices than those made with whole-grain flour. The bottom line is, a plethora of whole carbs exist.

We hope by now you are encouraged to think differently about food, in addition to realizing good nutrition and good-tasting "real" food (not "diet" food!) can indeed go hand in hand. We also hope we've shed some light on just how easy it can be to achieve and maintain a healthy body weight without deprivation dieting and without feeling hungry.

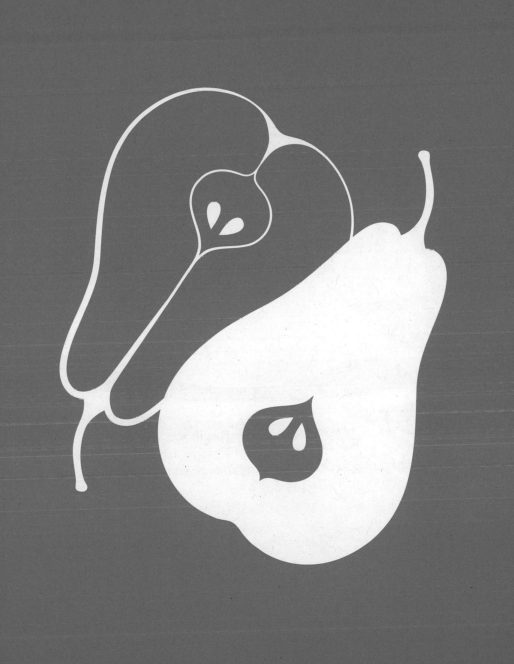

# the flexitarian lifestyle

· · · · · · · · · · · · · · · · · · · · · · · · · · · · · · · · · · · · · · · · · · · · · · · · · · · · ·

## eating vegetarian style part-time

**The term "flexitarian"** is new to the urban diction-
ary and means different things to different people. Here's what the definition
means to us: a flexitarian is an omnivore who maintains a predominantly
plant-based diet but still eats moderate-size servings of land and sea animal
foods one or two times a day (including fish, shellfish, eggs, dairy, meat,
and chicken). Why do things halfway? Why not just go all out and commit to
becoming a vegetarian or vegan? Mostly we fear encouraging a strict vege-
tarian/vegan-style diet is practically begging for all-out rebellion from the
general population. Having said that, if you eat a well-balanced plant-based
diet, you can pretty much eliminate meat from your diet and still be perfectly
healthy, assuming you also supplement with vitamin B12. But don't worry,
we're not suggesting you become a vegan.

In comparison, the flexitarian approach we support places a healthful and appealing emphasis on a wide variety of unrefined whole foods, ranging from grains, vegetables, nuts, seeds, fruits, beans, legumes, and soy, while offering an alluring allowance of animal foods. You won't feel deprived or shortchanged by adopting a flexitarian diet because there are so many options, even for the most passionate of meat lovers.

Environment and animal rights aside, there are four key health reasons for encouraging a predominately (but not entirely) whole foods, plant-based diet. In comparison to diets rich in animal foods, a whole foods, plant-based diet with moderate allowance for animal foods will 1) be substantially lower in saturated fat, 2) be richer in micronutrients such as antioxidants and phytochemicals, 3) contain substantially more fiber, and 4) be naturally less calorie dense. If such a diet also contains the optimal ratio of omega-3 to omega-6 fats, it will also be highly anti-inflammatory. This way of eating will help keep you slim, reduce the symptoms of a wide variety of inflammatory conditions, and offer protection against certain types of cancer, heart disease, type 2 diabetes, and high blood pressure. And for the scores of women who experience ovulatory infertility, findings from the Harvard-led Nurses' Health Study, which included more than 18,000 women, indicate that getting more protein from plants and less from animals can improve the chances of conception substantially; the study showed that replacing 25 grams of animal protein with 25 grams of plant protein was related to a 50 percent lower risk of ovulatory infertility.[1]

## Plant-Based Diets Help Keep Saturated-Fat Intake Low

The vast majority of saturated fat in the standard American diet is derived from animal foods. While many animal foods such as free-range chicken and their eggs, and lean cuts of meat from grass-fed beef offer important nutrients, others such as bacon, sausage, and luncheon meats virtually have no place in the diet because they contain too much saturated fat and too few nutrients to justify eating. In the recipes included in this book, we do use small amounts of saturated-fat-rich butter, cream, and full-fat cheese as flavor enhancers, but we are very careful to keep the total saturated-fat content of our recipes low. Saturated fat is harmful for a variety of reasons; it's notoriously harmful for heart health, and it also increases inflammation, which hinders your body's ability to burn fat and exacerbates the symptoms of a wide variety of inflammatory conditions ranging from arthritis to multiple sclerosis.

Eating a diet rich in saturated fat can also interfere with insulin function and contribute to insulin insensitivity, which means that every time you eat a carbohydrate/saturated-fat meal combo, you'll produce more fat-storing insulin than is desirable. This internal trend can pave the path to obesity and type 2 diabetes. Low-carb acolytes are notorious for consuming excessive amounts of saturated-fat-rich animal foods in the name of weight loss; but, ironically, the animal fats that low-carb dieters tend to consume in excess actually interfere with their body's natural fat-burning capabilities for other reasons too. For example, saturated fats ignite the activity of a protein called NF-Kappa B, which prevents the transport of glucose to your cells, thus triggering hunger and promoting inflammation, which slows metabolism. In comparison to meals rich in essential fats or monounsaturated fats, meals rich in saturated fats also produce lower levels of the satiety hormone leptin. The take-home message is that animal fat is not desirable. The less-saturated animal fat you eat, the better—for general health and weight management.

## Plant-Based Sources of Saturated Fat Are Healthier Than Animal Sources

Even if you were a strict vegan and ate zero animal foods, your diet is unlikely to be free from saturated fat. Plant-based sources of saturated fat include coconut, coconut oil, and coconut milk, palm kernel oil, cocoa butter, and palm oil. These plant-based saturated fats crop up in a number of commercially prepared products. For example, cocoa butter is found in commercial chocolate. Coconut and palm oils are found in anything from nondairy whipped toppings, microwave popcorn, and artificial coffee creamers to unhealthful vegetable shortenings, cookies, pies, and cakes. Most of the plant-based saturated fats found in packaged foods have been highly processed and exposed to chemical solvents, making them no healthier than the saturated fat from animals. The exception is whole food coconut, coconut milk, and unrefined *extra virgin* coconut oil, which is both solvent and chemical free. Let's explain in more detail.

Unrefined whole coconut meat, coconut milk, and coconut oil do have a lot of saturated fat. However, not all saturated fats are equal, and the saturated fats from coconuts actually have a different biochemical makeup than the saturated fats found in animal foods. Epidemiological studies strongly suggest the composition of saturated fat found in *unprocessed* coconut foods is not as harmful to heart health as the saturated fat from animal foods.[2] So, even though many people automatically assume *all* saturated fats increase the risk of heart disease, population studies of people living in the Pacific Islands and Asia, whose diets are naturally very high in coconut oil, show surprisingly low incidences of cardiovascular disease among the region. In 1992, researchers reviewed some of the epidemiological and experimental data regarding coconut-eating groups and noted that the available population studies show dietary coconut oil does not lead to high-serum cholesterol nor to high coronary heart disease mortality or morbidity.[3] Of course, it's imperative to put things into perspective and point out that the people of the Pacific Islands and Asia who enjoy coconut foods eat a predominantly whole foods diet consisting of a wide variety of unrefined foods.

There's even more good news about coconuts; unlike the saturated fat from animal foods, plant-based coconuts and extra virgin coconut oil that has not been refined will contain those beneficial phytochemicals we talked about in the last chapter (remember, animal foods *do not* contain phytochemicals) in addition to antiaging antioxidants, especially vitamin E. Coconuts also contain lauric acid, which has very powerful antibacterial/antiviral properties and is well known to support a healthy immune system and even facilitate brain function. It's very important to purchase only cold-pressed, extra virgin coconut oil that is unrefined, unbleached, and undeodorized to ensure you are getting a high-quality fresh oil containing the wide array of nutrients found within the whole coconut. You can often tell the difference between a high-quality coconut oil and a cheaper quality oil by conducting your own unofficial "sniff" test; high-quality oils will have the distinctive pleasant tropical smell of coconuts in comparison to commercial coconut oils that have been refined, deodorized, and bleached, and thus have no pleasant tropical aroma.

## Plant-Based, Whole Foods Diets Are Rich in Phytochemicals

As we mentioned in the last chapter, only plant-based whole foods contain disease-fighting, anti-inflammatory, and metabolism-supporting phytochemicals. These substances are one of nature's most powerful antioxidants, and they work to prevent both the internal and external oxidation that accelerates visible and cellular aging. The prefix *phyto* literally means "plant," so phytochemicals are nutrients found only in plant foods. Again, animal foods contain zero phytochemicals.

Plant-based foods contain literally hundreds of different phytochemicals that work together on many different cellular levels to optimize health. They also enable your body to burn fat for fuel faster by stimulating PPARs (peroxisome proliferator-activated receptors). PPARs reduce fat-storing insulin levels and even lower cholesterol. Since these powerful health-promoting, metabolism-supporting nutrients work synergistically, it's important to eat a wide variety of plant-based whole foods each day in order to maximize your consumption. If you are eating a diet consistently high in animal foods, then the animal foods will be taking the place of phytochemical-containing, plant-based foods, which

# the freshest coconut oil in the world

**If you were** to look for a fine wine, you'd first want to select one from a top region, and then you'd want to ensure that every step of production, from the critical harvesting to the clarification (the final step before bottling, where the solid particles are removed from the wine), was top-notch. The same principles apply to selecting fresh oils, including coconut oil. We have come to rely on Barlean's Organic Extra Virgin Coconut Oil (http://www.barleans.com) for supplying the best-tasting coconut oil. In addition, we have personally met the Barlean family, and we know their commitment to quality. For example, they use only hand-selected and fresh-picked coconuts for their oil; coconuts that are immature or overripe or that have fallen to the ground are not used. Barlean's coconut oil is also carefully cold-pressed to preserve nutrients from the whole coconut and is processed without the use of chemical solvents or harsh mechanical filtration. You will taste the difference, guaranteed!

We feel coconut in moderation is certainly acceptable on an otherwise low-saturated-fat, whole foods diet. For example, we use small amounts of coconut milk to add flavor to certain ethnic foods, and we often substitute extra virgin coconut oil for butter in baking recipes to cut down on animal-based saturated fat. Extra virgin coconut oil is a great substitute for butter in many baked goods recipes because, just like butter, coconut oil is very heat stable, so it resists oxidation and can withstand high-heat temperatures. Luckily, a little bit of coconut oil or milk goes a long way to add luxurious flavor to foods, so we don't need to use much!

Finally, don't relegate coconut oil just to the kitchen! The oil is actually an ideal nourishment for your skin, as it helps protect against oxidation and the formation of free radicals. Ivy always keeps a jar in the bathroom and uses it as an all-natural alternative to pricey, chemical-laden, conventional beauty products for a body moisturizer, body scrub (she mixes the oil with brown sugar), face mask (she mixes it with raw honey), cuticle treatment, and eye-makeup remover. Coconut oil will naturally help your skin look smoother and younger for a fraction of the cost of your current beauty products!

is one reason why it's important to be conscious of limiting your intake of animal foods and actively look to increase your intake of plant-based foods.

## Choose the Highest-Quality Animal Foods

You should think quality over quantity when it comes to animal foods. Consider the diet of the animals you eat, because the animal's diet reflects the health of the animal, which ultimately affects the health of the person who eats it. By choosing organic animal products, you are taking one giant step toward quality and one giant step toward healthier animals. Keep in mind that nonorganic animal foods often contain considerably more toxins than nonorganic plant foods simply because they are higher up the food chain—the higher up the food chain you go, the greater the chance of acquiring toxins found in the environment. Toxic overload can contribute to inflammation and a host of other problems. Eating organic animal protein will reduce your exposure to pesticide residues, synthetic hormones, and antibiotics.

But consuming the highest-quality animal products goes a step beyond simply choosing organic. One of the reasons so many people in modern society have such an essential fatty acid imbalance is because the vast majority of animals we eat are from conventionally raised sources. Modern conventional farming is designed to quickly grow and fatten animals at a very unnatural rate; the animals eat a calorie-rich grain-based diet (rich in omega-6 fat) rather than the calorie-poor, but nutrient-rich, grass-based diet (containing a balanced ratio of omega-6 to omega-3 fats) that they would naturally consume in the wild. Inappropriately feeding animals a deviant diet of dry grain is a direct contributor to those animals developing pathogens such as E. coli (in cattle) and salmonella (in poultry). Mad cow disease is unknown among cattle fed entirely on pasture and hay.

You simply can't separate the health of the animal you eat from your own health. Cows evolved to eat grass not grains. When factory-farmed cows eat grains, they aren't as healthy as they would otherwise be, and unhealthy cows get sick (and need antibiotics). So, even if ranchers feed cows organic grain, it doesn't mean the grain is optimal for cow health; and, ultimately, it's not desirable for the cow-eating consumer's health either. The same logic applies to humans and sugar; if push comes to shove, we'd rather eat organic sugar over regular sugar, but eating organic-stamped sugar cubes will never be what the doctor ordered for good health. Since the composition of the fats present in eggs, chicken, and meat reflects the foods the animals consume, animal foods raised on conventional, commercial grain feeds (even organic grain feed!) have less than desirable fat profiles. Grain-fed beef and the milk from grain-fed cows contain considerably more pro-inflammatory omega-6 fat and markedly less omega-3 fat compared to grass-fed cattle; the total fat content in the grain-fed animals is approximately twice that of grass-fed counterparts, and the saturated-fat content is also notably higher. Grass-fed beef also contains CLA (conjugated linoleic acid), a "good" fat with promising research suggesting it might help protect against obesity, type 2 diabetes, and certain types of cancer, including breast cancer.[4] Many nutritional supplement companies have caught wind of the potential benefits of CLA and now produce synthetic versions, but we suggest you avoid synthetic CLA, as research shows these artificial supplements might actually do more harm than good.[5] The most natural and effective way to increase your intake of CLA is to eat the meat and dairy products of grass-fed animals.

Don't confuse grass-fed to mean organic though. While certified organic animals are fed 100-percent organic feed and cannot be given hormones or antibiotics for any reason, organic does not necessarily mean grass-fed. Ideally, you would choose organic, grass-finished, or 100-percent grass-fed beef. While chicken and pigs do rather well on grain diets, these animals are still healthier when they have adequate access and free range to green plants. This means looking for the words "free range" or, better yet, "pastured" or "grass-fed"—which means the animals had more than adequate access to green grass—when buying chicken, eggs, and pork. (Check out our resource section for information on where to buy healthful animal foods.)

## Striking a Balance

Becoming a flexitarian is all about striking a balance. It's also about options and opening yourself up to a fresh new world of culinary adventures. It's about exploring tasty new foods and testing trendy ethnic-cooking techniques. You'll have the freedom and flexibility to enjoy high-quality animal foods every single day, but you'll also eat more plant-based foods than you did in the past.

Here's how it works. First, you'll want to make sure you eat three balanced meals a day. At every meal you'll include a vegetable or fruit. You'll also add some sort of healthy plant-based fat at each of your three meals (such as avocados, nuts, seeds, nut butters, extra virgin olive oil, ground flaxseed or flax oil, walnut oil, etc.). You'll incorporate a serving of fiber-rich, whole food dense carbs (like potatoes with the skins on, beans, lentils, corn, barley, oatmeal, spelt, sprouted whole grain bread, and millet) at every meal too. Finally, you'll want to add a protein-rich vegetarian or low-saturated-fat animal food. Healthy animal foods that are low in saturated fat include fish, shellfish, lean cuts of meat from grass-fed beef, low-fat organic cheese, low-fat organic yogurt, low-fat organic kefir, omega-3 organic eggs from cage-free or pastured chickens, free-range or pastured organic chicken, and wild game such as bison, elk, and deer.

However, since you are trying to adopt the flexitarian lifestyle, you'll eat *at least* one vegetarian-style meal a day. This means you won't eat animal foods at breakfast, lunch *and* dinner—one of those three meals will be animal free. Assuming you aren't allergic to soy, you will find soy to be one of the easiest and most versatile substitutions for animal foods because it's the only nonanimal source of complete protein. Delicious soy foods include tofu, tempeh, edamame beans, soybeans, soy nuts, soy milk, and miso. But if soy is just truly not your thing, you can also form a complete protein by combining beans with brown rice, corn, seeds, wheat, or nuts, *or* by combining brown rice with beans, nuts, seeds, or wheat. Whatever you decide, be sure to eat three balanced meals and try to eat at least one vegetarian-style meal a day.

## Real World "Flexitarian" Eating

In part 2 of this book we offer plenty of quick and easy recipes using tofu, tempeh, beans, lentils, nuts, soybeans, and whole grains to help you get rolling with the flexitarian lifestyle we advocate. But, in the real world, it's not always practical to use an "official" recipe for every food you eat. Besides, being a flexitarian goes beyond adopting a few vegetarian meals. It encourages you to think outside the box by becoming flexible and creative with your cooking and eating. Real cooking isn't about obsessively following recipes; it's about developing a general understanding of food and about gaining a certain level of confidence in the kitchen. We certainly don't follow a recipe every time we eat a meal. In fact, a lot of times we just throw a few things together from the refrigerator (like leftovers), or we rely on store-bought, healthful, unprocessed foods as a base, such as a healthy soup or salad dressing made with all-natural ingredients, and then add a few fresh items to create an "almost homemade" dish. To show you just how easy it is to eat a healthy, whole foods diet and also add just one vegetarian-style meal a day to your diet, check out the three-day snapshot below of how Ivy typically eats and how she works her vegetarian-style meal into her flexible daily menu.

### Day 1

**Breakfast:** *Tofu Scramble* (page 106 or make up your own easy version) and one cup of coffee

**Lunch:** *Grilled organic mozzarella cheese and roasted carrots with fresh dill on toasted sprouted whole-grain bread* (Ivy had the roasted carrots with fresh dill for dinner the previous night, so she just stuffed the leftovers into a sandwich and added some cheese for a complete meal)

**Snack:** *Pumpkin Pie Smoothie* (page 99)

**Dinner:** *Baked salmon, spinach salad with roasted red pepper vinaigrette, corn on the cob, 1 glass of wine, and a small scoop all-natural organic ice cream*

## Day 2

**Breakfast:** *Crepes with Strawberry Filling (page 98) and one cup of coffee*

**Lunch:** *Black bean soup with low-fat crumbled feta cheese*

**Snack:** *Baby carrots dipped in store-bought hummus*

**Dinner:** Restaurant Seasons 52's (in Palm Beach Gardens) *Chef's Rustic Roasted Vegetable Plate with Grilled Tofu, Tabbouleh, and Autumn Corn Salad, 1 glass of wine and a few decadent bites of Old-Fashioned Carrot Cake*

## Day 3

**Breakfast:** *Individual Baked Omelet Soufflés with Leeks and Mushrooms (page 100) and 1 cup of coffee*

**Lunch:** *Corn on the cob, edamame beans, and Amy's All American Veggie Burger (Amy's-brand California Veggie Burger made without soy protein isolate or textured vegetable protein) topped with hummus and jarred roasted red peppers*

**Snack:** *1 LÄRABAR (which contains fruit, nuts, and spices—nothing else) and 1 cup of Starbuck's unsweetened Tazo Green Tea*

**Dinner:** *Pork Chops with Mole Sauce and Apples (page 154) with a side of Roasted Baby Carrots (155), 1 glass of Merlot, and Savory and Sweet Frozen Vanilla-Peach Custard (page 141)*

Hopefully this chapter has opened your eyes to a flexible and exciting new way of adding more vegetarian-style whole foods to your diet. We feel confident you can embrace the flexitarian diet with energetic enthusiasm simply by repeatedly reassuring yourself that animal foods are not off-limits. Remember, to strike a balance, be flexible, and be adventurous in your eating!

# fake and phony

### ignoring the health claims on processed food

**In general,** we like to focus on the positive and place emphasis on all of the numerous delicious whole foods you should eat rather than spend all of our effort bad-mouthing the nutrient-poor foods you shouldn't eat. However, the reality is that some foods are just so completely junky they simply deserve to be bad-mouthed—big time. We've decided "fake and phony" most accurately describes the junky foods you should avoid at all costs. Junk foods cheat you out of nutrition. Unfortunately, clever, profit-minded food manufacturers often mislead the customer into believing junk foods are health foods simply by splashing healthful-sounding buzz words on the front of food packages. A few examples of the sneaky misleading words we're talking about include "Made with Natural Flavors," "All Natural," "Zero Trans Fats," "Made with Whole Grains," "Cholesterol Free," "Low-Fat," "Sugar

Free," "Vegan," "Organic," etc. Not one of these descriptions assures that the food is, in fact, a nutrient-rich and healthy whole food. One of our biggest gripes with so many processed products advertised nowadays is the guise of healthfulness that comes at the expense of real whole food.

An overwhelming 90 percent of Americans' household food budget is spent on processed and packaged convenience foods, the majority of which are filled with additives and stripped of nutrients. Snatch a snack food from the grocery store shelf, reach for a box of cereal, or grab a frozen entrée from your freezer; read the ingredients—the endless list of nonnatural items is staggeringly shocking. While the seemingly simple solution would be to just avoid packaged foods altogether, we live in the real world, and we know just how challenging and time-consuming it can be to make every single meal from scratch. As we've mentioned previously, we're not food purists by any stretch, which means if there's an otherwise healthy, prepared, whole food item that tastes nearly as good as our homespun version (say, hummus, for example) you can bet we're gonna buy it and eat it. With the wide variety of tasty and truly healthful prepared and convenience items now available, you shouldn't feel guilty about taking shortcuts—we sure don't!

We often use packaged healthful foods (such as soups, sauces, or salad dressings) as a base and then mix in fresh ingredients for a more homemade taste. The catch is to know the difference between which foods are truly healthy and which ones are simply packaged and marketed to *appear* healthy. The goal of this chapter is to help you become a savvy in-the-know food shopper and learn to navigate the packaged food world with the confidence to know you are buying a healthy food rather than a junk food dressed up in a healthy-looking disguise.

## Read the Ingredients!!!

The ingredient list on a food label is the listing of each ingredient in descending order of predominance. The ingredient lists don't lie. The Nutrition Facts can be very misleading (more on that in a bit), but the ingredient list, by law, is truthful. The ingredient list on food labels is, without a doubt, the most important bit of information on the entire package. This means the ingredient list is more important than the total calories, total carbs, fiber, fat grams, sodium content, and cholesterol listed on the Nutrition Facts label. The ingredient list is where you'll find out what's really in the product and just how healthy it is—or isn't!

Healthful whole food ingredients are pretty clear cut; for example, peanuts are peanuts and tomatoes are tomatoes. We happen to have a jar of all-natural peanut butter in our pantry right now, and the ingredients include peanuts and salt. Can't get any simpler than that. We also have a jar of marinara sauce in our pantry, and the ingredients read as follows: imported Italian tomatoes, imported olive oil, fresh onions, salt, fresh garlic, fresh basil, black pepper, and oregano. Again, not one single unrecognizable ingredient—just pure and simple good food. However, this doesn't mean *all* brands of peanut butter and marinara sauce are healthy. For example, some peanut butters contain dreadful trans fats, and some marinara sauces are infused with high fructose corn syrup and soybean oil. Then, of course, there's the concern over ingredients you might not be familiar with such as ammonium sulfate, which, by the way, happens to be an inorganic chemical fertilizer that also serves double duty as a general-purpose food additive.

The rule here is to eliminate packaged foods containing ingredients you don't recognize as real food. The more complicated-sounding the ingredient is, the more likely it is not to be healthy. This means it's best to avoid foods containing ingredients such as artificial sweeteners with complex-sounding names like aspartame and saccharin, sugar alcohols with names like sorbitol, xylitol, and maltitol, MSG (which is short for monosodium glutamate), propyl gallate, potassium bromate, butylated hydroxyanisole (BHA), sodium nitrite, sulfites, hydrolyzed vegetable protein, FD&C colors, olestra, etc. You don't need to memorize a lengthy list to avoid these additives—just use common sense. If you don't recognize an ingredient as being a bona fide food, don't eat it. Ditch the chemical cuisine. It's really as simple as that.

## Four Empty-Calorie Ingredients to Avoid

While it is not necessary to memorize lists and lists of the "bad" chemical additives mentioned above, you should memorize and actively avoid four of the most highly prevalent, nonnutritive, empty-calorie ingredients used in packaged foods. The terrible four includes trans fats, omega-6-rich vegetable oils, refined flour, and refined sugars. These four ingredients are indeed fake and phony, especially because they can be completely misrepresented by marketing claims on food-package labels. For example, a food containing trans fats can still be advertised as "Cholesterol Free," even though trans fats are known to be more harmful than dietary cholesterol. They have been proven to increase total cholesterol, decrease "good" HDL cholesterol, increase "bad" LDL cholesterol, increase triglycerides, and impair artery dilation (all bad for your cardiovascular health!).[1] As another example, foods containing massive quantities of sugar can still be advertised as "Fat Free," even though sugars can be converted by your body into fat and even though sugar spikes insulin levels, making it more difficult for your body to burn fat for energy. Read on for the true 411 on the terrible foursome, including where they hide out and how to avoid them.

## Trans Fats

At one point, trans fats were praised as a "heart-healthy" alternative to saturated-fat-laden butter. Scientists now know better. In fact, in a 1993 study in the prestigious medical journal *Lancet*, almost 90,000 healthy women were followed for eight years. There was an astonishing 50 percent increased risk in heart attacks and deaths in those women who ate just 5.7 grams of trans fats a day versus those who ate 2.4 grams of trans fats a day.[2] Trans fats also increase inflammation and therefore exacerbate symptoms of a variety of conditions such as asthma, allergies, arthritis, fibromyalgia, and multiple sclerosis. And, of course, as we have mentioned before, anything that increases inflammation will slow your metabolism and make it more difficult for your body to burn fat for energy. On top of that, trans fats decrease sensitivity to insulin, making it easier for your body to store fat; and, if you store enough fat, you're more likely to develop type 2 diabetes. For young women desperate to have a baby, the bad news for trans fats worsens. Findings from an eight-year study following 18,000 women, led by doctors Walter Willett and Jorge Chavarro from the Harvard School of Public Health, showed that the more trans fat in the diet, the greater the likelihood of developing ovulatory infertility. The study saw an effect on fertility at daily trans fat intakes of just 4 grams—far less than the amount of trans fats the average American eating the standard American diet consumes in a typical day.[3]

According to the Institute of Medicine, the safe level of intake for trans fats is zero. These are the fats to assiduously avoid at all costs. Trans fats are clearly bad-boy players in the world of processed foods, and they are found in many vegetable shortenings, margarines, fried foods, and *any* packaged food product containing hydrogenated or partially hydrogenated oils in the list of ingredients. Although trans fats are listed on the Nutrition Facts, you can't completely trust the label for the absurd reason that government labeling laws allow foods containing one-half gram or less of trans fats per serving to state zero grams of trans fats on the Nutrition Facts. One-half gram is more than zero, and one-half gram here, one half gram there can add up over the course of a day, especially if you are eating more than a single serving of a food (which, of course, most people do). The simple solution is to carefully read the ingredient list and avoid all foods containing hydrogenated or partially hydrogenated oils.

## Omega-6-Rich Vegetable Oil

Omega-6-rich vegetable oils are classified as polyunsaturated fats and include corn oil, soybean oil, safflower oil, sunflower oil, sesame oil, cottonseed oil, and "pure" vegetable oil. In the past, nutritionists pretty much lumped all polyunsaturated oils into one category and deemed them healthy, simply because these oils are all low in saturated fat. Nutritionists once advised that since excessive intake of saturated fat was not optimal, vegetable oils naturally low in saturated fat were a heart-healthy alternative to saturated-fat-rich butter and lard, especially because polyunsaturated vegetable oils were known to lower cholesterol. While we have long known eating too much saturated fat isn't healthy, newer research proves not all polyunsaturated fats are nutritionally equivalent from a health standpoint. We now know eating an excessive amount of omega-6, polyunsaturated-rich vegetable oils will lower your good HDL cholesterol (the cholesterol that actually sweeps your arteries clean) and increase your bad LDL cholesterol (the cholesterol that clogs your arteries), thereby negatively affecting your cholesterol ratio and not providing nearly the heart protection researchers once thought. We also know an excess intake of omega-6 polyunsaturated fats, especially when not balanced with adequate omega-3 polyunsaturated fats, leads to a decreased sensitivity to insulin (thus making it more difficult for you to burn fat) and increased systemic inflammation, which further slows your metabolism and exacerbates the symptoms of numerous inflammatory conditions. Unbalanced essential fat intake has even been linked to serious degenerative conditions, including heart disease, several cancers, stroke, and vascular dementia.[4]

The ideal ratio of omega-6 to omega-3 fat is about two to four times more omega-6 fat than omega-3 fat. Yet most people in modern society eating a modern diet consume a very unhealthy fourteen to twenty times more omega-6 fat than omega-3 fat. This is partly due to food manufacturers replacing trans fats with omega-6-rich vegetable oils in an all-out effort to be able to market their products as "trans fat free." The ingredient list is especially important because a product marketed as "Trans Fat Free," "Cholesterol Free," or "Saturated Fat Free" can still be made exclusively from omega-6-rich (and undesirable) corn oil. Eating omega-6-rich corn oil (or any of the other conventional vegetable oils) does not protect you from heart disease nor does it help slim your waistline; omega-6-rich corn oil merely contributes unwelcome, empty, nonnutritive calories.

Ratios and empty calories aside, another reason to dislike vegetable oils is because the majority of conventional vegetable oils sitting on grocery store shelves and mixed into packaged foods are processed using very high temperatures. This is bad because heat damages the polyunsaturated fats within the vegetable oils, causing them to oxidize and turn rancid. The heat-refined vegetable oils are then exposed to chemical solvents and deodorizers to neutralize the rancid taste. On top of that, the antioxidants and phytochemicals found within the original whole food (such as the corn or soybean from which the oils were made) will have been burned out. This means vegetable oils are simply an empty-calorie, pro-inflammatory food with zero nutritional value.

What does this mean for you? It means you need to read the ingredient list on all packaged foods and avoid products containing corn oil, soybean oil, safflower oil, sunflower oil, sesame oil, cottonseed oil, and pure vegetable oil. Look instead for packaged foods made with extra virgin olive oil, canola oil, or high-oleic oils (including high-oleic canola oil, high-oleic sunflower oil, and high-oleic safflower oil). Extra virgin olive oil and expeller-pressed canola oil contain generous amounts of monounsaturated fats, which help optimize your cholesterol ratio and even boost your body's ability to metabolize omega-3 fats. Canola oil contains a significant amount of omega-3 fats, while olive oil is particularly rich in antioxidants as well as an anti-inflammatory substance called "squalene."

High-oleic oils are acceptable, as the grains that produce these oils have been transformed, through hybridization, to be low in omega-6 fat and high in monounsaturated fat. However, while high-oleic oils are light tasting and can withstand high-heat cooking, they don't contain all of the nutrients found within extra virgin olive oil or expeller-pressed canola oil, so they should be used in moderation. Look to incorporate more omega-3-rich oils such as flax oil and walnut oil into your no-heat recipes. (Just like omega-6 oils, the omega-3 oils are also heat sensitive so you don't want to cook with them.) And of course extra virgin olive oil remains one of your safest all-round oils for multiple purposes.

## Sugars

Sugar epitomizes the definition of an empty calorie. In simple terms, sugar is pure carbohydrate with zero vitamins, minerals, or enzymes to aid in its digestion. And, because large amounts of B vitamins and other nutrients are required to metabolize sugar, eating too much sugar can actually deplete your body of essential nutrients. Remember, you need nutrients to support a healthy metabolism. This means eating sugar exhausts your body of the nutrients it needs to burn fat for energy. And a nutrient deficiency means you're much more likely to experience those nagging, gnawing, harassing food cravings. Even worse, sugars also cause chemical reactions inside your body that promote inflammation. Sugar can quickly be converted into fat if it is not immediately burned for energy, and the type of fat your body manufactures from sugar is a very harmful type of fat—a specific saturated fat called "palmitic acid." This type of bad fat is directly linked to increased risk of heart disease. Plus, palmitic acid increases inflammation, which further slows your metabolism and exacerbates the symptoms of a wide variety of inflammatory conditions.

Insulin resistance is another complication of eating too much sugar. If you repeatedly eat large amounts of sugar, you force your pancreas to work overtime to produce and pump out large amounts of insulin, all in an effort to keep your blood sugar at a healthy level. (High blood sugar levels are not desirable for anyone.) Such chronic elevated levels of insulin can cause your cells to become insulin resistant over time, which not only compounds the initial injury you are doing to your metabolism when you eat large amounts of sugar but greatly increases your risk of heart disease and type 2 diabetes. Of course insulin resistance paves the road to obesity too. It is even linked to having low good HDL cholesterol (again, this is the good stuff that sweeps your arteries clean) and high triglycerides, which are independently associated with heart disease.

Although nutritionists recommend keeping sugar consumption below ten teaspoons a day, the average American knocks back an astonishing thirty-four teaspoons a day! That's the equivalent of an extra 544 empty calories of sugar a day. To put things into perspective, if you eliminated 544 calories a day from your diet for an entire year, you'd lose an astounding fifty-four pounds.

Most people think they aren't eating a lot of sugar simply because they don't eat dessert or they shy away from sweets. That is why you've really got to read the ingredient list. Sugar is an all-pervading ingredient in the packaged food world, and it is found in multiple foods you might think are healthy, including breakfast cereals, frozen entrées, salad dressings, yogurts, pasta sauces, and energy bars. Even worse, sugar is rarely listed as "sugar" on the ingredient list. Look for synonyms such as sucrose, maltose, glucose, dextrose, fructose, fruit juice concentrate, or natural cane juice. As a good rule of thumb, you specifically want to avoid any foods containing sugar in the form of corn syrup or high-fructose corn syrup, as these cheap sugars are inevitably a red flag, indicating that the food is unhealthy for other reasons too.

Becoming sugar savvy doesn't mean you need to completely abandon sugar or even dessert; it just means you should be conscious of reading ingredient lists and be aware of the many ways sugars can be hidden in what might seem like a healthy food. Yogurt is a great healthy-sounding example of a food that often has the nutritional breakdown of dessert. Ivy once watched the CEO of a company that manufactures a household yogurt brand brag on national television that his company's product developers were the first to ingeniously take a bland and boring food like yogurt and transform it into something truly delicious, thus taking responsibility for introducing yogurt as a mainstream food to the American public years ago. Ummm, yeah, we too could have added gobs of sugar (specifically, about 100 calories worth in your average 8-ounce serving of sweetened yogurt) and mass loads of artificial flavors, which is exactly what the ingenious food developers for this major company did, and then packaged the "improved" yogurt as a health food. Of course, this wouldn't have been very ethical of us since the "improved-tasting" yogurt is no more healthful than an ice cream cone. The point is, we're not convinced the product developers behind the modern sugar-laden yogurts did any of us any favors. In chapter 6 we'll chat a bit about how to keep your daily sugar consumption to less than the recommended ten teaspoons a day while still indulging your sweet tooth —without harming your health or expanding your waistline.

## Refined Flour

The biggest difference between refined flour and sugar is that refined flour has been enriched with synthetic nutrients. (Synthetic nutrients are not recognized or metabolized by your body in the same manner as the naturally occurring nutrients found within unrefined whole foods.) Phytochemicals and certain antioxidants are completely absent in "enriched" flours. Most refined flours have also been exposed to bleaching agents and chemical additives. Synthetic nutrients and bleach aside, refined flour behaves and is metabolized just like sugar in your body. This means refined flour will spike blood sugar levels, which, in turn, will open the insulin floodgates, which, of course, will put your body right into fat-storing mode. While refined flours are indeed made from otherwise healthful whole grains, the nutritional integrity of the whole grain is completely compromised during the refinement process, a process that strips whole grains of their intrinsic health-and weight-loss-promoting properties.

You should know a bit about how refined flour is made to fully appreciate how downright unhealthful it is. To process a whole grain into refined flour, the first step is to strip the nutrient and antioxidant "germ" from the whole grain. This is a big deal because the germ contains vital, naturally occurring vitamins, minerals, essential fats, and phytochemicals. In fact, the reason wheat germ is touted as being so nutritious is because it is a concentrated source of all the nutrients stripped from the whole grain! As an experiment, eat two table-spoons of wheat germ as a snack one day when you are slightly hungry (you can mix the wheat germ with a tablespoon of yogurt if that helps) and then jot down how satisfied and full you feel and for how long afterward. The next day, have a slice of bread made with enriched flour and again jot down your level of satisfaction and fullness, and how long you feel full. We'll bet you a hundred dollars to a nickel (a good bet if you lose!) that you'll feel substantially more full and significantly more satisfied after having the nutrient-rich wheat germ snack compared with the empty-calorie bread snack—even though the wheat germ contains just 50 calories and the slice of bread contains almost twice as many. That is one of the reasons we don't encourage people to count points and calories, because not all points and not all calories behave the same.

In addition to removing the nutrient-rich germ, the refinement process also strips the whole grain of its bran, which constitutes the fiber-rich outer layer of a whole grain. Fiber in bran is what slows the absorption of carbohydrates into the bloodstream and therefore helps keep blood sugar levels stable and fat storing insulin levels suppressed. Fiber is also what provides bulk and works mechanically to take up space in your stomach so you feel full on fewer calories. Without fiber, it's unbelievably easy to consume massive amounts of starch without feeling the least bit full. Not convinced? Try eating one cup of *sprouted* whole-grain pasta (which contains about 8 grams of fiber and 200 calories) and then jot down how full you feel and how long the fullness lasts. On a separate occasion, have regular white pasta (which contains about 1 gram of fiber for the same 200 calories) and again note your level of fullness. We guarantee the one cup of regular white pasta will barely make a dent in your appetite compared to eating the exact same number of calories from the sprouted whole-grain pasta, which is unbelievably filling. Without the fiber, the starchy carbohydrate from the whole grain is quickly absorbed and can rapidly be converted to fat. In simple terms, refined flour is just empty-calorie starch, the nutritional equivalent of sugar.

Here's a quick mental note: "Enriched" is a code word for junk-food flour. Enriched wheat flour is the most common variety of flour used in processed foods, including breads, cereals, pastries, crackers, pizza crusts, and many other baked goods. Carefully read the ingredient list on the back of the packaged foods you buy, and then step away from the commercially prepared bread, crackers, and cereal boxes. Put down the foods containing enriched flour or any of the following highly refined flours: all-purpose flour, bleached flour, bread flour, cake flour, durum flour (often used to make noodles and pasta), high-gluten flour, pastry flour, or semolina (used to make standard pasta). Walk away from the junk.

Flour and baked-good enthusiasts, don't despair: plenty of alternatives to refined flour are widely available. Look for *whole-grain* flours, which contain the nutrient-rich germ and the fiber-rich bran from the entire whole grain. The key word to look for is "whole" on ingredient lists. For example, you want to choose a product made with *whole*-wheat flour rather than just wheat flour. (Wheat flour is made from wheat, but it certainly doesn't mean the flour contains all of the nutrients and fiber found within the whole wheat berry!) Don't be tricked by the words "natural," "organic," "seven-grain," "multigrain," or "enriched." Again, look carefully for the word "whole."

Another word that identifies baked goods and pastas as being made from the *entire* whole grain, and therefore healthful, is the word "sprouted." In fact, sprouted whole-grain breads and sprouted whole-grain pastas are often completely flourless and offer an *excellent* alternative to many conventional flour-based foods. We typically choose sprouted whole-grain breads and pastas over those made with whole-grain flour simply because sprouted grains are nutritionally superior. During the sprouting process, the vitamins, minerals, and availability of protein within the whole grain increase substantially. And that's not all; the sprouting process also naturally increases the protein content and decreases the calories and carbohydrates found within the original whole grain. In other words, sprouted whole grains are a nutrient-rich but rather low-calorie food. Of course sprouted whole-grain foods contain a lot of fiber too, which means they are *exceptionally* filling. And because sprouts are living, growing food sources, they have a rich supply of enzymes that your body is readily able to assimilate.

What about for home baking? You'll still want to use flour for baking, but you can substitute *whole*-grain flour for refined, all-purpose flour called for in the majority of recipes. Luckily, a plethora of healthy whole-grain flours exist from which to choose. Regular whole-wheat flour is a good start, but lots of other whole-grain flours are out there, so don't feel pigeonholed into using just plain whole-wheat flour. Here are a few of our favorites:

**Whole-Amaranth Flour.** This flour has a mild but distinctly sweet, nutty, malt-like flavor. It's a high-protein flour that doesn't contain gluten, so it's usually best mixed with wheat flour in recipes where a leavening agent is needed. One part amaranth flour may be used for every three parts wheat flour. However, in the preparation of flatbreads, pancakes, and pastas, 100 percent amaranth flour can be used.

**Whole-Barley Flour.** The mild and slightly sweet taste of barley flour is ideal for making wheat-free items such as pancakes, crepes, and even brownies. Again, if you want to make baked items where a leavening agent is needed, such as breads and muffins, it's best to mix barley flour with a little whole-wheat flour for the extra gluten.

**Whole-Corn Flour.** The natural bran, germ, and oils in the corn kernels are all kept intact with *whole*-corn flour, therefore retaining the fiber, protein, and vitamins within the "whole" corn. The fine light texture of whole-corn flour is delicious in corn bread, fish breading, multigrain recipes, and corn tortillas, and in any recipe that uses corn flour meal.

**Whole-Oat Flour.** This flour is made by grinding and sifting whole-oat groats in a natural stone mill. The proportions of the natural constituents of the oat groat remain unaltered, yet whole-oat flour is a dry free-flowing powder. Whole-oat flour is also surprisingly moist with just a hint of sweetness. It's simply delicious in breads, muffins, piecrusts, and cakes.

**Whole-Garbanzo and Whole-Fava Flour.** Bean flours provide protein for superb gluten-free baking. This combination of garbanzo and fava bean flour is great for making pizza crusts and breads, and it is a very high-fiber and nutrient-rich alternative to rice flour.

**Whole-Soy Flour.** If you're trying to sneak soy and fiber into your family's diet under the radar, whole-soy flour is a tasty and convenient way to do so. By using whole-soy flour, you can take advantage of the nutritional benefits of soy while stealthily hiding it in baked goods. We like to use soy flour in combination with whole-wheat flour, particularly for muffins and breads.

***White* Whole-Wheat Flour.** This has recently become our favorite all-purpose flour. In comparison to regular whole-wheat flour that is made from red wheat, white whole-wheat flour is made from a naturally occurring albino variety of wheat, which is lighter in color and has a sweeter, milder flavor (making it heavenly for many dessert recipes!). Yet, white whole-wheat flour offers the same nutritional goodness of its darker cousin. And, because white whole-wheat flour is less heavy than traditional whole-wheat flour, it can replace all-purpose white flour one to one in recipes. We've started using white whole-wheat flour almost exclusively in our baked good and dessert recipes, and the results are truly delicious. (Note: if you can't find white whole-wheat flour in your supermarket or natural foods store, you can order it online from King Arthur Flour company at www.kingarthurflour.com.)

**Whole-Wheat Pastry Flour.** This powdery flour, which is also every bit as healthful as regular whole-wheat flour, is made from a soft red winter wheat or a soft white winter wheat and makes a great alternative to heavier traditional whole-wheat flour in recipes where you want a lighter texture.

**Coconut Flour.** Delicious and naturally sweet, this gluten-free flour contains 67 percent fiber, the highest percentage of fiber found in any flour. While certain sweet baked goods such as muffins, pies, and cakes can be made using 100 percent coconut flour, you can generally replace 20 percent of the wheat flour in standard recipes with coconut flour. However, because of its high fiber content, coconut flour requires much more liquid than other flours. You'll need to use an equivalent amount of liquids to the amount of coconut flour used. If the batter seems too thick, just add more liquid to thin it out to the desired consistency.

## Don't Let Marketing Claims Fool You

The overriding take-home message from this chapter is to read the ingredients on the foods you buy and to pay no attention to the advertising on the front of the package. In other words, don't fall for the marketing hype. While marketing claims such as "Organic," "All-Natural," or "Vegetarian" all sound healthfully alluring, you just can't count on these descriptions to guarantee a nutritiously superior product. The U.S. Food and Drug Administration—the federal agency that regulates the labeling of all foods and beverages except meat, poultry, and alcohol—has no formal definition for natural or all-natural, and we doubt that they plan on creating one anytime soon. We can't really blame the agency too much because, when it comes down to it, people need to rely on common sense with some things. If a food comes directly from Mother Nature, like an apple from a tree, then it is all natural. If you have a sports or energy bar wrapped in a package, then it's not likely to be as healthful as the apple. There are no sports or energy bar farms last time we checked.

We especially need to emphasize that not all organic foods are healthy. Sure, we are aware of some of the latest research showing increased nutrient content in organic foods—including the four-year, European Union–funded study of organic and conventional crops grown in side-by-side plots that showed levels of antioxidants 20 to 40 percent higher in organic foods such as wheat, tomatoes, potatoes, and cabbage. With results of studies such as this, people are especially taken aback when we tell them the organic food they are eating isn't healthy. Organic not healthy? How could that be? Don't mistake us to be anti-organic by any stretch, we're just saying the "Organic" stamp of approval doesn't encompass all aspects of good nutrition. While certain atrocious ingredients such as MSG, hydrogenated oils, and artificial sweeteners are incompatible with the organic ethic, organic is not always synonymous with healthy. Many organic, all-natural, vegetarian-packaged and processed foods still contain lots of refined sugar, refined vegetable oils, and refined flour. This means organic processed food is *still* processed food.

There is no question that people today are extremely interested in foods they think are better for them—and many consumers will pay a pretty penny for all-natural and organic foods they *think* are healthy. Almost like an instant replay of what happened during the fat-free-crazed 1990s, today people are flocking to products advertised as "all natural" and "organic," and gobbling them up without a second thought. Anyway you slice it, fat-free cake and all-natural organic cake are *still* cakes. Of course, marketing specialists who work for food manufacturing companies are keenly aware of the natural and organic foods trends, and they are positioning and advertising their products to take full advantage of consumer naiveté. For example, Ivy was in line in the grocery store the other day and observed a couple watching their on-the-verge-of-being-too-plump, but absolutely adorable curly-haired toddler happily munching away on a cookie from a box that loudly splashed the words "ORGANIC! VEGAN!" The mother of the curly-haired little girl proudly turned to the father, exclaiming how pleased she was that little Katie liked these organic, vegan *healthy* cookies. Knowing full well that a cookie is a cookie, Ivy was trying to be optimistic that maybe this family had discovered a fabulously healthy, organic vegan brand of cookies that just so happened to be free of sugar, refined oil, and refined flour. She quickly ran back to the cookie aisle to scan the ingredients on the cookie box containing the oh-so-healthy cookies the little girl was so happily munching away on. Sure enough, the cookies were still just a sweet-laden dessert, not at all a suitable snack for a toddler. Here are the ingredients Ivy found on the cookie box, along with a note about the nutritional qualities in boldface:

**Organic chocolate chips:** (organic cane sugar, organic cocoa paste, organic cocoa butter, non-GMO soy lecithin, organic vanilla)—Strike one! Just to set the record straight, the *only* health-promoting ingredient in chocolate chips is the cocoa; the cane sugar and the saturated-fat-rich cocoa butter are anything but healthy. If you want the antioxidant benefits of chocolate, eat unsweetened cocoa powder.

**Walnuts:** these are very nutrient-rich and super healthy. Gold star ingredient!

**Organic unbleached white flour:** this is the nutritional equivalent of sugar. Strike two!

**Organic maple syrup:** this is sugar. Strike three!

**Organic evaporated cane juice:** this is sugar. The cookie had already struck out, but this would be strike four.

**Organic soybean oil:** this is a highly refined empty-calorie, pro-inflammatory oil. Strike five.

**Filtered water:** this is fine, obviously.

**Pure vanilla extract:** just a natural flavoring, perfectly fine.

**Soy lecithin:** this is an acceptable emulsifying substance.

**Organic unsulphured blackstrap molasses:** this is sugar. Strike six.

**Organic orange zest:** this is just the rind from the orange and is perfectly acceptable.

**Sea salt:** this is also fine.

The ingredient list above proves the organic cookie is still a cookie, but it's a cookie dressed up in a healthy-looking disguise. A much healthier and more nutritious snack for little Katie—a snack that had the *true* spirit of natural and organic—would have been something like an antioxidant-rich organic apple and a small handful of omega-3-rich organic walnuts. But, of course, such real foods don't come in fun-looking packages, and since moms today are practically computer programmed to buy foods from boxes, a "real" snack often isn't even considered. We're not saying you can't buy prepared foods, but the bottom line is you need to read the ingredients. *Always.* The landscape of modern-day grocery store aisles is thick with all sorts of junk food concoctions misleadingly advertised as health foods. While the advice from the nutrition bureaucrats and diet police might sound like a snore, the simpler the list of ingredients, the better. Simple is good. But simple isn't everything either. The simple foods also need to be nutritious! Which means simple foods like flour, sugar, and refined vegetable oil should be avoided as much as possible. Go for simple, nutrient-rich, unprocessed ingredients. Focus on the nutrients. It's really that simple.

# satisfaction guaranteed

## curing food cravings and hunger pangs

**Hunger derails** even the most virtuous of healthy eating efforts. It doesn't matter whether you are trying to "diet" for good health or a trim waistline; if your diet leaves you feeling hungry, you won't stick to it in the long run. Of course, hunger pangs go hand in hand with food cravings, so if you're hungry, chances are high you'll also be plagued by those pesky food cravings. While food cravings are often a sign of a nutrient deficiency (not necessarily a calorie deficiency), rarely do we crave the nutrient-rich foods our bodies really need. For example, magnesium is found in whole foods such as raw nuts, fruits, and legumes, but a magnesium deficiency can lead to a full-blown chocolate craving. (Chocoholics are all too familiar with how damaging this craving can be!)

The best way to stick to a healthy eating program is to control hunger while simultaneously avoiding nutrient deficiencies. This chapter will teach you to combine whole foods in such a way to optimize nutrition *and* stabilize blood sugar levels, therefore controlling hunger, curbing food cravings, and increasing satiety.

## Tortoise-Like Digestion Is a Good Thing

As previously discussed, if you want a healthy metabolism, you'll need to supply your body with some of the raw substances it needs, including nutrients—and lots of them! You'll also need to be sure those nutrients are coming from easily assimilated whole foods sources, too, and not just synthetic vitamin pills. However, if you want to take absolute maximum advantage of the ability of a whole foods diet to literally cure food cravings, suppress hunger, and accelerate weight loss, you'll want to combine whole foods in such a way that every time you eat, your meal is *slowly digested*.

The slower your foods are digested, the longer you'll stay full and the less hungry you'll feel. Slowly digested meals also minimally raise blood sugar levels, which means they help tame insulin, the fat-storing hormone. In comparison, eating foods that are digested and converted to sugar quickly causes a rapid rise in your blood sugar level, which will cause your pancreas to secrete large amounts of insulin that can, over time, lead to loss of sensitivity to insulin (we discussed insulin resistance in chapter 4). In a nutshell, insulin resistance occurs when your pancreas becomes exhausted from overstimulation due to eating too many quickly digested foods over and over again for a long period of time. Insulin resistance is a precursor for obesity, high blood pressure, heart disease, elevated triglycerides, and, of course, type 2 diabetes.

Scientists have known about the importance of keeping blood sugar levels stable and the benefits of eating slowly digested foods for a long time now. In fact, in 1981 the glycemic index (GI) concept was first developed by a team of scientists at the University of Toronto, Canada, to help determine which foods were best for people with diabetes. While diabetes is the infamous disease responsible for making "blood sugar" a household term, current medical thinking and research suggest that stable levels of blood sugar benefit health for *all of us*, while frequent irregularities in blood sugar are a contributing factor to many maladies, including heart disease and obesity. So, even though the glycemic index was initially created for diabetics, it became popular as a mainstream dietary tool for people looking to shed pounds, protect against heart disease, increase energy levels, and even improve physical performance during sports activities.

# A Few Words about the Glycemic Index

Basically, the glycemic index is a numerical system of measuring how quickly a carbohydrate-containing food turns to blood sugar. The slower the carbohydrate-containing food is digested, the slower it will be turned into sugar and the less hungry you will be after eating. Slowly digested carbohydrates have a low GI number below 55 (good), and quickly digested carbohydrates have a high GI number above 70 (bad). As an example, an apple has a low GI of 38 while a French baguette has a very high GI of 90. In this example, the apple actually happens to be a healthy nutrient-rich food that coincidentally has a low GI ranking, and the French baguette just so happens to be a highly refined nutrient-poor food that has a high GI ranking. But, don't be fooled into thinking all low GI foods are healthy and all high GI foods are junk. For example, nutrient-rich red-skinned potatoes have a very high GI of 88, while a pastry has a low GI of 59. The take-home message is that the GI ranking of a food does *not* indicate the healthfulness or nutritional value of the food. According to the GI, the following foods are equal choices simply because they have similar GI ranks.

- Pizza and plain unsweetened yogurt
- White pasta and carrots
- Bananas and potato chips
- Watermelon and white bread made with enriched flour
- Baked potato and glucose

Obviously pizza is not a nutritionally equivalent alternative to plain unsweetened yogurt, and watermelon is certainly healthier than white bread, but the point is that the GI does not recognize nutritional values in food. The most extreme example in the list above is the comparison between a baked potato and glucose. Glucose provides zero nutrients. Yet a 150-gram, small baked potato with the skin on contains only about 150 calories and approximately 4 grams of fiber plus almost 50 percent of your daily vitamin C requirement, 20 percent of your daily potassium needs, and vitamin B6. The foods listed above demonstrate how nutrient-poor foods that have a low GI ranking may appear in a falsely favorable light and vice versa. Unhealthful, nutrient-poor, low-GI foods are as numerous as poppy seeds on a bagel (and, FYI, the majority of bagels aren't healthy either!). But more on the pitfalls of the GI in just a bit.

The glycemic index was indeed a fantastic breakthrough in the early 1980s because, up until that point, the diet for people with diabetes was based on a complicated system of carbohydrate exchanges or portions. Although the final destiny of all carbohydrates except fiber is to be converted to sugar, the old-fashioned carbohydrate exchange system assumed all starchy foods produced the same effect on blood sugar levels, even though some earlier studies had already proven this was not correct. We now realize not all carbohydrates are digested at the same rate. The glycemic index was a very important new tool for diabetics because it allowed them to choose foods that were slowly digested, therefore resulting in a gradual rise and fall in blood sugar response. This allowed them better control of their disease. And since then, research has proven the glycemic index can be a helpful tool for nondiabetic and otherwise healthy people, since controlling blood sugar levels can facilitate hunger-free weight loss, help lower cholesterol, decrease triglyceride levels, and reduce the risk of heart disease.

Today, diet books and weight-loss programs based on the glycemic index abound, but the glycemic index does have some pretty steep pitfalls that are important to understand. First, the GI only addresses one aspect of nutrition—carbohydrates. You can't possibly determine a food's nutritional value by looking at the GI ranking. Another problem is that the test scientists use to determine the GI ranking of a food is not necessarily performed using typical portion sizes. All GI tests are based on 50 grams of carbohydrates, which isn't always a normal-size portion for every carbohydrate-containing food. Since *quantity* greatly affects the glucose response of carbohydrates eaten, this is a big downside to the GI system. Here's how scientists determine the GI of a food: ten or more volunteers are given a serving of a carbohydrate-containing food with 50 grams of digestible (net) carbohydrates. Scientists then take blood samples every fifteen minutes to test how long it takes the 50 grams of carbohydrates to turn into blood sugar. The subject's response to the carbohydrate being tested is then compared with the subject's sugar response to 50 grams of pure glucose. Since glucose is standard, it is the reference food, and the testing of glucose on the subject's blood sugar levels is done on a separate occasion. Then, the average blood sugar response from eight to ten people will determine the GI value of that particular carbohydrate-containing food. Sound complicated? It is! And, because the testing method uses 50 grams of carbohydrate as the standard, foods that are not normally eaten in 50-gram carbohydrate portions are not accurately reflected on the GI. For example, carrots rank high on the GI, but the typical three-ounce serving of carrots contains just 7 grams of net carbohydrates. It's not accurate to say carrots have a true high GI, because it's practically impossible to eat twenty-one ounces of carrots (the amount needed to obtain the 50 grams of net carbs used to measure the GI of a food).

One of the newer advancements developed to fix some of the intrinsic problems associated with the GI is to look at a meal's glycemic *load* (GL). The GL takes into consideration the GI of the food and the *amount* or *quantity* of carbo-hydrates eaten. The GI was created to help account for differences in serving size, since the quantity of carbohydrates eaten greatly affects the body's blood sugar response. Similar to the GI, the higher a food's GL, the more your blood sugar will spike, the more insulin will be released, and the less control you'll have over your appetite. But again, the GL doesn't determine whether the food is nutrient rich or nutrient poor! Besides, just like the GI, the GL is also complex in addition to requiring time-consuming mathematic calculations. We're get-ting woozy just thinking about it!

Personally, we find the GI charts and GL calculations to be both a major bother and an interruption in our already hectic lives. We're sure many of you can relate. We'd rather opt for a simple no-brainer approach to controlling our blood sugar levels and have some spare time to simply enjoy our meals. We think simple is good.

## The Simple No-Brainer Approach to Balancing Blood Sugar

Here's the deal: the glycemic index only concerns carbohydrates, yet the digestion of *all* carbohydrates—whether or not they have a high or low GI—can be slowed by mixing in some fat and protein. In other words, if you eat a baked potato all by itself, then your baked potato is going to be quickly digested, and you'll likely feel hungry after eating it speedy quick. However, if you eat your potato with a little bit of protein, such as some cheese or chicken, and add a little bit of fat, such as extra virgin olive oil, then the entire digestion of your potato will be slowed, and you'll feel full and satisfied for considerably longer. The longer you feel full and satisfied, the less likely you will be to consume excess calories later in the day. Let's add that eating your potato with some protein and fat is a much tastier way to eat too!

So, the no-brainer (and tasty) approach to balancing blood sugar levels is simply to eat balanced meals containing a serving of carbohydrates, protein, and fat. Mom was right! Eating balanced meals is essential to obtaining opti-mal health. By eating the proper balance of macronutrients (carbs, fats, and protein) at every meal, you'll improve blood sugar control, reduce insulin secre-tion, and naturally suppress your appetite. This means that you'll need to eat a serving from each of the following categories at breakfast, lunch, and dinner:
• **Nutrient and Fiber-Rich, Dense Whole Food Carbohydrates.** Choose "whole" carbohydrates in their most unrefined and least processed form. Also, since fiber greatly slows digestion, you should eat more fiber-rich carbohydrates. Bulky and fiber-rich, unrefined carbohydrate foods are very

satisfying and extremely filling. This means choosing beans, lentils, peas, corn, barley, oatmeal, spelt, potatoes, sprouted whole-grain breads and sprouted pastas, millet, and brown rice. We classify these foods as "dense" carbohydrates because they have less water and more calories in comparison to fruits and vegetables, which we put in their own category.

• **Vegetables and/or Fruits.** The vast majority of fruits and vegetables consists primarily of carbohydrates, but because they have so much water and fiber and so few calories, we don't classify them under the "dense" carbohydrate category. Vegetables and fruits are the ultimate low-energy density foods that will have a profound effect on improving satiety and controlling blood sugar. Such a wide array of vegetables and fruits exists, and we can't possibly list them all here—but all vegetables and fruits are healthy, and all are loaded with a wide spectrum of antioxidants and phytochemicals. Also, because fruits and vegetables are naturally packaged with so much fiber, their carbohydrate calories are slowly absorbed. However, if maximum appetite control is what you're after, and you really want to capitalize on nutrition for the fewest calories, make an all-out effort to eat more vegetables than fruit. For example, you might have a serving of fruit with your breakfast, but then for lunch and dinner try to eat vegetables. You can't go wrong increasing your vegetable intake.

• **Heart-Healthy, Low-Saturated Fat Protein.** Protein-rich foods definitely increase satiety and help control blood sugar levels when eaten as part of a balanced diet. In fact, studies show people are significantly less hungry when they eat adequate amounts of protein. However, you don't need to go overboard with protein; rather, you just need to be sure to include *some* protein at every meal. Only choose protein-rich foods that are also low in saturated fat. Healthful choices include fish, soy (such as tofu or tempeh), lean cuts of meat, omega-3 eggs, skinless white-meat turkey and chicken, and shellfish.

• **Flavor-Enhancing Anti-Inflammatory Fats.** Fat greatly enhances the flavor of foods and helps a healthy diet taste much better. Plus, fat significantly slows digestion, therefore helping control blood sugar levels as part of a well-balanced meal. Fats are also important for the absorption of certain nutrients, including fat-soluble vitamins A, D, E, and K as well as antioxidants such as lycopene. However, you don't need to go overboard adding fat to your meals, just a little dab will do. More fat than the equivalent of two tablespoons of oil in any one meal is too much. (Note: Two tablespoons of oil contains about 22 grams of fat.) Also, keep in mind some proteins naturally contain fat, such as salmon, eggs, and cheese, so you wouldn't want to add a lot of extra oil to meals containing these foods. However, other protein foods such as chicken are very low in fat, so they allow more room for adding healthful fat (such as stir-fried chicken with cashews). Finally, it's very important to choose anti-inflammatory fats for optimal health. Adding globs of butter, trans-fat-laden margarine, or processed vegetable oils won't do a body good. Examples of nutritious fats to add include extra virgin olive oil, nuts, seeds, all-natural nut butters, avocados, dry-roasted or raw nuts and seeds, flaxseed, flax oil, and walnut oil.

## Thirteen Additional No-Brainer Tips for Balancing Blood Sugar

Finally, as you consider the strengths and weaknesses of the GI/GL, it's important you don't lose sight of the original goal. *What you are really trying to do is control blood sugar levels and boost nutrient intake.* In addition to eating balanced meals, the following tips will further help control blood sugar levels, suppress your appetite, and ensure optimal nutrition.

**1.** Replace highly processed grains and sugars with whole grains in their most unprocessed and natural form. You'll get more nutrients, antioxidants, and phytochemicals, and the natural unrefined carbohydrates are much more difficult to overeat.

**2.** Avoid sugary beverages (including juice), which are notorious for being quickly digested.

**3.** Eat fish regularly and take a high-quality, pharmaceutical-grade fish oil supplement (1–3 grams a day) to promote blood sugar regularity and improve insulin sensitivity.

**4.** Supplement your diet with chromium and magnesium for healthy blood sugar control.

**5.** Consider having a glass of wine during or before meals; some research shows moderate alcohol consumption improves insulin sensitivity and reduces the risk of type 2 diabetes (see chapter 6).

**6.** Avoid eating carbohydrate-only snacks (such as fruit, pretzels, or crackers)—mix in some healthy fat (such as nuts) and/or a little bit of protein (such as a hard-boiled omega-3 egg).

**7.** Eat more fiber-rich carbohydrates, since fiber greatly slows digestion and maximizes satiety.

**8.** Make an effort to eat more vegetables; vegetables are loaded with fiber, plus they contain a wide variety of disease-fighting and anti-inflammatory phytonutrients that support a healthy metabolism and body.

**9.** Eat potatoes with the skins on (the skins have the fiber); avoid mashed potatoes unless they include the skins.

**10.** Eat more temperate fruits that are fiber-rich such as berries, cherries, apples, and pears. Tropical fruits such as pineapple, mango, and bananas are not as fiber rich and therefore not as filling or satisfying.

**11.** Avoid packaged foods that contain added sugars near the top of the ingredient list.

**12.** Eat more beans! All beans naturally have a very low GI ranking, and they contain lots of fiber plus protein too.

**13.** One of the biggest dietary changes you can make is to eat more whole grains and fewer products made with flour. Remember, *true* whole grains include foods such as wild rice, oats, barley, quinoa, millet, and wheat berries. It's best to choose flourless, sprouted whole-grain breads and pastas over those made with flour too. This is because when whole grains are pulverized into flour, whether it's into whole-grain flour or not, their surface area expands dramatically, providing a huge starchy area on which your enzymes can work. Consequently, the conversion to sugar happens very quickly. You can be pretty sure you're eating a natural grain with a low GI ranking if you have to chew it or if you can see grains or pieces of grains in the food. The more your jaw has to work, the better. If you cut down on all products made with flour and increase consumption of grains in their natural state, you will have a much easier time controlling your weight and improving your overall health and nutrition status.

The tips in this chapter should help you enjoy your meals without the need to use a calculator, check a GI chart, or do any other unnecessary, bothersome extra thinking. We think mealtime should be a celebration of good food, not a lesson in advanced mathematics. Rest assured, when you choose nutrient-rich "whole foods" wisely, balance them properly, and prepare them deliciously, you'll experience a most satisfying meal guaranteed to leave you hunger free and energized for hours.

# pure indulgence

....................................................

## enjoying wine, coffee, and even dessert . . .

**Whether it's due** to a narcissistic preoccupation with appearance or to a very unhealthy obsession with health, many people eschew what the diet "officials" have labeled dietary evils altogether. Well, we're not one of them. Sure, behaviors such as smoking are just so bad and so fundamentally harmful to your health that we can't justify any indulgence whatsoever. However, puffing away on a mini death tube stuffed with tobacco cannot possibly be classified in the same category as enjoying a glass of wine, sipping an espresso, or relishing a small scoop of organic ice cream. In fact, we indulge in wine, coffee, and dessert on a daily basis. Obviously we care about our health; it's just that we've learned the psychological pitfalls of strict dietary puritanism. We've also learned certain dietary vices actually have proven health benefits. In other words, some of your favorite guilty pleasures might actually improve your quality of life. (Or, at the very least, make life a little more enjoyable!) In this chapter, we'll share our tolerance and strategies for satiating your desires while still keeping both your good health and waistline in mind. Cheers!

# A Wine Lover's Guide to Informed Indulgence

Thomas Jefferson, who, by the way, lived to the ripe old age of eighty-three—almost double the average life expectancy of someone from his era—believed "good wine is a necessity of life." It's no longer a flight of the imagination that moderate wine consumption is the perfect pairing to a whole foods diet for long-term health promotion. Actually, any alcohol, including hard liquor and beer, enjoyed in *restrained moderation* (this means one or two drinks a day), has the potential to enhance health. We do favor wine over beer and hard liquor simply because wine contains the most antioxidants and the least amount of empty-sugar calories; beer contains some antioxidants but considerably more sugar than wine, while hard liquor contains zero sugar but, of course, zero antioxidants. The powerful antioxidants in wine, called polyphenols, are derived from grapes and are actually made more potent by the aging process of wine, which is why sipping plain old grape juice just won't pack the same polyphenol punch as a glass of vino. Sipping grape juice also isn't much fun, but we suppose that's a biased personal observation based on our experience at children's birthday parties.

Oh, and while you have surely heard some exciting media buzz on resveratrol, which is actually a type of polyphenol specifically found in red wines such as Cabernet Sauvignon and Syrah, the latest promising research indicates this substance extends the lives of lab rats by 30 to 50 percent due to the possibility of resveratrol mimicking the effect of a low-calorie diet. The resveratrol study would, of course, need to be conducted on humans before any definitive conclusions could be made, but the research done so far is certainly intriguing.[1]

Another reason we favor wine over other alcoholic beverages boils down to taste. While any food-science specialist will tell you alcohol is one of only two natural substances known to convey the flavor of food most effectively (FYI, the second substance is fat), wine enhances the flavor of your food far better than beer or hard liquor. Wine simply adds a gustatory pleasure to mealtime that other beverages have a hard time competing with. Having said that, even we admit certain foods, including chili and burgers, cry out for a good-quality gourmet beer, which we do indulge in from time to time. We also occasionally enjoy a good dry martini or vodka with a splash of orange juice. (We completely avoid the out-of-this-stratosphere, calorie-rich, sugar-spiked "umbrella" liquor drinks, though.)

Taste and specific preferences aside, alcohol has genuine health benefits that can't be denied. The science of self-indulgence is becoming increasingly more substantiated as new research proves legitimate long-term health benefits to moderate alcohol consumption beyond the obvious, immediate relaxing effect. Most of us can appreciate that having a glass of wine at the end of a hard day is an enjoyable way to unwind and de-stress, so it should come as no surprise that alcohol has been used medicinally throughout recorded history. What is a little surprising, considering how many diet books and nutrition gurus go out of their way to bad-mouth the substance, is that the health benefits of moderate alcohol consumption have long been known. In fact, one of the earliest scientific studies on the subject was published in the *Journal of the American Medical Association* in 1904.[2]

Research now shows moderate drinkers tend to have better health and live longer than those who are either abstainers or heavy drinkers. On the basis of its extensive review of research, the National Institute on Alcohol Abuse and Alcoholism (NIAAA) reported that moderate drinkers have the greatest longevity.[3] It also found that moderate drinking is beneficial to heart health, resulting in a sharp decrease in heart disease risk (40–60 percent). This is especially important because cardiovascular disease is the number one cause of death in the United States, and heart disease kills about one million Americans each and every year. You'd think, wouldn't you, that eating a good diet, exercising, and maintaining a healthy body weight would provide more benefit than moderate drinking? Not. Actually, the moderate consumption of alcohol appears to be more effective than just about every other lifestyle modification factor used to lower the risk of heart and other diseases.[4] Only cessation of smoking is proven more effective. Additionally, other medical research suggests that adding alcohol to a healthful diet is more effective than just following the diet alone. And the American Heart Association has reported moderate consumption of alcohol to be associated with dramatically decreased risk of stroke among both men and women, regardless of age or ethnicity.[5]

But the benefits are not limited, important as they are, to reductions in heart disease and stroke. Sensible drinking surprisingly appears to improve insulin sensitivity and thus helps prevent type 2 diabetes.[6] Even more startling, moderate drinkers have been found to be more resistant than abstainers to five strains of the common cold virus. Those who consumed two to three drinks daily had an 85 percent greater resistance to the common cold, those drinking one to two drinks daily had a 65 percent lower risk, and those who drank less than daily had a 30 percent lower risk than abstainers.[7] Harvard researchers have also found moderate drinkers to be almost one-third less likely to suffer Peripheral Artery Disease (a significant cause of death among the elderly) than those consuming less than one drink per week.[8]

All the health benefits might sound wonderful, but what about the calories? People always tell us they avoid wine so they can save the calories for dessert, or that they would rather eat their calories than drink them. Surely you must wonder about the "unarguable" truth of the calorie-intake theory and how drinking all those extra calories in wine might recalibrate your weight. Devout calorie counters will tell you in a New York minute that each glass of wine has approximately 100 calories. And, according to the calorie-in, calorie-out premise, those extra 200 calories a day (the equivalent of a mere two glasses of wine a day) add up to an additional 1,400 calories a week or 73,000 calories a year that would cause you to gain an astonishing eighteen pounds in a year if you didn't compensate by adding additional exercise or reducing 200 calories elsewhere from your diet. Well, what if we told you that the alcohol calories in wine are not metabolized in the same way as the calories derived from carbs, fats, and protein? Read on.

First, according to valid scientific medical research, even though alcohol does contain calories, drinking alcohol does not contribute to weight gain.[9] Whatever the reasons, the consumption of alcohol is not only *not* associated with weight gain but, believe it or not, is often associated with weight loss in women. The medical evidence of this is based on a large number of studies of thousands of people around the world. Some of these studies are very large; one involved nearly 80,000 and another included 140,000 subjects. The reason alcohol doesn't increase weight is not exactly clear cut, but research suggests alcohol energy is not efficiently used. Some research indicates the alcohol may actually enter a futile cycle where it is not metabolized in the same way as macronutrients (fat, protein, and carbs). Alcohol also appears to increase metabolic rate significantly, thus causing more calories to be burned rather than stored in the body as fat.[10] Other research reported in the *American Journal of Clinical Nutrition* has found the consumption of sugar to decrease as consumption of alcohol increases.[11]

Now that we have seemingly gone out of our way to tout moderate wine consumption as an enjoyable and acceptable part of a healthy lifestyle, we do not condone excessive drinking. Here's the deal. If you can easily limit your intake of wine to one or two glasses a day, you don't allow your intake to escalate, and you also don't find yourself craving three and four glasses, then (in all likelihood) you are *probably* a safe drinker. In our experience, "unsafe" drinkers are those who find moderate drinking extremely difficult. Unsafe drinkers also often have distinct personality changes when they drink, and their drinking habits interfere with, rather than enhance, their quality of lives. Unsafe drinkers often binge drink or drink so much that they regret it the next day. Only you know in your heart whether you have the combination of genetics and personality to be a safe and responsible drinker. If not, we'd advise you to avoid drinking at all costs, because the benefits of alcohol intake absolutely don't outweigh the risks of over-consumption. But, if you can safely tolerate wine, then we are confident you'll find a glass or two will contribute to your mealtime (presumably dinner) ritual. As a good French friend of ours stated over dinner one night, "There's just something about a glass of wine that just makes the whole meal feel special." We agree!

# Wake Up and Smell the Coffee

Coffee, the once bane and bugaboo of health consciousness everywhere, is now enjoying its blue-ribbon comeback award as a health promoter. For as long as we can remember, we got our morning zip and pep straight from our coffee mugs, and we fully admit we can't even fathom starting our day without first schlepping to our trusty coffeemaker. (We happen to like Dunkin' Donuts Coffee best!) But in addition to the jolt, we also thoroughly enjoy the taste of a smooth, full-bodied cup of joe. Taste aside, no doubt the caffeine in coffee is what most people, including us, are after when they say they "need a cup of coffee." Caffeine is a central nervous system stimulant drug. But besides its energizing effects, coffee has been linked to an increasing number of impressive health benefits. While many studies have desperately tried to link caffeine and coffee to increased risks of cancer, high blood pressure, and heart disease, these claims have (thankfully, in our coffee-loving opinions) been unfounded. In fact, enough high-quality studies have been performed that we can confidently say drinking up to twenty-four ounces of coffee a day is safe.

While everyone knows coffee contains caffeine, java lovers will surely get a smug jolt upon learning coffee happens to be the number one source of anti-oxidants in the American diet (followed by tea and bananas). Java came out the antioxidant top dog on the combined basis of both antioxidants per serving size and frequency of consumption.[12] While it may come as a surprise that coffee has antioxidants, it's even more surprising that some of them become even more potent during the roasting process. It has been found that chlorogenic acid, a property in the chemical makeup of coffee, is a strong antioxidant that helps in the reduction of oxidative tissue stress.

A cup of joe also improves memory, creativity, and mental function. (If you are a devout coffee connoisseur, you probably didn't need us to tell you that.) However, legitimate studies on aging show that, in addition to improving memory, coffee helps older people think more quickly and even have better reasoning. Studies also show coffee reduces the risk of Alzheimer's and Parkinson's diseases. While researchers are not sure why, they theorize that the caffeine in coffee has a beneficial impact on neurotransmitters that are involved in both diseases.[13] By the way, we don't recommend drinking decaffeinated coffee, because many brands are decaffeinated using chemical solvents that can leave a toxic residue. If you are going to drink coffee, then drink it the way nature intended, caffeine and all.

Other intriguing health benefits associated with coffee include a decreased risk of colon cancer, kidney stones, and gallstones.[14] Coffee also appears to improve sensitivity to insulin and thus reduce the risk of type 2 diabetes.[15] And while you're probably not thinking of it as a mood booster, recent studies have even shown that coffee functions as an antidepressant, raising the spirits of people who regularly drink coffee. Coffee and depression studies have found that drinking coffee reduced the rate of suicide in the large demographic populations observed.[16] And finally, a Japanese study actually showed coffee consumption was associated with a decreased risk of dying from *all causes*.[17] That last study alone is enough to keep our morning coffee mugs full.

## How to Indulge in Sweet Nothings Guilt Free

This is not the part of the book where we're going to tell you candy is dandy and dessert should be a guiltless pleasure. By definition, desserts are sweet and therefore contain sugar, which we already know is anything but salubrious. So, while we can't advise you to leave your dietary conscience at the back door once the dessert tray arrives (even if a European chocolate torte happens to be among the display), we can give you some sensible strategies for how to incorporate sweet treats into your diet. Because, while everybody loves dessert and nobody loves the calories, we believe everyone should still be able to indulge their sweet tooth daily.

In all honesty, it would take extraordinary willpower and, in our opinion, result in unnecessary deprivation to deny ourselves dessert all in the name of good health. Further, if you are sticking to the otherwise nutrient-rich whole foods diet we've talked about in the last five chapters, then you certainly have room for some sweet nothings at some point in the day. We say "sweet nothings" because most desserts provide zero in the nutrition department; they simply add extra, unwanted empty calories. Most desserts also contain a lot of saturated fat. Even worse, commercially prepared desserts are often chockful of those misbegotten trans fats.

Our simple strategy is to still indulge in all-natural sweets while sneaking a little nutrition in wherever and whenever possible. For example, we add fruit and nuts to so many of our desserts that if a fruit or nut-less dessert is served to our son, he will immediately demand to know "where are the fruit and nuts?" Actually, one of our super-easy, family-favorite desserts is what we call "chocolate fruit pots." To make the chocolate fruit pots, we put frozen berries (blackberries, blueberries, or raspberries) or frozen cherries in a small microwave-safe ramekin (everyone gets their own little "pot") and top each serving of fruit with a spoonful of dark mini chocolate chips and about a tablespoon of good-quality *unsweetened* cocoa powder (such as Ghirardelli or Green and Black's Organic brand). Then we microwave the fruit and chocolate together for about 1 minute on high, or until the chocolate melts and the fruit is soft. We stir the chocolate in with the fruit so the cocoa combines with the melted chocolate chips to make a silky smooth sauce. We then add a few dollops of all-natural vanilla ice cream and a smattering of finely chopped nuts (macadamia nuts, peanuts, almonds, pecans, walnuts, or whatever we have on hand) for the finishing touch. Voilà! The concoction delivers a double dose of luxurious chocolate in a velvety rich sauce combined with fruit-flavored undertones, creamy ice cream, and crunchy nuts. It's amazingly good and beyond easy to make. But, if you take the time to dissect it, our "dessert" is hardly sinful. It's got fruit, nuts, unsweetened cocoa, and just a smidgen of ice cream and chocolate. What's really so bad about that?

Presumably you will want a little more variety in your desserts beyond the chocolate fruit pots from time to time, which is why we've dedicated an entire chapter to sweets at the end of the book. (Don't forget to check out some of the desserts sprinkled throughout the menus section of the book; Warm Pistachio Pudding is one of our absolute favorites!) With a little knowledge and a few ingenious modifications and substitutions, you can effortlessly create all-natural and substantially healthier—even tastier—indulgences to enjoy, guilt free. Of course, a well-stocked pantry is essential to pumping up the nutritional profile of your desserts. Here's the inside scoop on health-ing up your sweet treats:

• Replace milk with soy milk or organic plain yogurt in dessert recipes. Or try grass-fed milk (such as Natural by Nature brand).

• Eliminate margarine and highly refined vegetables oils. Use high-oleic oils when you want a mild-flavored oil to replace vegetable oil (such as high-oleic canola, sunflower, or safflower oils) or experiment with more flavorful extra virgin olive oil, which can add a surprisingly welcome savory addition to many baked dessert recipes.

• To retain the buttery flavor of butter without the extra saturated fat and without resorting to trans-fat-laden butter alternatives, reduce butter in your recipes by one-half, but don't eliminate it entirely. Look for grass-fed organic butter.

• Consider puréed tofu, white soybeans, applesauce, ground flaxseed, prune purée, or baby food puréed fruit in place of empty-calorie oils.

• Reduce the sugar by a half cup but don't cut it out altogether.

• Even better than simply reducing the sugar in a recipe, why not replace sugar with unpasteurized raw honey? Since honey is sweeter than sugar, you need to use less, one-half to three-quarters of a cup for each cup of sugar. (Note: For each cup of sugar replaced, you should also reduce the amount of liquid in the recipe by one-quarter cup. In addition, reduce the cooking temperature by 25 degrees F since honey causes foods to brown more easily.) While honey is still very calorie dense, it also contains antioxidants, essential minerals, seven vitamins of the B complex group, amino acids, enzymes, and an array of phytochemicals. If you are going to use honey, be sure to use raw, unheated, unpasteurized honey as opposed to the conventional processed stuff you buy at the grocery store. Refined honey has been exposed to high-heat temperatures that destroy many of the phytochemicals, enzymes, and essential nutrients found in raw honey. Also, as many health benefits that honey possesses, it is crucial you *not* feed honey-containing products or use honey as a flavoring for infants under one year of age; honey may contain Clostridium botulinum spores and toxins that can cause infant botulism, a life-threatening paralytic disease.

• Try agave nectar instead of sugar. While it's called "nectar," agave is really more like a light syrup with a pleasant neutral flavor. All-natural agave nectar is made from the agave plant and has a surprisingly low glycemic level, even though it is sweeter than sugar. When substituting this sweetener in baking recipes, you'll want to reduce the liquid slightly, maybe by as much as one-third. You'll also want to reduce your oven temperature by 25 degrees to avoid over-browning.

• Use spice for sugar. To enhance the perception of sweetness, many recipes benefit from spices such as cinnamon, nutmeg, cardamom, allspice, pumpkin pie spice, or cloves. Orange or lemon zest can also boost flavor when sugar is reduced. *Pure* vanilla, lemon, and almond extracts are also excellent sugar-free flavor boosters that simultaneously add richness and depth to numerous desserts.

• Adding liqueurs is another great way to add richness to your desserts. Try amaretto, brandy, Kahlúa, rum, and bourbon.

• Celebrate the natural sweetness of nutrient-rich and fiber-rich fruits. We always make a fruit-based dessert whenever possible. Instead of sugar, why not try flavorful orange juice concentrate as a natural sweetener?

• Add crunch and satisfaction with nuts. You'll intensify their flavor if you toast the nuts first.

• Fiber up the flour. Making your own baked goods allows you more freedom to try healthy substitutions. Use white whole-wheat flour or whole-wheat pastry flour instead of all-purpose flour, or add a quarter cup of ground flaxseed in place of a quarter cup of flour. Try tossing in some wheat germ or oatmeal too. Coconut flour and amaranth flour are both slightly sweet, nutrient-rich flours ideal for desserts and definitely worth experimenting with.

• Add instant espresso to chocolate recipes to intensify the rich flavor of cocoa.

• Use dried fruit in place of half the chocolate chips in a recipe.

• Use unsweetened cocoa powder in place of sweetened cocoa powder.

• Use plain full-fat unsweetened yogurt instead of sour cream.

We should also mention portion sizes because, when it comes to dessert, super-sizing isn't a good thing. As a general rule of thumb, rich desserts such as cheesecake, brownies, and cakes should be no larger than about one inch thick and half the size of your palm (not including thumbs and fingers!). Lighter desserts such as cobblers and mostly fruit-based desserts can be slightly bigger. Creamy desserts such as puddings, ice cream, and mousse should be no more than about half a cup. For whatever it is worth, we've found it's really the first few bites of dessert that hit the spot for us anyway; believe it or not, you actually don't need to eat the whole piece of chocolate cake in order to get the satisfaction you'd get from eating half.

By now you have a good handle on the whole foods philosophy. Hopefully the final tips and strategies for self-indulgence shared in this chapter will help you look forward to living the whole foods way and squeezing your share of pure enjoyment out of each and every day and each and every bite (or drink!). Life is filled to the brim with endless delicious and nutritious possibilities. Let's move on to the recipe section.

# simple speedy recipes

**Get your feet wet** by preparing individual recipes using whole foods ingredients. Fuss-free, flavor-forward and easy to prepare, the collection of recipes in this section are specifically geared toward stress-less occasions, when you (in theory) have both the time and inclination to try something new. You'll find tempting recipes for weekend brunch munchies, filling one-dish wonders, and gratifying nutrient-spiked sweet treats. If you are new to cooking in general, you might even find you like life in the kitchen! But, whether you enjoy the actual process or just the end result, you're guaranteed to feel more confident about whole foods after cooking some of these recipes.

Please visit our Web site at www.wholefoodsdietcookbook.com to see recipe photos and additional recipes.

# brunch munchies

## recipes for the ultimate weekend luxury

**For our busy family,** starting the day over a leisurely gourmet breakfast with nothing on our morning "to-do" list ranks pretty high as an ultimate luxury. Gourmet breakfast meals are certainly not something we have the free time to enjoy on a daily basis, but we make a real effort to find the time on either Saturday or Sunday morning. During our crazy and sometimes sleep-deprived work week, we find we really look forward to having just one weekend morning when we know we'll get to slowly sip our coffee, stay in our bathrobes, relish reading the newspaper at a laid-back pace, and indulge in a delicious morning meal. No, it's not everyday, but it's nice to have a collection of tasty and healthy breakfast meals at your fingertips for those special mornings. In this chapter we've compiled a collection of our favorite family-friendly morning meals that fit our taste and lifestyle.

# rise-n-shine quesadillas with ricotta and honey-kissed peaches

We decided to give the classic Tex-Mex quesadilla a morning wake-up call by adding some distinctive breakfast flavors. While the word *quesadilla* literally means "cheesy little thing," our liberal interpretation includes the addition of nuts, fruit, and a drizzle of honey—ingredients that all blend unexpectedly well with cheese—in this case, ricotta. Also, by mixing the creamy ricotta with the almond butter, you substantially cut down on saturated fat while simultaneously ramping up the phytonutrient content. The end result is pure morning luxury in a deceptively healthy package. We'll rise and shine to that.

**Serves:** ❘❘❘❘

**Prep time:** ⏰

**Complexity level:** 🍎

- ¹/₄ cup almond butter
- ¹/₄ cup low-fat organic ricotta
- ¹/₂ teaspoon pure almond extract
- 4 (6-inch) sprouted whole-grain tortillas
- 2 firm peaches, thinly sliced
- ¹/₄ cup shaved almonds
- 4 teaspoons raw honey
- Cinnamon, to taste
- Canola oil cooking spray

**Mix** together the almond butter, ricotta, and almond extract in a blender; process until smooth and creamy.

**Divide** the almond butter–ricotta mixture in half and spread the mixture on two of the tortillas. Top each tortilla with peach slices. Divide almonds on top of the peaches, drizzle the honey on the peaches, and sprinkle with cinnamon to taste. Top with the remaining tortillas. Use your fingers to gently press the tortilla together.

**Spray** a cast-iron skillet with cooking spray; heat the skillet to medium-high. Place the tortillas on the skillet and then place a heavy object (such as a pot) on top of the tortillas. Cook until crispy and lightly browned, turning once. Remove and, using a sharp knife, cut each quesadilla into four triangular segments. Serve warm.

# frittata with roasted red peppers, scallions, and potatoes

We love omelets; we just don't love their delicate and tenuous nature. We're never particularly enamored with how every step must be done "just so," and we don't love how they never seem to turn out when we make them. What we do love are frittatas. Frittatas don't require the fine art of folding a sheet of egg paper over an assortment of fillings, but they'll still satisfy an omelet craving any day. Plus, frittatas can be surprisingly healthy, especially if you use omega-3 enriched eggs.

Serves:

Prep time:
Complexity level:

2 tablespoons extra virgin
  olive oil
2 shallots, finely chopped
6 small red potatoes, thinly sliced into
  rounds
3 cloves garlic, minced
Unrefined sea salt, to taste
Paprika, to taste
Black pepper, to taste
1 (12-ounce) can roasted red peppers,
  drained, patted dry with paper
  towels and finely chopped
6 cage-free organic omega-3 eggs
1/4 cup organic milk
1 tablespoon goat cheese
1/4 cup freshly grated organic
  Parmesan cheese
1/4 cup chopped scallions
1/4 cup chopped basil

**Heat** the oil over medium heat in a 10-inch ovenproof skillet (preferably cast-iron). Add the shallots and sauté until soft, stirring frequently, about 1½ minutes. Add the potatoes, garlic, salt, paprika, and pepper; sauté over medium heat until the potatoes are tender and golden, stirring frequently, about 15 minutes. Stir in the roasted red peppers. Preheat oven to 400 degrees F.

**In** a medium bowl, use an electric mixer to mix the eggs, milk, goat cheese, and Parmesan. Stir in the scallions and basil. Gently pour the egg mixture over the potato and roasted red pepper mixture, tilting the skillet so the egg mixture spreads evenly. Cover and cook over medium heat until the egg is almost set but the top is still runny, about 3–4 minutes.

**Place** the skillet in the heated oven and cook about 15 minutes, or until top is set. Remove from oven and allow frittata to cool 5 minutes before serving. To serve, use a spatula to loosen the frittata from the skillet; slide the frittata onto a cutting board and slice into four wedges. Serve at once.

# california-style crab and asparagus strata

While it may have a slightly pretentious-sounding name, this hearty brunch casserole doesn't entail a bit of preparation drudgery. In fact, it's the ideal breakfast when you have houseguests because it can be assembled in about 30 minutes the night before. Its enticing smell alone will lure any late-morning sleepers out of their beds before you can even get the coffeepot going.

**Serves:**

**Prep time:**
**Complexity level:**

Extra virgin olive oil cooking spray
8 slices whole-grain spelt bread, crusts removed
8 ounces fresh asparagus spears, cut into 1-inch pieces (about 2 cups)
6 ounces lump crabmeat
Unrefined sea salt, to taste
White pepper, to taste
$^1/_2$ cup chopped sun-dried tomatoes, packed in oil and drained
2 cups low-fat organic milk
$^1/_2$ cup low-fat organic ricotta cheese
2 tablespoons white whole-wheat flour
$^1/_2$ teaspoon baking powder
4 cage-free organic omega-3 eggs
2 teaspoons Dijon mustard
$^3/_4$ cup shredded low-fat organic cheddar cheese

**Lightly** spray an 8-inch-square ceramic baking dish with cooking spray. Place four slices of bread into the bottom of the dish. Arrange the asparagus evenly on top of the bread and then layer the crab on top of the asparagus. Season the asparagus and crab lightly with salt and pepper. Place the tomatoes on top of the asparagus. Arrange the remaining slices of bread on top of the tomatoes.

**Mix** milk and ricotta together; whisk in the flour, baking powder, salt, and pepper to taste. Add eggs and whisk until fully incorporated. Stir in the mustard. Pour the mixture over the bread and cover with aluminum foil; refrigerate overnight or for at least 5 hours.

**Bake** uncovered for 35 minutes at 350 degrees F. Sprinkle the cheese on top, increase the oven to 425 degrees, and bake for an additional 15 minutes, or until knife comes out clean when inserted near the center.

**To** serve, remove strata from the oven and let cool for several minutes. Cut strata into four square servings and enjoy!

# morning plum clafouti

Clafouti is actually a rustic French custard-like dessert (pronounced cla-FOO-tee) typically made with cherries, but plums contribute a more subtle flavor. (We've also made the dish with nectarines, which turned out every bit as tasty as the plum version.) Of course, we've lightened up our clafouti recipe considerably. We don't use any cream, and we've replaced the refined flour with white whole-wheat flour, reduced the sugar by three-fourths, and even added flaxseed. The finished product is surprisingly dessert-like and actually so nutritious that it makes for an ideal breakfast.

Serves: 4

Prep time:

Complexity level: 2

Canola oil cooking spray
1/4 cup plus 1 tablespoon brown sugar, divided
6 ripe plums, coarsely chopped into bite-size pieces
3 cage-free organic omega-3 eggs
2 teaspoons pure vanilla extract
1/2 cup white whole-wheat flour
1/4 cup ground flaxseed (such as Barlean's)
3/4 cup whole-milk organic plain yogurt
1/2 cup low-fat organic milk
Pinch of unrefined sea salt
Confectioners' sugar, for garnish

**Preheat** the oven to 375 degrees F. Spray an 8 x 8-inch gratin dish with the cooking spray; sprinkle the dish with one tablespoon brown sugar, then swirl the sugar so it coats the inner surfaces. Lay the plums in the dish, cut sides down, piling the plums on top of each other in layers.

**In** a medium-size bowl, use an electric mixer to whisk the eggs until foamy. Add the remaining 1/4 cup brown sugar and beat for 45 seconds. Mix in the vanilla extract.

**Add** the flour and flaxseed, and continue to beat until ingredients are well blended. Add the yogurt, milk, and salt. Pour the batter over the plums and bake for about 40 minutes, or until the top is nicely browned and a knife inserted in the middle comes out clean.

**Set** the clafouti on a wire rack to cool for 10 minutes. Sift confectioners' sugar on top, slice, and serve.

# crêpes with strawberry filling

These foolproof yet incredibly delicate crêpes have an intriguing faint nutty flavor with just a hint of sweet lemony undertones while maintaining an unbelievably light and airy texture. The batter can be prepared in advance and stored for up to 24 hours in a sealed container in the refrigerator, reducing the actual crêpe preparation time to minutes.

**Serves:**

**Prep time:**

**Complexity level:**

3 tablespoons grass-fed organic butter, melted
2 cage-free organic omega-3 eggs
1$^1$/$_2$ cups low-fat organic milk
1 teaspoon pure lemon extract
2 tablespoons plus 2 teaspoons water
1 cup white whole-wheat flour
$^1$/$_3$ cup ground flaxseed (such as Barlean's)
Canola oil cooking spray
3 cups finely chopped strawberries
2 tablespoons all-natural strawberry preserves
Confectioners' sugar, for garnish
$^1$/$_2$ cup shaved almonds, for garnish

**Place** the butter, eggs, milk, lemon extract, and water into a blender and process for 30–45 seconds, or until mixture is smooth and creamy. Add the flour and flaxseed and blend for 45 seconds.

**Spray** a large nonstick skillet generously with cooking spray and heat to medium-high; pour ¼ cup of the batter into the griddle and tilt the pan in a circular motion so the batter spreads out evenly. Cook the crêpe for about 2 minutes, until it lifts easily from the sides. Loosen with a spatula, turn, and cook on the other side for about 30 seconds. Transfer the crêpe to a large plate and place wax paper on top. Repeat process until all of the batter is gone. (Note: after each crêpe is cooked, remove the skillet from the heat, wipe it with a paper towel and spray cooking spray on the surface.)

**Place** the strawberries in a bowl and toss gently with the preserves:

**To** serve, place a few tablespoons of the strawberry mixture on the edge of each crêpe, roll the crêpes and top with confectioners' sugar and almonds. Serve warm.

# pumpkin pie smoothie

This richly flavored smoothie delivers zesty spice overtones while the intrinsic sweetness of the banana takes the place of added sugar. By using a frozen banana, you'll end up with a slushy ice cream–like smoothie that could almost compete in the dessert category. Pure chilled bliss.

Serves:

Prep time:
Complexity level:

1/4 cup canned pumpkin purée
3/4 cup whole-milk organic plain
   yogurt
2 tablespoons ground flaxseed (such
   as Barlean's)

1 frozen banana, cut into thick slices
1 teaspoon agave nectar
1/4 teaspoon cinnamon
1/8 teaspoon allspice
1/8 teaspoon nutmeg
1/4 teaspoon pure vanilla extract

**Combine** all ingredients in a blender. Whip until smooth and creamy. Serve at once.

# to-die-for chocolatey peanut butter banana shake

This shake didn't start out as a breakfast recipe. Ivy first came up with the concoction one night after dining out, and our son complained about not being allowed to order a milkshake for dessert. Ivy wanted him to have something nutritious. Long story short, he asked for it again the next morning, and the rest of the week.

Serves:

Prep time:
Complexity level:

2 frozen bananas, cut into chunks
1 teaspoon pure vanilla extract
1 cup full-fat organic plain yogurt or kefir
1 cup silken tofu, drained

2 tablespoons all-natural peanut
   butter
4 teaspoons raw honey
1/4 cup good-quality unsweetened
   cocoa powder

**Put** all ingredients in a blender and blend for one full minute. Pour into two glasses and serve at once.

# individual baked omelet soufflés with leeks and mushrooms

• • • • • • • • • • • • • • • • • • • • • • • • • • • • • • • • • • • • • • • • • • • • • • •

Leeks, an underutilized member of the onion family, always sound so elitist and sophisticated. Here, we've breathed new life into the already classy leek simply by shredding them. Although these soufflés look impressive, they truly are such a cinch to make; mix the ingredients together, pop them in the oven, and let the eggs do their thing.

**Serves:** | | | |

**Prep time:** 🕐

**Complexity level:** 🍎 🍎

Extra virgin olive oil cooking spray
1 stalk leeks, washed and sliced into
   1-inch rounds
1 tablespoon extra virgin olive oil
2 cloves garlic, minced
4 ounces gourmet mushroom blend
   (such as shiitake, crimini, baby bella,
   oyster, etc.)
Unrefined sea salt, to taste
White pepper, to taste
$1/2$ cup frozen petite peas
2 tablespoons chopped fresh basil
6 cage-free organic omega-3 eggs
$1/2$ cup crumbled low-fat feta cheese,
   divided

**Preheat** oven to 375 degrees F. Spray 4 (1-cup) jumbo muffin cups with cooking spray.

**Working** in small batches, place the sliced leek rounds into a food processor and pulse to shred. Set the shredded leeks aside.

**Heat** the oil in a large nonstick skillet to medium-high. When oil is hot, add the garlic and sauté for 1 minute. Add the shredded leeks and sauté for 2–3 minutes, or just until soft. Add the mushrooms and sauté for 2 minutes, or just until wilted. Season the leeks and mushrooms with salt and pepper to taste. Add the peas and cook for 1 minute. Gently stir in the basil. Remove the skillet from the heat.

**Place** the eggs, ¼ cup of the feta cheese, plus salt and pepper to taste in a blender; mix on high for 30 seconds.

**Divide** the leek-mushroom mixture into the centers of the 4 prepared jumbo muffin cups. Carefully pour the egg mixture on top of the vegetables, dividing the mixture evenly among the cups. Bake for 15 minutes.

**Remove** the omelet soufflés from the oven and divide the remaining ¼ cup feta cheese onto the top of each soufflé. Return the soufflés to the oven and bake for an additional 5–8 minutes. The omelet soufflés will be puffy and slightly brown when done. Allow to cool for 5–10 minutes and serve warm.

# almond butter and pear french toast with sweet pear syrup

• • • • • • • • • • • • • • • • • • • • • • • • • • • • • • • • • • • • • • • • • • • •

Here's a novel take on traditional French toast. Bosc pears are perfectly matched with the almond and cinnamon in this sophisticated remake of a morning staple. Our secret to infusing the French toast with a mild spicy pear flavor is to use baby food jars of puréed pears whisked with the eggs. (Don't gag; baby food is the ideal creamy consistency, and it saves you from the drudgery of boiling and puréeing the pears.)

**Serves:**

**Prep time:**
**Complexity level:**

2 small baby food jars pear purée,
  divided
1 cage-free organic omega-3 egg
$1/2$ teaspoon pure almond extract
Cinnamon, to taste
Unrefined sea salt, to taste
2 tablespoons almond butter
2 slices sprouted whole-grain bread
2 teaspoons grass-fed organic butter
2 tablespoons brown sugar
1 fresh Bosc pear, thinly sliced

**In** a medium-size shallow bowl, whisk together 2 tablespoons of the pear purée, egg, almond extract, cinnamon, and salt.

**Spread** 1 tablespoon of the almond butter on each slice of bread. Dip both sides of the bread into the egg-pear mixture.

**Heat** the butter in a large nonstick skillet to medium-high; tilt the pan so the butter coats the entire bottom surface (use a paper towel to spread the butter around if necessary). When the butter is hot, add the egg-dipped toast and cook 2–3 minutes on each side, or until golden. Place each slice of French toast on a serving plate.

**To** make the pear syrup, whisk together 1/4 cup pear purée with 2 tablespoons brown sugar and cinnamon to taste.

**Top** each piece of French toast with thin slices of fresh pear and drizzle the pear syrup on top. Serve at once.

# breakfast date, apple, and pecan loaf with apple-nut butter spread

This apple, date, and pecan-laced loaf is delicious alone, but it's absolutely incredible when smothered with the luxuriously decadent apple-nut butter spread, which, by the way, has fewer calories per tablespoon than peanut butter and less sugar than a serving of jam.

**Serves:** | | | | | | | | |

**Prep time:** ⏰

**Complexity level:** 🍎

Canola oil cooking spray
1/2 cup brown sugar
1/4 cup high-oleic canola oil
1 cage-free organic omega-3 egg
1 1/2 cups plain unsweetened soy milk
1/2 cup ground flaxseed (such as Barlean's)
2 cups white whole-wheat flour
3 1/2 teaspoons baking powder
1/2 teaspoon unrefined sea salt
1 teaspoon cinnamon
1 cup chopped dates
1 cup chopped dried apples
1/2 cup coarsely chopped pecans
1/2 cup prepared all-natural apple butter (look for a brand made without high-fructose corn syrup)
1/2 cup almond butter

**Preheat** oven to 350 degrees F. Spray a 9 x 5 x 3-inch loaf pan with cooking spray.

**In** a large bowl, combine the sugar, oil, and egg; mix thoroughly. Stir in the soy milk.

**In** a separate bowl, mix together the flaxseed, flour, baking powder, salt, and cinnamon. Add the dry ingredients to the wet ingredients and stir thoroughly to combine. Mix in the dates, apples, and pecans.

**Pour** the mixture into the prepared loaf pan. Bake for 40–45 minutes, or until the top of the loaf is slightly browned and a toothpick inserted in the middle comes out clean. Allow loaf to cool on a wire rack for 10–15 minutes before slicing.

**Make** the apple-nut butter by combining the apple butter with the almond butter and mixing ingredients with a fork until smooth and creamy. (Note: Apple-nut butter can be stored in an airtight container in the refrigerator for up to one week.) Slice the bread, spread with a dollop of apple-nut butter, and serve.

# blake's gingerbread pancakes with molasses cream syrup

We named these rich, toasty, and slightly spicy gingerbread cakelike pancakes after our son, Blake, who can never get enough of them. The somewhat lengthy ingredient list here might make you think these pancakes are a major ordeal to make; they aren't. P.S. If you want to do something extra special for your kids, cut the gingerbread pancakes out with a gingerbread cookie cutter before serving.

**Yields 10 pancakes**

**Prep time:** 🕐
**Complexity level:** 🍎 🍎

### GINGERBREAD PANCAKES
1¹/₂ cups white whole-wheat flour
¹/₂ cup plus 2 tablespoons ground flaxseed (such as Barlean's)
1 teaspoon cinnamon
¹/₂ teaspoon ground ginger
¹/₂ teaspoon ground cloves
¹/₂ teaspoon nutmeg
1 teaspoon baking powder
1 teaspoon baking soda
1 teaspoon espresso granules (or instant coffee)
2 cage-free organic omega-3 eggs
¹/₂ cup canned pumpkin (unsweetened pumpkin purée)
1 cup water
2 teaspoons pure vanilla extract
¹/₄ cup plus 2 tablespoons molasses
¹/₂ cup full-fat organic plain yogurt
Grass-fed organic butter, divided

### MOLASSES CREAM SYRUP
¹/₄ cup molasses
¹/₄ cup full-fat organic plain yogurt

### PANCAKES
**In** a medium-size mixing bowl, whisk together the flour, flaxseed, spices, baking powder, baking soda, and espresso granules.

**In** a small bowl, beat the eggs and blend in the pumpkin, water, vanilla extract, molasses, and yogurt. Add the wet ingredients to the dry ingredients and mix thoroughly.

**Heat** a nonstick skillet to medium-high and lightly rub the skillet with a thin coat of butter. When the butter is hot, ladle about ¼ cup batter into the center of the skillet. Cook for about 2 minutes each side, or until both sides are golden brown. Repeat process with remainder of the batter.

### SYRUP
**Whisk** together molasses and yogurt. Drizzle molasses cream syrup on top of pancakes just before serving. Serve pancakes warm.

# ricotta-orange cloud pancakes with brandied orange sauce

· · · · · · · · · · · · · · · · · · · · · · · · · · · · · · · · · · · · · · · · · ·

If you don't have ricotta on hand, you can substitute cottage cheese, but we personally prefer the fresh, creamy, and smoother consistency of ricotta. Whichever cheese you choose, the end result is a feathery heaven-like pancake. And, while the pancakes are delish naked, the brandied orange sauce is certainly not an afterthought; the sauce infuses the pancakes with flavor, moisture, and lavish richness that simple syrups can't begin to compete with.

Serves:

Prep time:
Complexity level:

### BRANDIED ORANGE SAUCE
1 teaspoon grass-fed organic butter
1 orange, cut into bite-size chunks
3 tablespoons brandy
2 tablespoons raw honey
1 tablespoon mascarpone cheese

### RICOTTA-ORANGE CLOUD PANCAKES
3/4 cup low-fat organic ricotta cheese
3 cage-free organic omega-3 eggs
   plus 1 egg white, separated
1 tablespoon grass-fed organic butter,
   melted
1 tablespoon high-oleic canola oil
2 tablespoons orange juice
1/2 cup white whole-wheat flour
2 tablespoons brown sugar
1/2 teaspoon cinnamon
1/2 teaspoon pure vanilla extract
1/2 teaspoon unrefined sea salt
1 tablespoon orange zest plus orange
   rind curls for garnish
Canola oil cooking spray

## SAUCE
**Melt** the butter in a small saucepan over medium-high heat. Add orange chunks and sauté for 2 minutes. Add the brandy and sauté 20–30 seconds more.

**Pour** the brandied oranges into a food processor or blender. Add the honey and mascarpone cheese. Process for 1 minute, or until ingredients are well blended. Set sauce aside.

## PANCAKES
**Place** ricotta cheese, egg yolks, butter, oil, and orange juice in a blender or food processor; process until ingredients are well blended. Add flour, sugar, cinnamon, vanilla extract, and salt. Scrape the mixture into a medium-size bowl and stir in the orange zest. Let mixture rest for 5 to 10 minutes.

**In** a separate bowl, whip the 4 egg whites until they are stiff but not dry. Gently fold the egg whites into the batter.

**Spray** a large nonstick skillet with cooking spray; pour the batter by 1/4 cupfuls onto the hot skillet. Cook pancakes until golden brown on both sides. Divide the pancakes among four plates, drizzle with the brandied orange sauce, and garnish with orange rind curls. Serve at once.

# baked whole-grain millet and lemon custard cups

Loveable and lightly sweetened lemony custard cups are enhanced with the taste and texture of whole-grain millet, making them perfect for a morning meal and a much more interesting alternative to the tiresome cereal and milk combo.

**Serves:**

**Prep time:**
**Complexity level:**

2 cups cooked millet (see cooking process at right)
Canola oil cooking spray
3 cage-free organic omega-3 eggs
1 cup plain unsweetened soy milk
1/4 cup raw honey
1/4 teaspoon unrefined sea salt
1 teaspoon lemon extract
1 teaspoon lemon juice
1 teaspoon lemon zest
1 tablespoon extra virgin coconut oil (such as Barlean's)
3/4 cup golden raisins
1/4 cup ground flaxseed (such as Barlean's)

**Cook** the millet one of two ways: 1) Put 1 cup millet and 2 cups water in a rice cooker and cook millet for 45 minutes, or 2) Cook millet on the stovetop: bring 2 cups of water to a boil, add the millet, reduce heat to a simmer and cook, stirring occasionally, for approximately 30 minutes.

**Preheat** oven to 350 degrees F. Spray four 3/4-cup ramekins with cooking spray.

**In** a large bowl, beat eggs; add soy milk and honey, and mix well. Add the salt, lemon extract, lemon juice, lemon zest, and coconut oil, and blend thoroughly. Stir in the cooked millet, breaking any clumpy pieces with a fork. Stir in the raisins and flaxseed. Pour mixture into prepared ramekins and set cups inside a large shallow baking pan containing 1 inch boiling water.

**Bake** for 55 minutes, or until puffy and slightly browned. Serve warm or cold. (Note: Custard cups will keep for up to 3 days if covered with foil and refrigerated.)

# tofu scramble with poblano chiles, cheddar, and chili-tomato sauce

While there is no one way to make a tofu scramble, in our very biased opinion, this one is tops. For whatever reason, Ivy usually makes this more often for dinner than for brunch. When she makes it for dinner, she serves it with a simple green salad and warm, sprouted, whole-grain tortillas. For breakfast it is more than plenty served as is.

**Serves:** | | | |

**Prep time:** ⏰

**Complexity level:** 👿 👿

1 pound firm tofu, drained and pressed dry with paper towels
2 tablespoons plus 1 teaspoon extra virgin olive oil, divided
1 teaspoon paprika
Unrefined sea salt, to taste
$^1/_2$ cup finely chopped Spanish onion
3 cloves garlic, minced
$^1/_2$ teaspoon oregano
$^1/_2$ teaspoon chili powder
1 (14-ounce) can petite diced tomatoes, drained
2 teaspoons grass-fed organic butter
1 poblano chile pepper, seeded and diced
$^1/_4$ cup diced red onion
2 tablespoons chopped fresh cilantro
$^1/_2$ cup low-fat organic shredded cheddar cheese

**Crumble** tofu and pat dry again with paper towels (the drier the tofu the better). Place tofu in a medium-size bowl and add 1 teaspoon oil, paprika, and salt to taste. Set tofu aside.

**Heat** the remaining 2 tablespoons oil in a large skillet over medium heat; add onion, garlic, oregano, and chili powder to the skillet and cook for 5–6 minutes, or until onion is soft. Add the tomatoes, cover, and simmer for 5 minutes. Remove tomato sauce from the heat and set aside to cool. When cool, season sauce with salt to taste and transfer to a blender; process until smooth and creamy. Set sauce aside. Wipe the skillet clean with a paper towel.

**Heat** the butter in the same skillet to medium-high. Add the poblano chiles and red onion; cook for 5–6 minutes, or until onion is soft. Stir in the crumbled tofu and cook for 2–3 minutes, or until tofu is heated through. Season with salt to taste. Remove skillet from heat. Immediately sprinkle cilantro and cheese on top of the hot tofu, cover skillet with a lid, and allow cheese to melt (about 2 minutes).

**To** serve, spoon tofu onto serving plates and top with the chili-tomato sauce.

# espresso banana and macadamia nut muffins

· · · · · · · · · · · · · · · · · · · · · · · · · · · · · · · · · · · · · · · · · · · · · · · · · · · · ·

These indulgent morning muffins have just a tiny hit of espresso plus a smattering of cocoa for a rich and full-bodied flavor. They are loaded with nutrients and fiber so they'll keep you powered and going strong all morning long. The potassium-rich bananas provide most of the sweet flavor, so there's barely any added sugar. To transform the muffins into a totally decadent dessert, simply add ½ cup of mini-chocolate chips to the batter just before baking.

**Yields 12 muffins**

**Prep time:** 🕰
**Complexity level:** 🍎

Canola oil cooking spray
1½ cups white whole-wheat flour
¼ cup steel-cut oats
¼ cup ground flaxseed (such as
   Barlean's)
2 teaspoons baking powder
¼ teaspoon unrefined sea salt
1 teaspoon instant espresso
3 teaspoons high-quality unsweetened
   cocoa
2 tablespoons sugar
¼ cup extra virgin coconut oil (such
   as Barlean's)
¼ cup raw honey
½ cup low-fat organic plain yogurt
3 very large ripe bananas, mashed
2 cage-free organic omega-3 eggs,
   lightly beaten
½ cup chopped macadamia nuts

**Preheat** the oven to 375 degrees F. Position the racks low in the oven. Spray 12 muffin tins with cooking spray.

**In** a large bowl, combine flour, oats, flaxseed, baking powder, salt, espresso, cocoa, and sugar. Whisk to combine.

**In** a separate bowl, mix the oil, honey, yogurt, bananas, and eggs. Add the dry ingredients to the wet. Stir to combine. Add the macadamia nuts and mix well.

**Spoon** batter into prepared muffin tins. Bake for about 20 minutes, or until a toothpick inserted in the middle comes out clean. Cool in the tin for 10 minutes. Remove and eat!

# one-dish chic

• • • • • • • • • • • • • • • • • • • • • • • • • • • • • • • • • • • • • • •

## soups, stews, casseroles, and salad entrées

**We've found one** of the easiest and least stressful ways to feed our hungry family is with our repertoire of one-dish meals. Using just one skillet, large salad bowl, casserole dish, or pot, you can put together a complete and balanced healthy meal that minimizes both cooking time and the very noncreative (not fun!) culinary cleanup. And who says simple can't be sumptuous? In this chapter, you are preparing hassle-free one-dish meals that emphasize good taste and fabulous flavors. And rest assured, it would take considerably more time to hop in the car and get takeout than it would to prepare any of the meals in this chapter!

# roasted vegetable and tofu lasagna

Spend just a few extra well-worth-every-minute minutes to pre-roast the vegetables before assembling your lasagna. Why pre-roast? Because roasting adds a completely new flavor dimension to the vegetables; the roasting process brings out the natural sweetness of vegetables while intensifying their flavor better than any other cooking method. To conceal the tofu, blend it with low-fat ricotta and add extra richness and creaminess with a touch of cashew-nut butter, which imparts phytochemicals plus the smooth velvety texture you'd get from full-fat dairy products without the saturated fat. All this without compromising flavor. (The other ingredients overpower the mild nutty undertones of the cashew-nut butter.) You'll notice we eliminate the extra step of precooking the lasagna noodles since the noodles will soften during the cooking process when smothered in sauce.

Serves: |||| ||||

Prep time: 🍎

Complexity level: 🍎🍎🍎

Extra virgin olive oil, for brushing
2 eggplants, cut lengthwise into
    $1/4$-inch strips
2 zucchini, cut lengthwise into
    $1/4$-inch strips
Paprika, to taste
Unrefined sea salt, to taste
Black pepper, to taste
1 (12-ounce) jar roasted red peppers,
    rinsed, drained, patted dry, and
    sliced

1 cage-free organic omega-3 egg
2 tablespoons cashew-nut butter
1 cup organic low-fat ricotta
7 ounces ($1/2$ of a 14-ounce block) of
    extra-firm tofu, drained and patted
    dry
$3/4$ cup grated Asiago cheese, divided
2 cloves garlic, chopped
$3/4$ cup chopped fresh basil
1 (24-ounce) jar good-quality,
    prepared marinara sauce, divided
9 whole-wheat lasagna noodles
$3/4$ cup shredded, low-fat organic
    mozzarella cheese

**Preheat** the oven to 400 degrees F. Lightly brush two baking sheets with extra virgin olive oil. Arrange the eggplant and zucchini strips on top of the baking sheet. (Don't overcrowd the vegetables.) Lightly brush the vegetable strips with more extra virgin olive oil and season to taste with paprika, salt, and pepper. Roast the vegetables for 15 minutes. Remove from the oven and set aside to cool.

**Lower** the oven temperature to 375 degrees F. In a large bowl, gently toss the cooled vegetables with the red peppers. Set vegetables aside.

**Place** the egg, cashew-nut butter, and ricotta in a food processor or blender; process until smooth and creamy. Add the tofu, Asiago cheese, and garlic, and process until well blended. Add the basil and pulse to combine. Season with salt and pepper

**To** assemble the lasagna, spread ¾ cup of marinara sauce in bottom of a 13 x 9-inch baking dish coated with cooking spray. Arrange 3 noodles over the tomato sauce and spread ½ cup of the marinara over the noodles. Divide half of the vegetable mixture over the marinara. Spread half of the ricotta-tofu mixture over the vegetables. Sprinkle vegetables with ¼ cup mozzarella. Spread ½ cup marinara on top of the mozzarella.

**Arrange** 3 noodles on top of the mozzarella and spread ½ cup marinara over the noodles. Cover marinara-smothered noodles with remaining vegetable mixture and top with remaining ricotta mixture. Cover ricotta mixture with remaining 3 noodles. Spoon 1 cup of marinara sauce over the noodles and sprinkle remaining ¼ cup Asiago and ¼ cup mozzarella on top.

**Bake** lasagna, uncovered, at 375 degrees F for 50 minutes. Remove lasagna from the oven and allow to sit for 15 minutes before serving. (Note: Lasagna can be made up to 3 days in advance.)

# calamari salad with basil aioli and golden croutons

We happen to be big calamari fans. Unfortunately, almost every time we eat out, our only option is a fried calamari concoction of some sort, which is why we opt to eat calamari at home instead. This particular salad combination is one of our favorites, as the mellow-flavored calamari is perfectly paired with plump and juicy kalamata olives, peppery arugula, and sweet fragrant basil aioli offset by slightly salty sun-dried tomatoes. The golden crispy croutons contribute the crunch you'd otherwise get from frying the calamari.

**Serves:** | | | |

**Prep time:**

**Complexity level:**

### GOLDEN CROUTONS
1 1/2 cups whole-grain spelt bread
  cubes (crust removed)
2 tablespoons extra virgin olive oil
Unrefined sea salt, to taste
Black pepper, to taste

### BASIL AIOLI
3 cloves garlic, chopped
2 tablespoons lemon juice
1/3 cup canola oil mayonnaise
1 tablespoon extra virgin olive oil
1 teaspoon Dijon mustard
1/3 cup packed fresh basil (you can
  also substitute fresh dill)
1/4 teaspoon unrefined sea salt
Pepper, to taste

### SALAD
3 cups mixed salad greens
3 cups arugula leaves
1/2 cup chopped sun-dried tomatoes
  marinated in extra virgin olive oil
1/2 cup chopped kalamata olives
1/2 cup finely chopped red onion
Unrefined sea salt, to taste
Pepper, to taste

### CALAMARI
1 tablespoon extra virgin olive oil
3 cloves garlic, chopped
1 1/4 pounds calamari tubes, cut
  crosswise into 1/4-inch-wide rings,
  cleaned and patted dry
Unrefined sea salt, to taste
Pepper, to taste

## CROUTONS

**Preheat** oven to 400 degrees F. Toss the bread cubes in oil, sprinkle with salt and pepper, and spread on a baking sheet. Toast the cubes until golden, about 10 minutes, turning once. Set croutons aside to cool.

## AIOLI

**In** a food processor, add all ingredients and process until mixture is smooth and creamy. Set aioli aside.

## SALAD

**In** a large serving bowl, add the salad greens, arugula, tomatoes, olives, and red onion. Gently toss salad ingredients, season with salt and pepper, and set aside.

## CALAMARI

**Heat** the oil in a large skillet over medium heat. Add garlic and cook for 30 seconds. Add calamari and pan-fry in a single layer, without tossing, until the calamari are golden on the bottom, about 3–4 minutes.

**When** the calamari are just about cooked, stir in the aioli. Cook calamari for an additional minute. Pour the warm calamari and aioli mixture on top of the salad ingredients. Season with more salt and pepper. Add the croutons. Let the salad sit for 4–5 minutes to slightly wilt the greens. Serve family style.

# -simmered red lentil dal with pan-grilled tofu

This twist of a traditional Indian dish, which is usually served over basmati rice, incorporates pan-grilled tofu for a boost of texture, taste, and nutrition. We've used red lentils since they cook up considerably quicker than their green and brown cousins. This is ideal leftover food because the flavor is even better the next day after the spices have a chance to mix, mingle, marry, and intensify.

**Serves:**

**Prep time:**
**Complexity level:**

1 pound (drained, total weight) of
  cubed super-firm tofu*
Unrefined sea salt, to taste
Paprika, to taste
Ground ginger, to taste
2 tablespoons extra virgin olive oil
2 tablespoons extra virgin coconut oil
  (such as Barlean's brand)

4 cloves garlic, minced
1 tablespoon grated fresh ginger
1 Spanish onion, finely chopped
1 cup finely chopped carrots
1 pound dry red lentils
2 teaspoons cumin
2 teaspoons curry powder
$1/2$ teaspoon cardamom
$1/2$ cup organic coconut milk
$1/2$ cup tomato paste
1 quart organic vegetable broth
$1^1/2$ cups water
2 teaspoons brown sugar

*Note: Nasoya brand offers packages
of 8-ounce extra-firm cubed tofu;
you'll need to buy two packages for
this recipe

**Pat** the cubed tofu pieces dry with paper towels (the drier the better!). Place tofu cubes in a shallow bowl and season to taste with salt, paprika, and ginger.

**Heat** olive oil in a large nonstick skillet to medium-high; when oil is hot and begins to shimmer, add the tofu cubes and cook for 3–4 minutes, tossing frequently. Remove tofu from the skillet and set aside.

**Add** the coconut oil to the skillet and heat to medium-high; when the oil is hot, add the garlic and ginger, and sauté until fragrant, about 1 minute. Add the onion and sauté for 4–5 minutes.

Add the carrots and sauté 3–4 minutes, or until soft. Season the vegetables with salt to taste.

**Add** the dry lentils to the vegetables and toss to coat the lentils with the oil. Mix in the cumin, curry powder, and cardamom.

**In** a small cup, whisk together the coconut milk with the tomato paste; pour coconut-tomato mixture over the spiced lentils and mix well.

**Set** a timer for 25 minutes. Add 1 cup of the vegetable broth and cook, stirring frequently to keep the lentils from sticking to the skillet, until liquid is absorbed. Continue adding the vegetable broth 1 cup at a time, stirring the lentils frequently. When the vegetable broth is gone, add the water, ½ cup at a time, until all liquid is absorbed and lentils are soft. (The lentils should take approximately 25 minutes to cook.) Stir in the brown sugar. Taste and adjust the seasonings, adding more salt if necessary.

**Stir** in the cooked tofu and cook for 1–2 minutes. Serve at once.

# whole-grain pilaf with shiitake mushrooms, almonds, and asiago cheese

Vegetarians will especially love this wholesome and hearty fall-inspired entrée dish, which proves whole grains need not be frugal or boring. The whole grain we've used here is triticale, a hybrid blend of wheat and rye, but you can also substitute spelt if you like.

**Serves:** | | | |

**Prep time:**

**Complexity level:**

2 cups dry triticale
4 cups organic vegetable broth
3 tablespoons extra virgin olive oil, divided
3$^1$/$_2$ ounces fresh shiitake mushrooms, sliced (take care not to wet the mushrooms!)
Unrefined sea salt, to taste
1$^1$/$_2$ cups sliced fennel, stalks, and fronds
1 tablespoon grass-fed organic butter
1 shallot, finely chopped
3 cloves garlic, minced
2 teaspoons thyme
Juice from 1 lemon
$^3$/$_4$ cup shaved almonds
1 cup grated Asiago cheese

**Put** the triticale and vegetable broth in a rice cooker and cook for 50 minutes. Allow cooked triticale to sit, covered, in the rice cooker for 10 minutes before removing. (Alternately, you can cook the triticale stovetop by simmering the grains in the broth for up to one hour, or until triticale is soft.) Put the triticale in a strainer to drain off any excess liquid; set aside.

**Heat** one tablespoon oil in a large nonstick skillet to medium-high; when oil is hot, add mushrooms and sauté for 3 minutes, or until they just begin to wilt. Season lightly with salt. Pour the remaining 2 tablespoons oil on top of the mushrooms and add the fennel. Cook the fennel for 2–3 minutes. Add the butter, shallot, garlic, and thyme, and cook 2–3 minutes.

**Add** the cooked triticale to the skillet with the vegetables. Mix in the lemon juice. Cook the grains with the vegetables for 5 minutes. Remove the skillet from the heat. (Triticale can be made up to 2 days in advance and stored in a covered container in the refrigerator. Reheat in the microwave or oven just before serving.) Before serving, toss the shaved almonds in with the triticale and vegetables. Serve each portion with ¼ cup grated Asiago cheese on top. Serve warm.

# slow-cooker fiery cajun creole with seafood trio

Cajun cuisine has a real affinity for seafood. By using the slow cooker in combination with customary Cajun spices, you'll intensify and deepen the flavor of the stew tremendously. As one of the seafood options, we use monkfish, nicknamed "tenderloin of the sea," for its meaty, sweet, firm texture; it's a wonderful substitute for pricey lobster. However, feel free to use lobster in place of monkfish if you'd like.

**Serves:** | | | | | |

**Prep time:**

**Complexity level:**

1 tablespoon grass-fed organic butter
2 tablespoons extra virgin olive oil
2 onions, chopped
4 cloves garlic, minced
1/4 teaspoon unrefined sea salt, plus more to taste
2 tablespoons white whole-wheat flour
1 cup free-range organic chicken broth
2 (14.5-ounce) cans diced fire-roasted tomatoes with juices
1 red bell pepper, chopped
1 yellow bell pepper, chopped
3 tablespoons tomato paste
4 scallions, chopped
1/2 teaspoon dried oregano
1/2 teaspoon dried thyme
2 teaspoons paprika
1 teaspoon grated lemon zest
1/4 teaspoon cayenne pepper
1/2 teaspoon crushed red pepper flakes
1/2 teaspoon black pepper
1/4 cup chopped fresh parsley
3/4 pound monkfish or lobster, cut into 1/2-inch cubes
1 pound scallops, drained, rinsed, and patted dry
1 pound large shrimp, peeled and deveined

**Heat** the butter and oil in a large skillet to medium-high; when butter melts and oil is hot, add the onion and garlic, and sauté 4–5 minutes, or until onion is soft. Season lightly with salt. Whisk in the flour and stir until well blended.

**Transfer** the onions to a 5- or 6-quart slow cooker. Add the chicken broth, tomatoes, bell peppers, tomato paste, scallions, oregano, thyme, paprika, lemon zest, cayenne pepper, red pepper, black pepper, 1/4 teaspoon salt, and parsley. Stir all ingredients together until well combined. Cook on high heat for 2 1/2 to 3 hours or on low heat for 5 1/2 to 6 hours.

**If** not already on high heat, turn the slow-cooker temperature to high and add the monkfish and scallops. Cook for 15 minutes. Add the shrimp and cook for an additional 15 minutes. Serve warm.

# south-of-the-border tofu triangles

• • • • • • • • • • • • • • • • • • • • • • • • • • • • • • • • • • • • • • • • • • • • • • • •

Inspiration for this Mexican-flavored dish came one night after Ivy had a bout of insomnia and stayed up into the wee hours of the night, watching a late-night cooking show featuring a dish for curried tofu. The curried tofu sounded tempting enough, but it used way too much oil, heavy cream, and coconut milk to make its way into this particular recipe collection. Besides, it seems tofu is always teamed with coconut and curry—been there, done that. This dish flies you south of the border for a super tasty entrée featuring sultry flavors with just a speck of spicy kick.

**Serves:** | | | |

**Prep time:** ⏰

**Complexity level:** 🍎 🍎 🍎

1 (14-ounce) block of extra-firm tofu
Unrefined sea salt, to taste
Cumin, to taste
1 cage-free organic omega-3 egg, beaten
$1/4$ cup whole-grain corn flour
2 tablespoons extra virgin olive oil, divided
1 Spanish onion, sliced
4 cloves garlic, minced
$1/2$ cup prepared hummus

1 (4.5-ounce) can chopped green chiles
Pinch of cayenne pepper
1 (28-ounce) can diced fire-roasted tomatoes, drained and patted dry with paper towels
1 green bell pepper, chopped
2 (15-ounce) cans black beans, rinsed with water and drained
1 cup shredded, low-fat organic cheddar cheese

**Remove** the tofu block from its package and pat dry with paper towels. Slice the tofu block into 12 triangle segments. (Note: Slice the block of tofu into thirds lengthwise and then make an "X" on top of the three rectangular blocks, which will yield 12 triangle segments.) Drain excess water from the tofu by placing the tofu triangle segments between two clean dish towels and putting a heavy pan on top. Let the heavy pan sit on top of the tofu for at least 15 minutes.

**Season** the dry tofu triangles on both sides with salt and cumin. Dip the seasoned tofu into the beaten egg and then dredge the tofu lightly in the corn flour.

**Pour** 1 tablespoon oil into a large nonstick skillet and heat to medium-high. When the oil is hot, add the tofu to the pan and sear for 3–4 minutes

per side, or until both sides are slightly browned. Transfer the tofu to a plate and set aside.

**Pour** the remaining tablespoon of oil into the same skillet (do not clean between uses) and add the onion; sauté for several minutes over medium-high heat and then add the garlic. Continue sautéing for several more minutes or until onion is tender. Season with salt.

**In** a small bowl, whisk the hummus and green chiles together; add a pinch (or two) of cayenne pepper. Pour the chile-hummus mixture into the skillet with the onion and season with a bit more salt to taste. Simmer for 1 minute.

**Add** the tomatoes and bell pepper to the skillet; simmer for 6–8 minutes. Add the black beans and cook 2–3 minutes. Add the previously seared tofu to the skillet and sprinkle with cheese. Cover the skillet with a lid, turn the heat off, and let cheese melt for 2–3 minutes before serving.

**To** serve, divide the tofu with the vegetables and sauce into 4 large shallow bowls. For an extra hearty meal, consider serving the tofu and vegetables over steamed brown rice. Serve warm.

# chicken sausage stew with leeks and millet

This moving medley of millet, barley, and lean chicken sausage accented with fresh lemon juice and the slight citrus undertones of marjoram yields scrumptious contrasts in taste and texture. We speed things up by precooking the whole grains together while the other ingredients are being assembled.

**Serves:** | | | |

**Prep time:**

**Complexity level:**

3 cups water
3/4 cup pearl barley
1/2 cup millet
2 tablespoons extra virgin olive oil
1 tablespoon grass-fed organic
   butter
4 cloves garlic, finely chopped
2 stalks leeks, thoroughly cleaned
   and sliced into thin rounds
2 cups finely chopped carrots
8 ounces baby Bella mushrooms
Unrefined sea salt, to taste
White pepper, to taste
12 ounces cooked lean organic free-
   range chicken sausage, cut into
   1/2-inch rounds
3 tablespoons chopped fresh
   marjoram
1 quart all-natural, free-range
   chicken broth
1 cup Chardonnay
Juice from 1 whole lemon
3/4 cup freshly grated Parmesan
   cheese

**Combine** the water, barley, and millet in a rice cooker; set the timer for 25 minutes. (Alternately, you can cook the whole grains stovetop: pour the measured water into a medium-size saucepan, bring to a boil, and add the barley and millet. Reduce the heat to medium-low, cover and simmer the whole grains for 25 minutes, stirring occasionally.) Set the precooked whole grains aside while you prepare the rest of the ingredients.

**Heat** the oil and butter in a large saucepan to medium-high heat; add the garlic and leeks, and sauté 3 minutes, or until leeks begin to soften. Add the carrots and cook 2–3 minutes, or until they are just tender. Add the mushrooms and sauté until just softened, about 2 minutes. Season vegetables with salt and pepper.

**Stir** the chicken sausage in with the vegetable mixture. Add the marjoram and gently toss with the vegetables and chicken sausage.

**Add** the precooked whole grains to the saucepan with the vegetables and chicken. (Carefully break up any clumps of whole grains that may have formed.) Pour the chicken broth and Chardonnay over the vegetables and whole grains. Bring the liquid to a boil, reduce heat to low, cover, and simmer for 10–15 minutes.

**Squeeze** the fresh lemon juice into the stew and gently stir. Let the stew sit for 10–15 minutes before serving. To serve, ladle the stew into serving bowls and top with freshly grated Parmesan cheese. Serve warm.

# flounder and spinach bake topped with anchovies and red cream sauce

You either love anchovies or you hate them. But when you slow-cook them in a little bit of oil, the briny flavor mellows into something slightly nutty and very pleasant overall. We don't recommend making this dish without anchovies, but almost any mild, white, delicately flavored fish such as tilapia or orange roughy can be substituted for the flounder.

**Serves:**

**Prep time:**
**Complexity level:**

Extra virgin olive oil cooking spray
1 (10-ounce) package frozen chopped spinach
1 pound fresh small flounder, tilapia, or orange roughy fillets
Unrefined sea salt, to taste
White pepper, to taste
1/4 cup sun-dried tomatoes packed in extra virgin olive oil, chopped, plus 1 teaspoon of the tomato-infused oil
1 (2-ounce) can flat anchovies, packed in extra virgin olive oil, chopped
4 cloves garlic, minced
3/4 cup loosely packed jarred fire-roasted red peppers, drained and patted dry
1/2 cup prepared hummus (made with extra virgin olive oil and tahini)
1 tablespoon organic Neufchâtel cream cheese
1/3 cup freshly grated Parmesan cheese

**Preheat** the oven to 350 degrees F. Spray an 8 x 8-inch casserole with cooking spray. Set casserole aside.

**Remove** the frozen spinach from its container and place in a microwave-safe bowl; microwave on high for 4 minutes, or until spinach is completely thawed. Use cheesecloth, clean kitchen towel, or paper towels to press the liquid out of the spinach. (The drier the spinach, the better!) Arrange the spinach across the bottom of the prepared casserole.

**Season** both sides of the fish fillets with salt and pepper. Arrange the fish fillets evenly over the spinach.

**Place** the tomatoes with their oil and the anchovies in a small skillet and heat on medium. Gently sauté for 2–3 minutes, stirring constantly. Add the garlic and sauté for an additional minute. Spread the tomato-anchovy mixture evenly on top of the fish fillets.

**Place** the red peppers, hummus, and cream cheese in a blender and process until smooth and creamy. Pour the red sauce over the fish fillets. Sprinkle the Parmesan cheese on top. Bake for 25 minutes. Remove casserole from oven and allow to cool 10 minutes before serving. Serve warm.

# grown-up mac-n-sharp cheddar cheese with butternut squash purée

Foodies all know mac-n-cheese has made a major comeback. While it's still not exactly a three-forks kind of dish, it's no longer relegated to kid-centric menus either. Gourmet versions of the comfort-food staple are popping up in posh restaurants across the country. But most mac-n-cheese, even the gourmet versions, still aren't exactly health-friendly. By puréeing canned white soybeans with butternut squash, you'll get a rich, creamy, and lusciously textured nutrient-rich purée that blends perfectly with the sharp cheddar (which you won't need much of, thanks to the butternut squash purée acting as a flavor booster and filler too).

Serves: | | | |

Prep time: 🕰️
Complexity level: 🍎🍎🍎

1/2 cup canned white soybeans, rinsed and drained
1/2 cup frozen butternut squash, thawed
2 tablespoons organic Neufchâtel cream cheese
3/4 cup plus 2 tablespoons 1-percent low-fat organic milk, divided, plus more if necessary
2 tablespoons plus 2 teaspoons extra virgin olive oil, divided
1/2 onion, chopped

4 cloves garlic, minced
1/4 cup sliced sun-dried tomatoes marinated in extra virgin olive oil, drained
1 tablespoon fresh thyme
Unrefined sea salt, to taste
White pepper, to taste
1 tablespoon whole-wheat pastry flour or white whole-wheat flour
1 cup shredded organic sharp cheddar cheese
3 cups cooked whole-wheat elbow macaroni
Extra virgin olive oil cooking spray
1/4 cup wheat germ
1/4 cup freshly grated Parmesan cheese

**Preheat** oven to 400 degrees F.

**Place** soybeans, butternut squash, cream cheese, and ¼ cup plus 2 tablespoons of milk in a blender; purée until smooth and creamy. Set aside.

**Heat** 1 tablespoon of oil in a large nonstick skillet over medium-high heat; add onion, garlic, and tomatoes, and sauté 4–5 minutes, or until onions are soft. Mix in the thyme, salt, and pepper. Remove vegetables from the skillet and set aside. Wipe the skillet clean with a paper towel.

**Heat** the remaining tablespoon oil in the skillet over medium-high heat; whisk in the flour and stir constantly, until the mixture resembles a thick paste but has not browned, about 30 seconds. Add the remaining ½ cup milk and cook, stirring every now

and then, until the mixture thickens, about 2 to 3 minutes. (Note: If mixture is too thick, dilute with more milk as needed.) Blend in the soybean and butternut squash purée and stir until ingredients are well combined. Add the shredded cheese and continue stirring until cheese melts. Stir in the onion mixture. Mix in the macaroni. Season with salt and pepper.

**Spray** an 8 x 8-inch casserole with cooking spray. Transfer the macaroni-and-cheese sauce to the casserole.

**In** a small bowl, mix together the remaining 2 teaspoons of oil, wheat germ, and Parmesan cheese. Sprinkle the topping onto the macaroni casserole. Bake, uncovered, for 10 minutes. Remove from oven and allow casserole to cool for 10 minutes before serving. Serve warm.

# volcano ahi tuna rolls with avocado, edamame, cucumber, and wasabi

We can't take full credit for inventing these volcano dynamos, which look like a layered salad but sport a striking resemblance in taste to a sushi roll. Inspirational credit goes to one of our favorite local casual restaurants, The Yard House, a small-scale chain boasting the world's largest selection of draft beer. While we never actually asked for the official Yard House recipe, named "Spicy Tuna Roll" on the menu (but served as a gigantic, perfectly formed round layered salad), our version is pretty darn good and tastes remarkably similar to the Yard House real deal.

Serves: |||||

Prep time:

Complexity level:

2 Hass avocados, peeled and chopped into bite-size chunks
Unrefined sea salt, to taste
1 1/2 pounds sushi-grade ahi tuna steaks, cut into 1-inch chunks
1 tablespoon freshly grated ginger
3 scallions, finely chopped
1 teaspoon crushed red pepper
1/4 cup plus 1 tablespoon canola oil mayonnaise (such as Hellmann's), divided

2 tablespoons soy sauce
1 teaspoon prepared wasabi paste, divided (you can get a small container of this from the sushi deli section in your local supermarket)
2 teaspoons sesame oil
2 cucumbers, peeled, seeded, and finely chopped
1 1/2 cups frozen edamame beans, thawed
Shredded carrots, for garnish

**Place** the chopped avocados in a small bowl and mash lightly with a fork. Season with salt. Set aside.

**Working** in small batches, place the tuna chunks in a food processor, and pulse a few times to break the pieces into a consistency that somewhat resembles ground beef. (Note: take care not to overprocess the tuna.) Add the tuna to a mixing bowl and mix in the ginger, scallions, red pepper, ¼ cup of mayonnaise, soy sauce, ½ teaspoon wasabi paste, and salt to taste. Mix the ingredients with clean hands to thoroughly combine.

**Heat** the oil in a large nonstick skillet to medium-high heat; add the tuna mixture and lightly stir-fry for no more than one minute. Quickly remove the tuna from heat and allow to cool several minutes. Using your hands, form the cooled tuna into medium-size round patties. Set tuna patties aside.

**In** a medium bowl, add the cucumber, edamame beans, remaining mayonnaise, and remaining wasabi paste. Gently toss ingredients together and season with salt to taste. Divide the cucumber-edamame mixture into four equal piles on four individual serving plates. Shape each pile with your hands into a round circular shape roughly the same size as the tuna patties.

**Carefully** pile one tuna patty on top of each of the four cucumber-edamame stacks. Lightly spread the chunky avocado spread on top of the tuna patties. Garnish with shredded carrots. Serve immediately or refrigerate for up to 2 hours

# baked eggplant rollatini with tofu, ricotta, and parmesan

• • • • • • • • • • • • • • • • • • • • • • • • • • • • • • • • • • • • • • • • • • • • • • •

Our version of eggplant rollatini offers pure lavishness with considerably less saturated fat than traditional versions. The inclusion of tofu is undetectable and right at home in the creamy cheese filling. (Note: The marinara sauce you choose has a major influence over the taste of this dish, so don't skimp by buying a cheap brand. (If you want to make your own sauce, two different basic marinara recipes are on pages 134 and 218.)

**Serves:** | | | |

**Prep time:** 🕐
**Complexity level:** 🍎 🍎 🍎 🍎

**Extra virgin olive oil cooking spray**
**2 medium eggplants**
**Unrefined sea salt, to taste**
**1 tablespoon extra virgin olive oil,**
  **plus more for brushing**
**1/2 onion, finely chopped**
**1/4 cup finely chopped shallots**
**5 cloves garlic, finely minced**
**1/4 cup finely chopped basil leaves**
**1/4 teaspoon nutmeg**
**1 cage-free organic omega-3 egg,**
  **lightly beaten**
**1/4 cup low-fat organic ricotta**
  **cheese**
**3/4 cup freshly shredded Parmesan**
  **cheese, divided**
**1/4 cup wheat germ**
**1/4 cup finely chopped walnuts**
**7 ounces extra-firm tofu, drained**
  **and crumbled**
**2 cups good-quality, all-natural**
  **prepared marinara sauce**

**Preheat** oven to 425 degrees F. Spray a 9 x 13-inch baking dish with cooking spray.

**Line** two large baking sheets with foil; spray foil with cooking spray.

**Cut** both ends off the eggplants. Cut the eggplants lengthwise into 1/2-inch-thick slices. Arrange slices on the foil-lined baking sheets. Lightly brush with olive oil and season with salt. Roast for 10 minutes. Remove eggplant from the oven and set aside to cool.

**Lower** oven temperature to 325 degrees F.

**Heat** 1 tablespoon oil in a large skillet. Add the onion, shallots, and garlic; sauté for 4–5 minutes, or until onion is soft. Stir in basil, nutmeg, and salt to taste. Set onion mixture aside.

**In** a medium bowl, mix together the egg, ricotta, 1/2 cup of the Parmesan, wheat germ, walnuts, and tofu. Add the onion mixture and mix thoroughly until all ingredients are well blended.

**Arrange** 2–3 tablespoons of the onion-cheese mixture at the narrow end of each eggplant slice and roll it up. Arrange the rolls in the prepared baking dish with the seams facing down. Pour tomato sauce over the rolls and sprinkle the remaining 1/4 cup Parmesan on top. Bake for 20–25 minutes. Allow eggplant rolls to cool for 10 to 15 minutes before serving. Serve warm.

# winter greens salad with oranges, blackberries, and goat cheese medallions

This completely ingredient-driven salad cleverly combines tastes and textures for a chic luncheon entrée or light dinner. To give the salad a whole new personality, you can replace the distinctly muted winter greens we recommend with pungent and spicy arugula. Whatever you do, don't try to substitute the pistachio oil in the vinaigrette. Crisp, intense pistachio oil adds a luxurious contribution to an otherwise simple dressing. Pistachio oil happens to be super rich in heart-healthy monounsaturated fats, the same fats found in extra virgin olive oil. Also, if you are serving this for a luncheon, we've found mimosas to be the most complementary beverage. Enjoy!

**Serves:**

**Prep time:**
**Complexity level:**

1/3 cup pistachio oil
2 teaspoons Dijon mustard
3 tablespoons fresh lemon juice
2 teaspoons raw honey
1/4 teaspoon unrefined sea salt, plus
   more to taste
1/8 teaspoon coarsely ground black
   pepper
1 1/4 cups shelled dry-roasted
   pistachios
1 (8-ounce) goat cheese log, cut into
   1-ounce rounds (dental floss works
   best for slicing goat cheese)
1 large head frisée, leaves torn into
   bite-size pieces
1/2 head radicchio, thinly sliced
4 Belgian endive, thinly sliced
2 oranges, cut into bite-size pieces
2 cups blackberries

**Preheat** oven to 350 degrees F. In a blender, add the oil, mustard, lemon juice, honey, salt, and pepper; purée until smooth and creamy. Set vinaigrette aside.

**Place** the pistachios in a food processor and process into fine crumbs. Roll the 8 goat cheese medallions in the pistachio crumbs, pressing so the pistachios adhere to the cheese. Reserve the remaining pistachio crumbs for later.

**Place** the goat cheese medallions on a baking sheet and bake for 3–4 minutes, or until cheese is just warm and soft. (Be careful not to bake the goat cheese too long or it will melt into a gooey mess!)

**In** a large serving bowl, combine the frisée, radicchio, and endive. Gently toss in the oranges and blackberries. Toss the lettuce and fruit with the vinaigrette to taste. Divide the salad among 4 large plates. Top each salad with 2 pistachio-crusted goat cheese medallions. Sprinkle remaining pistachio crumbs on top of each salad. Serve at once.

# lamb, barley, and red wine stew

In this rustic stew, the Merlot helps tenderize the lean lamb meat and give it an almost buttery texture while imparting a rich and aromatic flavor. The savory vegetables and earthy texture of whole-grain barley are perfect complements.

Serves: | | | | | |

Prep time: 🕐

Complexity level: 🍎🍎

Canola oil cooking spray
3 pounds boneless, pasture-raised lamb leg roast, trimmed of all visible fat and cut into bite-size pieces (Note: Once the lamb is trimmed of all visible fat, you should have about 2 pounds of useable meat)
Unrefined sea salt, to taste
Coarsely ground black pepper, to taste
2 tablespoons extra virgin olive oil
1 yellow onion, diced
1$^1$/$_2$ cups peeled and sliced carrots
4 cloves garlic, minced
1 pound fresh small white mushrooms, sliced
3 tablespoons whole-wheat flour
2 cups Merlot
2 cups water
1 cup uncooked barley
2 tablespoons orange juice concentrate
1 bay leaf
$^1$/$_4$ cup chopped parsley

**Spray** a Dutch oven with cooking spray and heat to medium-high. Meanwhile, season the lamb pieces generously on all sides with salt and pepper. When the Dutch oven is hot, add the lamb and cook about 6 minutes, until brown on all sides. Remove the lamb with the juices from the pot and set aside.

**Pour** olive oil in the pot and add the onion, carrots, and garlic; reduce the heat to medium and cook, stirring constantly, until the vegetables are softened, about 5 minutes. Season with salt and pepper. Add the mushrooms and cook, stirring, an additional 2 minutes.

**Sprinkle** the flour evenly over the vegetables and cook, stirring, for about 1 minute until well blended. Gradually pour in the Merlot and water, stirring constantly. Bring the liquid to a boil. Season with more salt and pepper.

**Add** the barley, reserved lamb with juices, orange juice concentrate, and bay leaf to the pot. Simmer, uncovered, for 35 minutes, stirring frequently and scraping up any browned bits from the bottom of the pot. Add the parsley and cook an additional 5 minutes. Let the stew cool for 10 minutes before serving.

# tofu cubes in spicy toma[...]
# orange garlic sauce

• • • • • • • • • • • • • • • • • • • • • • • • • • • • • • • • • • • • • • • • • • • • • • • •

Everyone needs a repertoire of recipes for out-of-the-ordinary fast food—recipes that deliver taste, satisfaction, nutrition, and minimal involvement. This particular dish, which, by the way, serves two rather than four, is a fast-food family favorite, probably because it's considerably more unusual than most express-lane meals. The tofu keeps a rather low profile while the tangy tomatoes combine beautifully, and unexpectedly, with the sweet orange segments.

**Serves:**

**Prep time:**
**Complexity level:**

3 tablespoons extra virgin olive oil
12 cloves garlic, peeled and lightly
    mashed
2 (14.5-ounce) cans diced fire-roasted
    tomatoes, with juices
1 orange, cut into $^{1}/_{2}$-inch chunks
$^{1}/_{4}$ teaspoon cayenne pepper
$^{1}/_{2}$ teaspoon paprika, plus more to
    taste
1 teaspoon brown sugar
Unrefined sea salt, to taste
1 (14-ounce) block extra-firm tofu,
    drained, patted dry with paper
    towels and cut into $^{1}/_{2}$-inch blocks
2 teaspoons grass-fed organic butter

**Heat** the oil in a large skillet to medium-high; add the garlic and cook, stirring, for 1 minute. Add tomatoes, orange chunks, cayenne pepper, paprika, brown sugar, and salt. Adjust heat so the mixture simmers and cook uncovered, stirring occasionally, for 20 minutes. Transfer tomato sauce to a large dish and set aside.

**Season** the tofu cubes by tossing in a generous amount of paprika plus salt to taste.

**Wipe** the skillet clean with a paper towel and add the butter; melt butter over medium-high heat. Add the seasoned tofu to the skillet and cook for 3–4 minutes per side, or until tofu is lightly golden. Add the sauce back to the skillet and gently stir to combine. Cook to heat the sauce for 1–2 minutes. Serve warm.

# orange-glazed sea scallop salad with macadamia nuts and citrus vinaigrette

If you've ever vacationed in Florida, this citrus and seafood combo will bring you back. If you already live in Florida, you'll feel right at home with every bite. As native Floridians, we've always had an affinity for tropical foods, especially those combining fish with fresh fruit. Here, the oh-so-simple-to-make orange glaze permeates the already slightly sweet scallops and sets the tone for a most memorable salad. It's ideal for effortless backyard summer dining.

**Serves:**

**Prep time:**

**Complexity level:**

1 tablespoon grass-fed organic butter
3 tablespoons extra virgin olive oil, divided
2 cloves garlic, crushed
4 slices sprouted whole-grain sourdough bread cut into bite-size pieces (crusts removed)
Unrefined sea salt, to taste
Freshly ground pepper, to taste
6 cups baby mixed greens (such as arugula, chervil, chickweed, dandelion, and oak leaf), washed and spun dry
4 kiwi fruit, peeled and sliced
2 oranges, cut into bite-size chunks
1/2 red onion, finely sliced
1 cup finely chopped macadamia nuts
1/3 cup flax oil (we recommend Barlean's brand)
2 tablespoons fresh lime juice
2 tablespoons marmalade
3 tablespoons orange juice concentrate, divided
20 large fresh sea scallops, drained, rinsed, and patted dry

**Heat** the butter and one tablespoon oil in a large skillet over medium-high heat. Add the garlic and sauté for 30 seconds. Gently toss in the bread pieces, season with salt and pepper, and cook, stirring frequently, until golden brown. Set croutons on paper towels to cool.

**In** a large serving bowl, add the mixed greens, kiwi slices, orange chunks, red onion, and macadamia nuts. Gently toss ingredients together. Season salad ingredients with salt and pepper to taste. Set salad aside.

**In** a small cup, whisk together the flax oil, lime juice, marmalade, and 2 tablespoons orange juice concentrate. Set aside.

**Season** the scallops with salt. Pour the remaining 2 tablespoons oil in a large skillet and heat over high. Once the oil is very hot, add the scallops, flat side down. Sear scallops for about 2 minutes before flipping (don't flip scallops until you see a nice caramel crust on the underside). Flip scallops and cook for 1 additional minute. Deglaze the pan with the remaining orange juice concentrate.

**To** assemble salad, pour the vinaigrette on top of the salad greens and lightly toss to coat. Divide salad greens among 4 plates. Top each salad with 5 scallops. Arrange croutons on top of the salad. Let salads sit at room temperature for about 5 minutes before serving. (This will allow the heat from the scallops to slightly wilt the greens.)

# tex-mex polenta pizza with chipotle-black bean hummus and rotisserie chicken

Health concerns aside, we've never been huge fans of take-out pizza; we like our pizza pies to boost originality, personality, and pizzazz. Here, traditional pizza gets a major wake-up call as we've swapped the usual wheat-based crust for hearty polenta—deep-dish style—and traded the conventional tomato sauce for a Tex-Mex smoky chipotle–black bean hummus. The flavors and textures deliver a winning combination sure to satisfy. Even better, it's super easy to make!

**Serves:**

**Prep time:**

**Complexity level:**

Extra virgin olive oil cooking spray

2 cups water

1 cup cornmeal (polenta)

2 tablespoons plus 1 teaspoon extra virgin olive oil, divided

1/2 teaspoon unrefined sea salt, plus more to taste

1/4 teaspoon black pepper

1 (15.5-ounce) can black beans, rinsed and drained

1 chipotle pepper (buy chipotle peppers in a can)

2 cups shredded carrots (to save time, buy bagged preshredded carrots)

Cumin, to taste

6 ounces shredded rotisserie chicken

1 cup shredded, low-fat organic mozzarella cheese

1 cup chopped fresh cilantro leaves

**Preheat** oven to 400 degrees F and coat an 8½-inch springform pan with cooking spray.

**In** a medium saucepan, bring water to a boil. Whisking constantly, slowly add the cornmeal and 1 tablespoon oil. Reduce heat to low and cook, stirring, until the polenta starts to pull away from the sides of the pan, 4–5 minutes. Stir in salt and pepper. Remove from heat. Spread the polenta over the bottom of the prepared pan, using a spoon to form a raised edge. Set aside for 10 minutes to set.

**Meanwhile,** in a food processor or blender, purée the black beans, remaining oil, and chipotle pepper until mixture is smooth and creamy. Using the back of a spoon, spread the chipotle–black bean hummus on top of the polenta. Layer the shredded carrots on top. Season carrots with cumin to taste. Scatter the chicken on top of the carrots and sprinkle the mozzarella on top of the chicken.

**Bake** polenta pizza for 15 minutes. Remove from oven and sprinkle the chopped cilantro on top. Return polenta pizza to the oven and bake for an additional 5 minutes. Allow polenta pizza to cool for 10 minutes before removing from the springform pan. Cut into wedges and serve warm.

# slow-cooker mexican-style vegetarian stuffed peppers

For whatever reason, stuffed peppers always look so impressive, festive, and fun. These exquisite-looking, stuffed jumbo jewels are also a great way for tempeh to hide out in a medley of south-of-the-border flavors, interesting textures, and bright colors. One stuffed pepper is pretty much a meal by itself, but you could always add a side salad or some vegetable-based soup.

**Serves:** | | | |

**Prep time:** ⏰
**Complexity level:** 🍎 🍎

1 tablespoon extra virgin olive oil
4 cloves garlic, minced
1/2 onion, finely chopped
1 (8-ounce) package tempeh, crumbled
Unrefined sea salt, to taste
1 teaspoon paprika
2 pinches cayenne pepper
1 teaspoon cumin
1 cup frozen corn kernels, thawed
1 1/2 cups good-quality, all-natural prepared marinara sauce
1 (4.5-ounce) can chopped green chiles
1/4 cup chopped fresh cilantro
1 (14.5-ounce) can black beans, rinsed and drained
4 red bell peppers, tops removed and seeded
1/2 cup shredded, low-fat organic cheddar cheese

**Heat** the oil in a large nonstick skillet to medium-high; add garlic and onion, and sauté until onion is just tender, about 3–4 minutes. Add the tempeh and sauté for 3–4 minutes. Season onion and tempeh with salt to taste. Mix in the paprika, cayenne pepper, cumin, and corn kernels.

**In** a small bowl, whisk together the marinara sauce and green chiles. Pour the marinara–green chile mixture into the skillet with the tempeh; mix well to combine. Stir in the cilantro and black beans.

**Stuff** the peppers with the tempeh mixture. Arrange the peppers in a 5- or 6-quart slow cooker. Cover and cook the peppers on high for 2 hours or on low for 4 hours. Remove the lid and top the peppers with the shredded cheese, replace the cover, and cook on high for 15 to 20 additional minutes. Allow peppers to cool 10–15 minutes before serving. Serve warm.

# slow-cooker summer citrus salmon with white wine

Like chicken, one can never have too many salmon recipes. To us, slow-cooker citrus salmon is the quintessential summer meal, perfect for balmy summer nights. Pair this dish with a crisp white wine and . . . life is good.

Serves: | | | |

Prep time: ⏰

Complexity level: 🍎

Extra virgin olive oil cooking spray
2 tablespoons extra virgin olive oil
1 medium red onion, chopped
2 stalks leeks, cleaned and sliced into 1-inch rounds
1/2 cup chopped marinated artichokes (marinated in extra virgin olive oil), drained and patted dry with a paper towel
1/4 cup chopped parsley
Unrefined sea salt, to taste
4 (6-ounce) salmon fillets, rinsed and blotted dry
1 orange, sliced
1 lemon, sliced
1 teaspoon grass-fed organic butter, melted
1/2 cup orange juice
1/2 cup Chardonnay

**Spray** the bottom and sides of a 5- or 6-quart slow cooker with cooking spray.

**Heat** oil in a large saucepan to medium-high. When the oil is hot, add the onion, leeks, and artichokes; sauté for approximately 5 minutes, or until onion and leeks are softened. Mix in the parsley and season the vegetables with salt. Arrange the vegetables on the bottom of the slow cooker.

**Season** the salmon with salt. Arrange the salmon on top of the vegetables. Arrange the orange and lemon slices on top of the salmon.

**In** a small bowl, whisk together the butter, orange juice, and Chardonnay. Pour the liquid over the fish and vegetables. Cover and cook the fish on high for approximately 1½ hours, or until fish is opaque and firm to the touch.

# made-from-scratch manicotti crêpes

This meal isn't really as fussy as the title might make it seem; it actually only requires a three-step prep. But, if you insist on taking a shortcut, you can cut the preparation time in half by purchasing a top-quality marinara rather than making your own. Our favorite brand of sauce is Rao's. We've used both Rao's Homemade Marinara and Homemade Roasted Eggplant Marinara sauces with great success in this recipe.

Serves:

Prep time:
Complexity level:

### BASIC MARINARA SAUCE
1/4 cup extra virgin olive oil
1 medium onion, finely chopped
3 cloves garlic, minced
1 carrot, peeled and finely chopped
1/2 teaspoon unrefined sea salt, plus more to taste
1/2 teaspoon white pepper, plus more to taste
1/2 teaspoon dried oregano
1 (28-ounce) can crushed tomatoes
3 tablespoons dry white wine
1/4 cup chopped fresh basil
1 teaspoon brown sugar

### CRÊPE BATTER
3 cage-free organic omega-3 eggs
1 1/2 cups water
1 cup white whole-wheat flour
1/4 cup ground flaxseed (we recommend Barlean's brand)
1/4 teaspoon unrefined sea salt
1 tablespoon extra virgin olive oil, plus more for brushing the skillet

### TOFU, SPINACH, AND RICOTTA FILLING
1 cup organic ricotta
1 cup crumbled firm tofu, patted as dry as possible with paper towels
2 cage-free organic omega-3 eggs, slightly beaten
1/4 cup shredded Parmesan cheese
1/3 cup chopped fresh parsley
1/2 teaspoon unrefined sea salt
1/2 teaspoon white pepper
1/4 teaspoon nutmeg
1 (10-ounce) package frozen chopped spinach, thawed, drained, and patted as dry as possible with paper towels
1 1/4 cups shredded low-fat organic mozzarella cheese, divided

## MARINARA SAUCE

**In** a heavy saucepot, heat the oil to medium-high. Add the onion and garlic, and sauté until onion is translucent, about 10 minutes. Add the carrot, season with salt and pepper, and sauté until all vegetables are soft, about 10 minutes.

**Add** the oregano, tomatoes, and wine. Simmer, uncovered, stirring occasionally, for 40–45 minutes. Remove from heat. Season sauce with additional salt and pepper to taste. Stir in basil and brown sugar. (Note: Sauce can be made ahead and either frozen or stored in the refrigerator in a covered container for up to 4 days.)

## CRÊPES

**Combine** the eggs, water, flour, flaxseed, salt, and oil in a food processor; process for 30–45 seconds, or until well blended.

**Lightly** brush an 8-inch nonstick skillet with olive oil and heat over moderate heat until hot. Ladle ¼ cup of the batter into the skillet, tilting and rotating skillet to coat the bottom. Cook until underside is just set and lightly browned, about 30 seconds; flip and cook the other side for another 20–30 seconds. Invert the crêpe onto a clean kitchen towel to cool completely. Make 10 more crêpes in the same manner, brushing skillet lightly with oil as needed.

## FILLING

**In** a medium-size bowl, add the ricotta, tofu, eggs, Parmesan, parsley, salt, pepper, nutmeg, spinach, and ½ cup of the mozzarella; gently stir to combine all ingredients.

**To** assemble the manicotti, preheat oven to 425 degrees F. Spread 2 cups of the sauce in a 9 x 13-inch glass baking dish. Spread 1 cup of sauce in a smaller 8 x 8-inch glass baking dish. Arrange 1 crêpe on a work surface and spread about ¼ cup of the ricotta filling in a line across the center, fold in sides to enclose filling, leaving ends open. Transfer crêpe, seam-side down, to either baking dish. Fill 9 more crêpes in the same manner, arranging them snugly in 1 layer in both dishes (approximately 7 in the larger dish and 3 in the smaller dish).

**Spread** the remaining sauce on top of the crêpes and sprinkle the remaining ¾ cup mozzarella on top. Tightly cover the dishes with foil and bake for 15–20 minutes. Remove manicotti from oven and cool on a wire rack for 5–10 minutes before serving. Serve warm. (Note: Manicotti can be made up to one day in advance and stored in a covered container in the refrigerator.)

# almost guilt-free treats

. . . . . . . . . . . . . . . . . . . . . . . . . . . . . . . . . . . . . . . . . . . . . . . . . . . . . . . .

## nutrient-spiked desserts

**Anyone with a sweet tooth** will tell you the dessert tray is by far the best and most exciting part of the meal. Health-conscious dessert lovers will be especially pleased to know the grand finale need not be a total nutritional nightmare either. This chapter proves savvy ingredient swaps and sneaky additions of healthful foods like fruit, wheat germ, nuts, nut butters, soymilk and tofu (yes, tofu) can indeed transform sweet treats into rich and satisfying splurges everyone can enjoy—might we add, guilt free.

# peanut butter blondie bars with chocolate chips

In our household, these simple, unfussy, crowd-pleasing treats rarely survive uneaten for more than two days. In fact, you might actually consider making a double batch to freeze. They really are so good that it's hard to imagine we intentionally kept the sugar to a minimum while simultaneously pumping them chockful of healthful ingredients, including peanut butter, omega-3 eggs, and a hefty dose of an all-star winner in the nutrition department—wheat germ. Mum's the word, though, as we assure you that nobody will suspect there is anything healthy about them (including, and especially, the kids!).

Serves: | | | | | | | | | | | | |

Prep time:

Complexity level:

Canola oil cooking spray
1 cup all-natural chunky peanut butter
3 cage-free organic omega-3 eggs
3/4 cup brown sugar
1/4 cup low-fat organic milk
2 teaspoons pure vanilla extract
1 teaspoon aluminum-free baking powder
1 cup wheat germ
1/2 cup white whole-wheat flour
3/4 cup mini dark chocolate chips

**Preheat** oven to 350 degrees F. Coat an 8 x 8-inch square glass baking dish with cooking spray. In a medium-size bowl, combine the peanut butter, eggs, sugar, milk, and vanilla until smooth.

**Add** the baking powder and blend thoroughly. Mix in the wheat germ and flour just until blended. Stir in the chocolate chips.

**Scrape** the batter into the prepared pan and bake for 25 minutes, or until a knife inserted in the center comes out moist but clean. Remove the pan from the oven and use the back of a spoon to flatten and smooth the top. Let the blondie bars cool on a rack for at least 15 minutes before serving. Cut into 12 squares and enjoy!

# fresh raspberries with whipped cocoa and almond cannoli filling

If your quality of life is measured by how delicious your last dessert was, then here's the ultimate in dessert satisfaction (at fast-food speed!). Our cocoa and almond cannoli filling is similar to the sweet luscious cream you'll find inside the beloved Sicilian cannoli dessert—but we've added a chocolate and almond twist. We've also eliminated the wickedly unhealthful crispy fried pastry that traditionally accompanies the cream and substituted fresh fruit instead. Pure indulgence and almost instant satisfaction with zero guilt.

**Serves:** | | | |

**Prep time:** 🕐
**Complexity level:** 🍎

- ⅓ cup low-fat organic ricotta cheese
- ⅓ cup plus 2 tablespoons organic whipping cream, divided
- 3 tablespoons powdered sugar, divided
- 2 tablespoons unsweetened cocoa powder
- 3 teaspoons pure almond extract, divided
- 3 cups fresh raspberries (or use frozen raspberries that have been thawed in the refrigerator)
- ¼ cup finely chopped almonds

**In** a medium bowl, stir the ricotta cheese with 2 tablespoons of the whipping cream. In a medium mixing bowl, beat the remaining ⅓ cup whipping cream, 2 tablespoons powdered sugar, cocoa, and 1 teaspoon almond extract with an electric mixer until peaks begin to form. Carefully fold the ricotta into the cocoa–whipped cream mixture.

**In** a large bowl, gently toss the raspberries with the remaining 2 teaspoons almond extract and remaining tablespoon powdered sugar.

**Divide** the raspberries among four individual dessert bowls; top with dollops of ricotta mixture and sprinkle with chopped almonds.

# cocoa torte with bailey's whipped cream topping

Unlike most chocolate desserts, this understated yet sophisticated indulgence maintains a subtle rather than concentrated chocolaty presence. Recipe credit goes to Ivy's mom, Gail, who actually first created the recipe for Papa's eightieth birthday party (and, yes, it can most definitely be served as birthday cake).

**Serves:** ▮▮▮▮ ▮▮▮▮

**Prep time:** ⏰

**Complexity level:** 🍎

### COCOA TORTE
Canola oil cooking spray
$1/4$ cup water
2 teaspoons good quality instant espresso
$1/2$ cup dark chocolate chips
1 tablespoon grass-fed organic butter
9 pitted prunes
4 cage-free organic omega-3 eggs
1 teaspoon pure vanilla extract
$1/3$ cup plus 2 tablespoons white whole-wheat flour
$1/2$ cup brown sugar
1 teaspoon aluminum-free baking powder
$1/3$ cup high-quality unsweetened cocoa powder
1 Granny Smith apple, unpeeled and finely chopped
$3/4$ cup finely chopped pecans

### BAILEY'S WHIPPED CREAM TOPPING
$1/2$ cup organic whipping cream
1 tablespoon white sugar
2 tablespoons Bailey's Irish Cream liqueur

## COCOA TORTE
**Preheat** the oven to 325 degrees. Spray a 9-inch round springform pan with canola oil cooking spray.

**Pour** the water into a small saucepan and heat over medium-high. Add the instant espresso, chocolate chips, and butter, stirring to blend all ingredients. When butter and chocolate melt, add the prunes and reduce heat to low. Gently cook for 1 minute to soften prunes. Remove saucepan from the heat and set mixture aside to cool.

**Place** eggs in a blender and process for 1 minute, until pale yellow and frothy. Add the vanilla extract and chocolate-prune mixture; process for an additional minute, or until prunes are completely puréed.

**In** a medium-sized mixing bowl, mix together the flour, sugar, baking powder, and cocoa. Add the egg mixture and stir to combine. Stir in the chopped apples and pecans. Pour the batter into the prepared pan and bake in the center of the oven for 35 minutes, or until a toothpick inserted in the middle comes out clean.

**Remove** the torte from the oven, immediately run a knife around the inside of the rim of the springform pan, and unlatch the pan's ring. Allow the torte to cool for 10-15 minutes. Then, run a long metal spatula under the torte and gently slide onto a serving platter. Cut the torte into slices and serve with a dollop of Bailey's Whipped Cream Topping.

### BAILEY'S WHIPPED CREAM TOPPING

**Pour** the whipping cream into a large mixing bowl and use an electric mixer to whip the cream for several minutes until peaks begin to form. Add the sugar and liqueur, and beat for several more seconds, or until smooth and creamy. Serve with the Cocoa Torte.

# savory and sweet frozen vanilla-peach custard

This has become one of Ivy's favorite go-to signature desserts. Not only is it a no-brainer to make, thanks to the savory surprise factor from the ricotta and goat cheese, it's ideal when you want something truly unique. This blissfully creamy treat is best described as a cross between gelato and custard.

**Serves:**

**Prep time:**
**Complexity level:**

1/2 cup part-skim organic ricotta cheese
1/4 cup goat cheese
1 cup frozen peaches, semi-thawed
1/4 teaspoon pure lemon extract
1 cup organic vanilla ice cream

**Purée** the ingredients in a food processor or blender until smooth and creamy. (Note: you may need to interrupt the processing to stir the ingredients several times.) Scoop the custard into individual dessert bowls and serve at once.

# grand marnier chocolate mousse

Decadent and voluptuously creamy chocolate desserts inspire a deep sensual pleasure that's hard to put your finger on. This particular liqueur-spiked mousse is surprisingly quick and easy to prepare, thus yielding ultimate satisfaction in a hurry. The bitter chocolate makes a harmonious match with the smooth orange-infused sweetness of the Grand Marnier. Keep in mind that most liquor stores will carry miniature bottles of Grand Marnier, so don't feel you need to buy a huge bottle just for one recipe.

**Serves:**

**Prep time:**

**Complexity level:**

1/2 cup unsweetened plain soy milk
1 cup mini dark chocolate chips
16 ounces silken tofu
2 tablespoons unsweetened high-
   quality cocoa
2 tablespoons Grand Marnier liqueur
1/4 teaspoon pure orange extract
Pinch of fine unrefined sea salt

**Pour** the soy milk into a small saucepan and slowly bring to a simmer. Remove the saucepan from the heat and let it cool a bit.

**Meanwhile,** slowly melt the chocolate chips in a double boiler, stirring occasionally; or place the chocolate chips in a microwave-safe dish and heat on high for 40–50 seconds, or until the chocolate chips are very soft.

**Add** the melted chocolate to the warm soy milk and stir well. Mix in the silken tofu. (Don't be alarmed, the mixture will look curdled.) Transfer the chocolate-tofu mixture to a blender and process on high until smooth and creamy. Add the cocoa, Grand Marnier, orange extract, and sea salt, and process once more.

**Chill** the mousse in individual bowls for at least 1 1/2 hours before serving.

(Note: For a pretty presentation, chill the mousse in a large ziplock plastic bag; snip a corner of the bag and pipe the mousse in a circular motion into cordial cups, parfait glasses. or even large shot glasses.)

# grilled banana "split" with sweet cashew cream sauce

If you've repeatedly made a note to yourself to eat more fruit and nuts, this treat helps solve your healthy eating resolutions while keeping your taste buds happy. Instead of ice cream, we've topped our bananas with a moist, gooey cashew cream sauce. We then added a layer of flavor complexity to the dessert by grilling the bananas (an inspiration from a Thai street snack). Put together, the flavors of the grilled bananas and cashew cream sauce marry perfectly for a mouthwatering backyard treat. (Note: You can buy agave nectar, the low-glycemic sweetener we use in this recipe, at any natural foods store.)

**Serves:**

**Prep time:**
**Complexity level:**

4 firm bananas
Extra virgin coconut oil (such as Barlean's) for brushing
Cinnamon, to taste
2 teaspoons plus $1/2$ teaspoon pure vanilla extract, divided
$1/2$ cup raw cashews
2 tablespoons organic heavy cream
2 tablespoons agave nectar (or raw honey)
Fresh boysenberries, optional

**Heat** the grill to high.

**Prepare** the bananas by cutting off the ends with a knife. With the banana still in its skin, cut it in half vertically so it is in two long lengths.

**Lightly** brush the face of each banana with coconut oil; sprinkle with a generous amount of cinnamon and then drizzle 2 teaspoons of vanilla extract on top.

**Place** the banana halves cut-side-down on the hottest part of the grill. Grill the bananas for 2–3 minutes, or until the cinnamon forms a "crust" and the bananas are slightly charred. Remove the skins from the bananas, transfer the bananas to individual dessert plates, and place them in the freezer.

**Meanwhile,** place the cashews, heavy cream, agave nectar, and remaining $1/2$ teaspoon of pure vanilla extract into a mini food processor and purée until smooth and creamy. Top the bananas with the cashew cream sauce and freeze for another 20 minutes.

**Serve** cold with fresh boysenberries, if desired.

# 5-minute-emergency decadent chocolate dessert

· · · · · · · · · · · · · · · · · · · · · · · · · · · · · · · · · · · · · · · · · · · · ·

Desperate times call for desperate measures. This emergency dessert was created out of sheer desperation one night when Andy called on his way home from work with some fabulous news that definitely deserved a special treat. Since Ivy has an affair with all things chocolate, it seemed the most suitable main ingredient for the celebratory sweet treat. Yet, this is relaxed cooking at its best—the special but speedy sophisticated dessert is so good, you'll find yourself greedily licking every last bit from the bowl.

Serves:

Prep time:

Complexity level:

1/2 cup canned pumpkin purée
1/3 cup mini dark chocolate chips
1/3 cup unsweetened high-quality
  cocoa powder
1 tablespoon brown sugar
1/3 cup organic whipping cream
1/2 cup vanilla ice cream

**In** a medium-size bowl, stir together the pumpkin, chocolate chips, and cocoa powder. Heat in the microwave for 1½ minutes. Stir in the sugar. Set mixture in the freezer to cool.

**In** a clean nonreactive bowl, whip the whipping cream with an electric mixer until soft peaks form. Add the somewhat cooled chocolate-pumpkin mixture and whip for 30 seconds. Spoon mixture into serving cups and top each serving with ¼ cup vanilla ice cream. Serve at once.

# florida honey-orange blossom cheesecake

Fanatical cheesecake lovers will be overjoyed to know it's entirely possible to give this classic dessert a very healthy makeover with zero compromises in taste and zero sacrifices in beloved velvety texture. Here we've added nutrients in the form of wheat germ, tofu, and omega-3 eggs, and we've cut down substantially on sugar and saturated fat. In keeping with a tropical Florida theme, we also added a delicious flavor twist to the crust by incorporating extra virgin coconut oil.

**Serves:** ⌇⌇⌇⌇⌇ ⌇⌇⌇⌇⌇

**Prep time:** ⏰

**Complexity level:** 🍎 🍎

2 tablespoons extra virgin coconut oil, plus more to prepare pan
6 ounces biscotti
1/4 cup wheat germ
2 tablespoons grass-fed organic butter, melted
7 ounces soft tofu, patted dry with paper towels
3/4 cup part-skim organic ricotta, drained
1 (8-ounce) package organic Neufchâtel cheese
1/2 cup orange blossom honey (regular raw honey is okay)
2 teaspoons pure orange extract
Pinch of unrefined sea salt
3 cage-free organic omega-3 eggs
1/4 cup all-natural marmalade
1 tablespoon Grand Marnier liqueur

**Preheat** the oven to 325 degrees F. Lightly oil a 9-inch springform pan with coconut oil.

**Finely** grind the biscotti in a food processor or blender; add the wheat germ and process again. Add 2 tablespoons coconut oil and butter, and process until the crumbs are moistened. Press the crumb mixture onto the bottom (not sides) of the prepared pan. Bake the crust for 12 minutes. Cool completely on a cooling rack.

**Blend** the tofu and ricotta in the food processor until smooth and creamy. Add the Neufchâtel cheese, honey, orange extract, and salt, and process again. Add the eggs, one at a time, processing between each addition.

**Pour** the creamy cheese mixture over the crust in the pan. Bake the cheesecake in the middle rack in the center of the oven for 60 minutes.

**Transfer** the cake to a wire rack and cool for 1 hour.

**Meanwhile,** bring the marmalade and liqueur to a boil in a small saucepan, stirring constantly until smooth (flakes of orange zest will remain in the marmalade). Brush the cooled cheesecake with the jam mixture.

**Refrigerate** the cheesecake until cold, 4–5 hours. Remove the springform pan, cut the cake into wedges, and serve.

# mom's refrigerator almond butter pie with chocolate crust

This recipe is courtesy of Ivy's mom, Gail. It's nutty and rich but only mildly sweet. Feel free to expand your horizons by substituting peanut butter for the almond butter, if you like.

**Serves:**

**Prep time:**
**Complexity level:**

## CHOCOLATE CRUST
- 1 cup white whole-wheat flour
- 1/4 teaspoon unrefined sea salt
- 5 tablespoons good-quality unsweetened cocoa powder
- 1 tablespoon grass-fed organic butter
- 2 tablespoons extra virgin coconut oil
- 2 heaping tablespoons organic sour cream

## FILLING
- 1 (8-ounce) package Neufchâtel cream cheese
- 1 cup all-natural crunchy almond butter (or substitute all-natural chunky peanut butter)
- 1 teaspoon pure almond extract (eliminate if using peanut butter)
- 1/2 cup plus 4 tablespoons powdered sugar, divided
- 1 (8-ounce) container heavy whipping cream
- 1/4 cup slivered almonds (or chopped peanuts if using peanut butter)

## CHOCOLATE CRUST
**Preheat** oven to 375 degrees F.

**Sift** the flour, salt, and cocoa powder together into a large mixing bowl. Cut the butter and coconut oil into the flour using a pastry cutter or two knives. Mix in the sour cream (use your hands to blend thoroughly). Press the crumbs onto the bottom and sides of a 9-inch round pie dish. Bake the crust for 20 minutes.

**Remove** the crust from the oven and cool on a rack for several minutes. Transfer the crust to the refrigerator and cool for 15 minutes before filling.

## FILLING
**With** an electric mixer, blend the cream cheese, almond butter, and almond extract together until smooth. Add 1/2 cup plus 2 tablespoons of the powdered sugar and beat until well blended.

**Remove** the piecrust from the refrigerator and fill with the almond butter filling.

**In** a separate bowl, whip the whipping cream with an electric mixer until almost firm. Add the remaining 2 tablespoons powdered sugar and whip until soft peaks just begin to form.

**Frost** the almond butter pie with the whipped cream. Decorate with slivered almonds running along the edge of the pie plate.

**Refrigerate** the pie for 1 hour before serving. Serve chilled.

# children's yogurt cake with cashew-cream cheese frosting

Ivy first made this cake on Labor Day when our son was home from school, and he enthusiastically decided to pitch in and help prepare for a party we were having. He did an excellent job of mixing, measuring, stirring and, of course, licking. Once it was baked and frosted, our little guy desperately wanted to taste the finished product, and Ivy didn't have the heart to say "No." Needless to say, the cake was such a hit, she had to hurry and make a new one fast before our friends arrived. We call this a "children's" cake because it really is one of the best cakes to make for little kids. Not only do they gobble it up, but it's surprisingly low in sugar and rich in plenty of nutrients to fuel those growing little bodies and rumbling tummies!

Serves: |||| |||| ||||

Prep time: 🕐
Complexity level: 🍎

## CAKE
**1/3 cup high-oleic canola oil, plus extra for preparing pan**
**1 cup whole-milk organic plain yogurt**
**3/4 cup powdered sugar**
**2 cage-free organic omega-3 eggs**
**2 ripe bananas, smashed**
**1 teaspoon pure vanilla extract**
**1 tablespoon amber rum (don't worry, the alcohol cooks out)**
**2 cups white whole-wheat flour**
**1 1/2 teaspoons aluminum-free baking powder**
**1 teaspoon baking soda**
**Pinch of fine unrefined sea salt**

## FROSTING
**All-natural cashew nut butter (preferably fresh cashew nut butter with no added ingredients)**
**1/2 cup organic Neufchâtel cream cheese**
**1/4 cup powdered sugar**
**Juice from 1/2 lemon**
**2 tablespoons whole-milk organic plain yogurt**

## CAKE
**Preheat** oven to 350 degrees F. Grease the bottom and sides of a 10-inch springform pan with canola oil.

**In** a medium-size bowl, whisk the yogurt and sugar together. Add the eggs, one at a time, and blend thoroughly. Mix in the bananas, vanilla extract, rum, and remaining oil.

**Sift** the flour, baking powder, baking soda, and salt together. Stir the dry ingredients into the wet ingredients and mix well. Pour the batter into the prepared pan. Bake the cake for 30 minutes, or until a knife inserted in the middle comes out clean.

**Transfer** the cake to a wire rack and cool for 15–20 minutes before frosting.

## FROSTING
**Combine** all ingredients and, using a handheld mixer, whip together until smooth and creamy. Frost the cake when it cools. (Note: Cake is best served at room temperature.)

# spiced holiday drop "cake-cookies" with dried cranberries

Our son absolutely loves these cookies during the holiday season! He calls them "cake-cookies" because that's just what they are—a brilliant combination of cake and cookie rolled in one. (Could anything possibly be better?) They are shaped like cookies, but they have a lighter and more cakelike texture. The spice is pleasantly subtle, just enough to add contemporary culinary interest.

**Serves:** | | | | | | | | | | | | | | |

**Prep time:** ⏰

**Complexity level:** 🍎🍎

Canola oil cooking spray
1 cup white whole-wheat flour
1 cup old-fashioned oats
1 teaspoon baking soda
¼ teaspoon allspice
¼ teaspoon cinnamon
½ teaspoon unrefined sea salt
½ cup firmly packed dark brown sugar
4 tablespoons grass-fed organic butter, softened
2 tablespoon extra virgin coconut oil (such as Barlean's)
2 tablespoons almond butter
½ cup unsweetened applesauce
¼ cup canned pumpkin
1 cage-free organic omega-3 egg white
½ cup shaved almonds
½ cup dried cranberries

**Preheat** oven to 350 degrees F. Coat a large baking sheet with canola oil cooking spray.

**In** a medium bowl, combine the flour, oats, baking soda, allspice, cinnamon, and salt.

**In** a large bowl, beat the sugar, butter, coconut oil, and almond butter together with a handheld mixer until ingredients are well combined. Add the applesauce, pumpkin, and egg white, and mix for 1 minute. Stir in the flour mixture, almonds, and cranberries.

**Drop** the dough by heaping double tablespoonfuls onto the baking sheet, leaving about 1 inch between (you should have enough for 12 large-size cookies.) Bake for 15 minutes. Let "cake-cookies" cool on the baking sheet for 5-8 minutes, then use a spatula to lift and transfer them onto a serving platter. (Note: "cake-cookies" can be made 3 days in advance and stored in a ziplock bag in the refrigerator.)

# peach and blackberry cobbler

Ahhh, cobbler. What would a cookbook be without a cobbler recipe? While straight-up peach cobbler seems assiduously ubiquitous, the addition of unexpected black-berries delivers a little tang and a dash of excitement to this classic standby.

**Serves:**

**Prep time:**
**Complexity level:**

1/2 pound fresh blackberries
3 firm peaches, chopped (keep the skins on)
2 tablespoons frozen orange juice concentrate
1/3 cup plus 2 tablespoons brown sugar, divided
1/2 teaspoon pure almond extract
1 teaspoon brandy
2 cups plus 2 tablespoons white whole-wheat flour, divided
3 tablespoons cold grass-fed organic butter
2 tablespoons extra virgin coconut oil (such as Barlean's)
2 teaspoons baking powder
1/4 teaspoon unrefined sea salt
3/4 cup full-fat Greek-style yogurt
2 tablespoons confectioners' sugar

**Preheat** oven to 400 degrees F.

**Place** the blackberries, peaches, frozen orange juice concentrate, 1/3 cup brown sugar, almond extract, and brandy in a medium saucepan; heat mixture until orange juice concentrate melts and liquid just begins to boil. Whisk in 2 tablespoons of the flour and cook for 1 minute, stirring very gently. Spoon the fruit filling into an 8-inch square glass baking dish.

**Using** clean hands, pinch the butter, coconut oil, and 2 cups of flour together between your thumbs and forefingers until mixture becomes crumbly. Mix in the remaining 2 tablespoons of sugar, baking powder, and salt. Add the yogurt and mix with your hands to make a soft dough.

**Use** your hands to crumble the dough evenly over the fruit. Sprinkle the top with confectioners' sugar. Bake cobbler, uncovered, for 20 minutes, or until biscuit mixture turns a light golden brown. Allow cobbler to cool for 10 minutes before serving.

# menus for every occasion

**By now** you can define whole foods, and you've already dabbled in making whole foods recipes. It's time to ramp things up a few notches! This section shows you how to put everything together with a comprehensive collection of effortless everyday family meals, menus for entertaining, special occasion and holiday meals, and internationally themed soirees with wine flights and more. The whole foods recipes in this section take the guesswork out of meal planning and simplify everything that might seem complex or even mildly overwhelming about preparing a full-blown meal. You'll also discover just how easy and doable it is to make whole foods eating a part of your life . . . every day of the year!

Please see our Web site www.wholefoodsdietcookbook.com for photos of recipes and some additional recipes.

# weeknight dinners

quick and easy menus for weeknight dining

**These weeknight** meals aren't particularly fancy, and they certainly aren't intimidating, but they do have "family friendly" gourmet flair. In other words, even the palates of your not-so-sophisticated kids and teens will still be satisfied. This chapter was actually originally created for multitasking, stressed-out soccer moms (like Ivy!) who seem to have zero time to spare. To help take the "thinking" out of meal planning, we've assembled a complete menu of complementary dishes, so all you have to do is pick and choose your weekly menu, write the grocery list, and, of course—get cooking!

# pork chops with mole sauce and apples with roasted baby carrots

· · · · · · · · · · · · · · · · · · · · · · · · · · · · · · · · · · · · · · · · · · · · · · ·

**Serves:** | | | |

**Prep time:** ⏰

**Complexity level:** 🍎 🍎

## pork chops with mole sauce and apples

2 poblano peppers

1 medium onion, quartered

1 tablespoon plus 1 teaspoon extra virgin olive oil, divided (plus more for coating the pork chops)

½ teaspoon unrefined sea salt, plus more to taste

White pepper, to taste

½ cup dry-roasted pecans

1 teaspoon chili powder

2 teaspoons cinnamon

1 teaspoon cumin

2 tablespoons good-quality unsweetened cocoa powder

1 tablespoon tomato paste

1 tablespoon molasses

1 teaspoon white vinegar

4 (6-ounce) center-cut boneless pork loin chops (about ½ to ¾ inch thick)

3 Granny Smith apples, cored and sliced into ½-inch-thin rounds (keep the skins on)

Juice from 1 lemon

**Preheat** the oven to 400 degrees F.

### MOLE

**Place** the peppers and onion on a baking sheet and drizzle with 1 tablespoon of oil. Roast for 25 minutes, or until all vegetables are soft and slightly charred. Remove from the oven and set aside. Once the peppers are cool enough to handle, peel the skins and remove the seeds.

**Transfer** the peppers and onion to a food processor or blender; add the pecans, chili powder, cinnamon, cumin, cocoa powder, ½ teaspoon salt, tomato paste, molasses, and vinegar. Purée all ingredients until smooth and creamy. Set the mole sauce aside.

### PORK CHOPS

**Preheat** a grill or nonstick griddle pan over medium-high heat. Lower the oven to 350 degrees F.

**Lightly** coat both sides of the chops with a small amount of oil and season with salt to taste. Cook the chops for 2–3 minutes per side on the heated grill pan of your choice. Remove the chops from the pan and transfer to a baking sheet. Baste chops with a liberal amount of mole sauce and place in the oven to finish cooking. Bake for 8–10 minutes, or until apples are ready to come off the grill and pork is done.

**APPLES**

**Season** the apple rounds with lemon juice, a teaspoon of oil, and a little bit of salt. Cover grill pan surface with as many apple slices as possible and cook about 3 minutes per side. (Note: you don't want the apples to be too soft.)

## roasted baby carrots

**1 pound baby carrots, peeled**
**2 teaspoons extra virgin olive oil**
**2 tablespoons fresh marjoram**
**$1/2$ teaspoons unrefined sea salt**
**Pepper, to taste**

**Place** the carrots on a baking sheet and toss with oil, marjoram, salt, and pepper. In the preheated 400-degree F oven, place next to the peppers and onion that are being roasted for the mole sauce. Bake for 30 minutes, or until the carrots are slightly charred.

**Remove** the chops from the oven and top with apples and more mole sauce. Arrange the roasted carrots to the side of the pork chops. Serve at once.

# jamaican lime and curry-crusted salmon and white-raisin couscous pilaf with sautéed spinach

Serves: ▯ ▯ ▯ ▯

Prep time: ⏰

Complexity level: 🍎

## jamaican lime and curry-crusted salmon

Extra virgin olive oil cooking spray
1¹/₂ pounds salmon filet, skin removed
Old Bay Seasoning, to taste
Dried basil, to taste
Jamaican curry powder, to taste
¹/₂ cup panko crumbs (or whole-wheat panko crumbs by Ian's Natural Foods)
2 tablespoons unsalted grass-fed organic butter, sliced into very thin pieces
Juice from 2 limes

**Preheat** oven to 375 degrees F. Spray a 9 x 11-inch baking dish with cooking spray.

**Place** salmon in the baking dish. Sprinkle with a generous amount of Old Bay Seasoning, basil, and curry. Sprinkle panko crumbs on top. Arrange butter slices on top of salmon.

**Place** salmon in the oven and bake for 15 minutes, or until cooked through.

**Remove** salmon from the oven and squeeze lime juice on top. Let salmon sit 2–3 minutes before serving. Serve warm.

# white-raisin couscous pilaf

2 teaspoons grass-fed organic butter
2 tablespoons extra virgin olive oil,
 divided
3 cloves garlic, minced
1 red onion, diced
Unrefined sea salt, to taste
3/4 cup yellow raisins
1 1/2 cups dry whole-wheat couscous
1 1/2 cups water
Juice from 1 whole lemon

**Heat** the butter and 1 tablespoon oil in a large skillet over medium-high heat; add the garlic and sauté for 1 minute. Add the onion and sauté until tender, about 5 minutes. Season the onion with salt, add the raisins, and toss to coat.

**Mix** the dry couscous with the onion and raisin mixture; add the remaining tablespoon oil and toss to coat the couscous. Pour the water and lemon juice over the couscous and cook, stirring frequently, until couscous is done, about 5 minutes. Season couscous with more salt. Remove couscous from heat and cover to keep warm until serving time.

# sautéed spinach

3 tablespoons extra virgin olive oil
5 cloves garlic, chopped
2 shallots, finely chopped
1 1/2 pounds baby spinach leaves
Unrefined sea salt, to taste
White pepper, to taste
1/2 teaspoon nutmeg

**In** a very large Dutch oven, heat the oil over medium-high heat; add the garlic and shallots, and cook 3–4 minutes, or until shallots are soft. Add the spinach, cover, and cook for 2 minutes. Uncover spinach and season with salt, pepper, and nutmeg. Toss spinach with a large spoon and cook about 1 more minute, or until spinach is wilted.

# bulgarian-style lamb and pasta and brussels sprouts

Serves: | | | |

Prep time: 🕐

Complexity level: 🍎

## bulgarian-style lamb

2 pounds boneless, pasture-raised lamb
   stew meat, trimmed of all visible fat
Unrefined sea salt, to taste
White pepper, to taste
5–6 cloves garlic, sliced
1 lemon, freshly squeezed
2 tablespoons good-quality soy sauce
1 teaspoon Dijon mustard
1 teaspoon dried rosemary
1/4 cup good full-bodied red wine (don't
   use cooking wine!)
1/2 cup prepared hummus
1/2 cup full-fat organic plain yogurt

**Season** the lamb with salt and pepper; transfer lamb to a large ziplock plastic bag. To the bag, add cloves garlic, lemon juice, soy sauce, mustard, rosemary, and wine. Toss the liquid to coat the lamb. Transfer the ziplock bag with the lamb to the refrigerator and marinate for 1–4 hours (the longer the better).

**Remove** the lamb from the refrigerator and transfer the lamb and marinade to an 8 x 8-inch glass baking dish. Cover the dish with aluminum foil and slow-cook at 300 degrees F for 1 hour.

**Meanwhile,** whisk the hummus and yogurt together in a medium-size bowl. Set aside.

**When** the lamb is cooked through, add the lamb and marinade juices to the large bowl with the hummus-yogurt mixture. Add the Pasta and Brussels Sprouts (below). Gently mix all ingredients and toss to coat. Serve warm.

## pasta and brussels sprouts

2 1/2 cups water
1/2 teaspoon unrefined sea salt
2 pounds brussels sprouts
8 ounces dry-sprouted whole-grain
   penne pasta

**Bring** a large pot of salted water to a boil. When the water boils, add the brussels sprouts and cook for 5 minutes. Add the penne pasta to the boiling water with the brussels sprouts and cook for 5 minutes. Drain the brussels sprouts and pasta, and transfer to a large bowl. Season with salt and pepper. Gently toss the hummus-yogurt mixture in with the pasta and brussels sprouts and mix thoroughly.

# white bean–butternut squash ragout and polenta squares

● ● ● ● ● ● ● ● ● ● ● ● ● ● ● ● ● ● ● ● ● ● ● ● ● ● ● ● ● ● ● ● ● ● ● ● ● ● ● ● ● ● ● ●

Serves: ▎▎▎▎

Prep time: 🕐
Complexity level: 🍎 🍎

## white bean–butternut squash ragout

2 tablespoons extra virgin olive oil
1 large onion, diced
Coarse unrefined sea salt, to taste
3–4 cloves garlic, minced
1-inch piece gingerroot, peeled and
 minced
1 (12-ounce) package frozen butternut
 squash, thawed and drained of excess
 water
2 tablespoons all-natural creamy peanut
 butter
1 (14.5-ounce) can diced tomatoes,
 drained
2 (14.5-ounce) cans Great Northern beans,
 rinsed and drained
1 tablespoon finely chopped fresh sage
Pinch of cayenne pepper
1 cup shredded Gouda cheese

**Heat** oil in a heavy 3-quart saucepan over medium heat. Add the onion and a pinch of salt; sauté for 5 minutes, or until onion is softened. Add the garlic and gingerroot, and sauté an additional 2 minutes.

**Add** the butternut squash and peanut butter; stir to combine until peanut butter is well blended. Stir in the tomatoes, beans, sage, and cayenne pepper; cover and simmer over low heat for 15 minutes.

**Spoon** the ragout over the individual square-shaped polenta servings (below). Top the ragout with shredded Gouda cheese. Serve at once.

## polenta squares

3 cups water
1/2 teaspoon coarse unrefined sea salt
1 cup corn grits (polenta)
1 tablespoon extra virgin olive oil, plus
 more as needed

**Pour** the water and salt into a medium-size pot; bring water to a boil. Add the polenta and reduce heat to low;

cover and cook, stirring occasionally, for about 5 minutes. Stir in the oil.

**Oil** the bottom and sides of an 8 x 8-inch casserole; spoon the polenta into the casserole and let sit for 10 minutes, or until firm. When firm, cut polenta into four squares and place on individual plates.

# corn and quinoa risotto and mushroom and olive salad with truffle vinaigrette

Serves: | | | |

Prep time:

Complexity level:

## corn and quinoa risotto

3 cups free-range organic chicken broth
2 tablespoons extra virgin olive oil
3 cloves garlic, minced
1 leek, carefully rinsed, trimmed, and
   thinly sliced
½ cup Arborio rice
½ cup quinoa
Freshly ground coarse unrefined sea salt,
   to taste
Freshly ground black pepper, to taste
1 teaspoon dried thyme
¼ cup Chardonnay
1 (15.5-ounce) can diced organic
   tomatoes, drained
2 cups frozen corn kernels, semi-thawed
¾ cup freshly shaved Parmesan cheese

**Bring** the broth to a boil in a 2-quart saucepan over high heat. Reduce heat to maintain a steady simmer.

**Warm** the oil in a heavy 3-quart pan over medium-high heat; add the garlic and leek, and sauté until tender, about 4–5 minutes. Add the rice and quinoa, season lightly with salt and pepper, and sauté, stir-frying for about 2 minutes.

**Sprinkle** the thyme on top of the grains and add the Chardonnay; cook until dry. Ladle ½ cup of the hot broth into the pan with the grains and add the tomatoes, stirring constantly. Continue adding the hot broth, ½ cup at time, and continue stirring until the liquid has been absorbed before adding each subsequent ½ cup of water. Cook the grains over medium heat for about 25 minutes, or until all liquid is absorbed, stirring frequently so the grains do not stick to the pan.

**Remove** the pan from the heat and add the semi-thawed corn kernels; cover the pan and let the risotto sit for 15 minutes before serving.

**Serve** risotto warm with Parmesan cheese.

# mushroom and olive salad with truffle vinaigrette

1/4 cup black truffle oil
1/4 cup flax oil (such as Barlean's)
1/4 cup lemon juice
2 tablespoons canola oil mayonnaise
2 tablespoons orange juice concentrate
2 tablespoons distilled white vinegar
Freshly ground coarse unrefined sea salt, to taste
Freshly ground black pepper, to taste
8 ounces very fresh white button mushrooms, trimmed and thinly sliced
1/2 red onion, diced
10 ounces mixed baby greens (such as spinach, arugula, and Bibb lettuce)
3/4 cup thinly sliced fresh green olives marinated in garlic and extra virgin olive oil (available at a gourmet market olive bar)
1/2 cup drained and thinly sliced sun-dried tomatoes packed in olive oil

In a large salad bowl, whisk together the truffle oil, flax oil, lemon juice, mayonnaise, orange juice concentrate, vinegar, salt, and pepper.

Add the mushrooms and onion, and toss gently to coat. Add the greens and toss again. Top the salad with the green olives and sun-dried tomatoes. Serve immediately.

# ...west tofu burgers and ...cky beans with green ...iles and tomatoes

Serves: | | | |

Prep time: ⏰

Complexity level: 🍎 🍎 🍎

## southwest tofu burgers

¹/₂ cup shaved almonds
¹/₂ cup unsweetened plain soy milk
14 ounces extra-firm tofu, drained, crumbled, and patted dry with paper towels
³/₄ cup finely chopped shallots
2 cups frozen corn kernels, thawed
1 cup wheat germ
4 cloves garlic, minced
¹/₂ teaspoon unrefined sea salt
¹/₄ teaspoon cayenne pepper
1 teaspoon paprika
2–4 splashes Tabasco or other hot sauce
2 teaspoons cumin
2 tablespoons finely chopped cilantro
2 tablespoons extra virgin olive oil, divided

**Preheat** oven to 425 degrees F.

**Place** the almonds and soy milk in a blender and process until completely puréed. Add tofu and blend well.

**Transfer** mixture to a large bowl; add shallots, corn, wheat germ, garlic, salt, cayenne pepper, paprika, Tabasco, cumin, and cilantro. Combine until well blended.

**Form** the mixture into 16 small burgers (about 2 tablespoons each) and set aside on a large baking sheet.

**Heat** 1 tablespoon oil in a nonstick skillet over medium-high heat. Place 8 burgers on skillet and lightly brown 3–4 minutes per side. Transfer burgers to baking sheet. Repeat process with remaining 8 burgers. Bake burgers for 5 minutes. Serve warm.

## garlicky beans with green chiles and tomatoes

2 tablespoons extra virgin olive oil
¹/₂ red onion, finely chopped
8–9 cloves garlic, minced
Unrefined sea salt, to taste
1 pint cherry tomatoes, halved
2 (14-ounce) cans small red beans, rinsed with water and drained
1 (4.5-ounce) can chopped green chiles, drained
1 teaspoon ground cumin
2 pinches cayenne pepper
¹/₄ cup chopped fresh cilantro

**In** a large skillet, heat the oil over medium-high heat; add the onion and garlic, and cook, stirring, until the onions are tender, about 5 minutes. Season lightly with salt.

**Add** tomatoes and cook, stirring occasionally, until tomatoes are just tender, about 2 minutes. (Do not overcook or tomatoes will get mushy.) Gently stir in beans and green chiles, and cook an additional 2–3 minutes. Season with cumin, cayenne pepper, and a little more salt. Stir in cilantro and cook for one more minute. Serve warm.

# easy roasted orange roughy and slow-cooker ratatouille

Serves: | | | |

Prep time: ⏰

Complexity level: 🍎🍎

## easy roasted orange roughy

Extra virgin olive oil cooking spray
4 (6-ounce) orange roughy fillets, rinsed
and patted dry
1 tablespoon extra virgin olive oil
2 tablespoons lemon juice
3 cloves garlic, minced
1/4 teaspoon unrefined sea salt
2 teaspoons paprika
1/4 teaspoon coarse black pepper
1/4 teaspoon dried thyme

**Preheat** oven to 450 degrees F. Spray a large casserole with cooking spray. Place the fish fillets in a single layer in the casserole.

**In** a small bowl, whisk together the remaining ingredients. Drizzle the mixture on top of the fish. Roast the fish for 10–12 minutes, or until the fish flakes easily with a fork, about 10 minutes per inch of thickness. Remove the fish from the oven and serve with the ratatouille on top.

## slow-cooker ratatouille

1 whole head of garlic (about 15 cloves
garlic)
1/3 cup plus 2 tablespoons extra virgin
olive oil, divided
2 tablespoons balsamic vinegar
2 yellow bell peppers
2 tomatoes
1 zucchini
3 onions
1 eggplant
1 1/2 teaspoons unrefined sea salt
1 teaspoon coarsely ground black pepper
2 teaspoons dried oregano
1 cup packed chopped fresh basil

**Peel** the garlic and place the cloves in a small microwave-safe dish. Pour 2 tablespoons oil over the garlic, cover the dish with

a paper towel, and microwave on high for 1 minute, or until garlic is soft. Remove the garlic from the microwave and mash the cloves with a fork. Mix in the vinegar. Set aside.

**Cut** the vegetables into 1-inch chunks and place them in a large bowl. Season with salt, pepper, and oregano. Mix in the garlic and vinegar. Pour in the remaining 1/3 cup oil and toss to coat.

**Transfer** vegetables to a 5- or 6-quart slow cooker, cover, and cook on low heat for 6–7 hours. Add the basil 10 minutes before serving. Leaving the juices in the slow cooker, transfer the ratatouille with a slotted spoon to a large serving bowl. Let ratatouille cool for 10–15 minutes. Ladle a generous serving on top of the fish. Serve warm.

# tofu pockets with artichoke ricotta stuffing and pan-grilled corn with onions and almonds

Serves: ▌▌▌▌

Prep time: 🕰

Complexity level: 🍎🍎🍎

## tofu pockets with artichoke-ricotta stuffing

¹/₄ cup tahini

¹/₄ cup low-fat organic ricotta cheese

¹/₄ cup good-quality canned artichokes marinated in extra virgin olive oil, drained of excess oil

1 (8-ounce) package extra-firm tofu, drained and patted dry with paper towels

1 cage-free organic omega-3 egg, beaten

¹/₂ teaspoon Dijon mustard

Unrefined sea salt, to taste

White pepper, to taste

2 tablespoons extra virgin olive oil, divided

¹/₄ cup whole-wheat pastry flour or white whole-wheat flour

1 (12-ounce) can roasted red peppers, drained and patted dry

1 heaping tablespoon organic cream cheese

**Place** the tahini, ricotta, and artichokes in a blender or food processor and purée until creamy but not completely smooth. (The mixture should have some texture to it.)

**Cut** the tofu block into thirds lengthwise so that there are three thin

rectangular blocks. Then cut each block on the diagonal to form two triangles, ending with six triangles total. Starting at the apex of one triangular tofu block, carefully insert a thin sharp knife three-fourths of the way through the tofu triangle to create a pocket. (Take care not to cut through the triangle though!) Carefully stuff each pocket with the artichoke-ricotta stuffing.

**In** a wide bowl, lightly beat the egg with the mustard.

**Season** the tofu triangles on both sides with salt and pepper. Immerse the tofu in the mustard-egg mixture and then dredge in the flour.

**Heat** 1 tablespoon oil in a large nonstick skillet over medium-high heat. (Use a paper towel to distribute the oil evenly over the pan.) Working in two batches, place half of the tofu pockets in the hot skillet and sear for 2–3 minutes each side. Repeat process with the remaining oil and tofu pockets.

**To** make the purée, place the peppers and cream cheese in a blender and purée until smooth and creamy.

**Serve** warm, drizzled with red pepper purée.

## pan-grilled corn with onions and almonds

**4 ears corn, shucked**
**1 tablespoon extra virgin olive oil**
**1 medium-size red onion, finely chopped**
**Unrefined sea salt, to taste**
**Cayenne pepper, to taste**
**1/2 cup chopped fresh cilantro**
**3/4 cup shaved almonds**
**1 lime, cut in half**

**Stand** the corn up on a cutting board and use a knife to strip the kernels off the cob.

**Pour** the oil into a medium-size non-stick skillet and heat to medium-high. When the oil is hot, add the onion and sauté for 4-5 minutes, or until tender. Season lightly with salt and cayenne pepper. Add the corn and sauté for 3–4 additional minutes. Season again with salt.

**Remove** the skillet from the heat. Toss the cilantro and almonds in with the corn and onions. Squeeze the lime juice on top of the corn and serve at once.

# swordfish kabobs in herb sauce and mashed garlic "cauli-tatoes"

Serves: ❘❘❘❘
Prep time: 🕐
Complexity level: 🍎🍎🍎

## swordfish kabobs

**HERB SAUCE**
3 cloves garlic
³/₄ cup parsley
¹/₄ cup fresh oregano
2 tablespoons orange juice concentrate
2 tablespoons walnuts
Juice from 1 whole lemon
¹/₂ cup flax oil (such as Barlean's)
1/8 teaspoon cayenne pepper
Unrefined sea salt, to taste

**KABOBS**
¹/₄ cup extra virgin olive oil
¹/₄ cup orange juice concentrate
2 tablespoons balsamic vinegar
1 teaspoon dried oregano
¹/₄ teaspoon unrefined sea salt, plus more
    to taste
6 cloves garlic, minced (about
    1 tablespoon)
2 teaspoons ground paprika
2 pounds swordfish, cut into 1¹/₂-inch
    cubes
8 bamboo skewers
1 pint cherry tomatoes
2 orange bell peppers, cut into 1-inch
    pieces
1 (7-ounce) jar large Spanish green olives
    stuffed with pimentos

**HERB SAUCE**
**Place** all ingredients in a blender and process until smooth. Place herb sauce in a covered container and refrigerate for up to 2 days before serving.

**KABOBS**
**Combine** the oil, orange juice concentrate, vinegar, oregano, measured salt, garlic, and paprika in a large ziplock bag. Add the swordfish chunks, refrigerate, and marinate for at least 30 minutes (or up to 4 hours).

**Preheat** the broiler (or light the grill) and then soak bamboo skewers in water for 15 minutes. Alternate threading the swordfish, cherry tomatoes, peppers, and olives onto the bamboo skewers. Place the swordfish kabobs on a large nonstick baking sheet. Lightly season the swordfish and vegetables with salt and baste with the remaining marinade.

**Grill** or broil the skewers 6 inches from the heat source until the fish cubes are just cooked through and vegetables are lightly browned around the edges, about 8 minutes.

**To** serve, arrange the kabobs on a large serving platter and smother with the herb sauce. Serve remaining herb sauce in a small bowl in the center of the serving platter. Serve kabobs warm.

# mashed garlic "cauli-tatoes"

3 Idaho baking potatoes
1 medium-size head of cauliflower
3$^{1}/_{2}$ cups water
$^{1}/_{2}$ teaspoon unrefined sea salt
$^{1}/_{3}$ cup whole-milk organic plain yogurt
1 tablespoon organic cream cheese
1 tablespoon prepared hummus
7 cloves garlic, thinly sliced
1 tablespoon extra virgin olive oil
$^{1}/_{2}$ teaspoon unrefined sea salt
$^{1}/_{2}$ cup chopped parsley

**Pierce** the potatoes on all sides with a fork and bake at 400 degrees F for 1 hour.

**Meanwhile,** cut the cauliflower into small pieces. Bring a large pot of salted water to a boil, add cauliflower florets, and cook until tender but not mushy, about 10 minutes. Drain the cauliflower and rinse with cool water.

**When** cauliflower is cool enough to handle, place several florets in a blender or food processor. Add the yogurt, cream cheese, and hummus, and purée until smooth. Working in small batches, continue to add cauliflower florets to the blender/food processor and purée each batch until smooth.

**Place** the sliced garlic pieces in a small microwave-safe dish and pour the oil on top of the garlic; microwave the garlic on high for about 1 minute, or until garlic is soft. Set garlic aside.

**Once** potatoes are done, remove from oven and allow them to cool. Using clean hands or a potato masher, squash the potatoes (keep the skins on!). Place the squashed potatoes in a large bowl and continue squashing until they are fairly well mashed. (We don't suggest using an electric mixer as it might have a hard time with the skins.)

**Pour** the puréed cauliflower into the bowl with the potatoes and use a fork to thoroughly mix and mash the cauliflower purée in with the potatoes. Stir in the garlic and oil. Season with salt. Stir in the chopped parsley. Serve warm.

# gourmet tempeh burger melts with avocado-lime soup and asparagus and orange salad

Serves: ▮▮▮▮

Prep time: ⏰

Complexity level: 🍎🍎🍎

## gourmet tempeh burger melts

1 cup organic vegetable stock
8 ounces tempeh, crumbled
$^1/_2$ cup finely diced celery
$^1/_4$ cup finely diced Spanish onion
$^1/_2$ cup finely diced red bell pepper
$^1/_4$ cup prepared hummus
$^1/_4$ cup canola oil mayonnaise
1 tablespoon fresh lemon juice
2 teaspoons Worcestershire sauce
$^1/_4$ cup finely chopped Spanish olives
marinated in extra virgin olive oil and
garlic (look for fresh olives from the deli
or olive bar in your supermarket)
1 teaspoon paprika
Unrefined sea salt, to taste
$^1/_2$ cup shredded low-fat organic cheddar
cheese

**Preheat** oven to 400 degrees F. Line a baking sheet with parchment paper.

**Combine** the vegetable stock and tempeh in a medium-size cast-iron skillet and heat over medium-high heat; simmer tempeh for 10 minutes, or until liquid is absorbed. Remove skillet from heat and set tempeh aside to cool.

**Add** the cooled tempeh to a medium-size mixing bowl. Mix in the celery, onion, bell pepper, hummus, mayonnaise, lemon juice, Worcestershire, olives, paprika, and salt.

**Divide** the tempeh and vegetable mixture into 6 patties. (You'll either have leftovers or two people can eat 2!) Arrange the patties on the prepared parchment paper, using your hands to shape them. Divide the shredded cheddar cheese on top of the patties. Bake for 10 minutes, or until cheese is melted. Allow tempeh to cool for 5 minutes before carefully removing the patties with a spatula. Serve warm.

# avocado-lime soup

1 tablespoon extra virgin olive oil
$^1/_2$ Spanish onion, finely chopped
4 cloves garlic, minced
Unrefined sea salt, to taste
1 teaspoon cumin
2 or 3 pinches cayenne pepper
1 cup organic vegetable broth
$^1/_4$ cup fresh lime juice
7 ounces silken tofu
2 small ripe avocados

**Heat** oil in a medium saucepan to medium-high. Add onion and garlic, and sauté for about 8 minutes, until onion is soft. Season with salt, cumin, and cayenne pepper. Add the vegetable broth and lime juice. Simmer for 10 minutes. Remove from heat and transfer liquid to freezer; chill for 30 minutes.

**Meanwhile,** purée the tofu and avocados in a blender. Add chilled liquid to blender and process until mixture is smooth and creamy. Season with additional salt. Serve chilled.

# asparagus and orange salad with citrus vinagrette

$^1/_4$ cup orange juice concentrate
2 tablespoons white wine vinegar
$^1/_4$ cup flax oil (such as Barlean's)
2 tablespoons raw honey
2 cloves garlic, chopped
2 teaspoons chopped fresh tarragon
Unrefined sea salt, to taste
Freshly ground black pepper, to taste
2 cups water
1 pound asparagus
2 oranges, cut into bite-size chunks
2 shallots, chopped
$^1/_2$ cup finely chopped pecans

**Prepare** the vinaigrette by combining the orange juice concentrate, vinegar, flax oil, honey, garlic, and tarragon in a blender; process until smooth and creamy. Season vinaigrette with salt and pepper to taste.

**Bring** water to a boil in a medium-size saucepan. Add asparagus to the water and cook for 3–4 minutes, or until fork-tender. Drain asparagus, rinse with cool water, and transfer to an ice bath for 4–5 minutes to stop the cooking process.

**Remove** the asparagus from the ice bath, drain, and transfer to a medium-size serving bowl. Toss in the oranges and shallots. Season with salt and pepper. Drizzle the vinaigrette over the asparagus and toss to coat. Scatter pecans on top of asparagus. Let salad sit at room temperature for 10–15 minutes before serving.

# herbed arctic char (or salmon) with feta cornbread muffins and asparagus with sun-dried tomatoes

Serves: | | | |

Prep time: 🕐

Complexity level: 🍎 🍎

## herbed arctic char

¹/₂ cup chopped fresh dill
¹/₂ cup chopped fresh parsley
¹/₂ cup chopped fresh mint
¹/₄ cup canola oil mayonnaise
1¹/₄ pounds Arctic char (or salmon) fillets
Unrefined sea salt, to taste

**Preheat** the oven the 425 degrees F.

**In** a mini food processor, purée the dill, parsley, mint, and mayonnaise together.

**Season** the Arctic char (or salmon) fillets with salt. Place the fillets in a baking dish and spread the creamy herb mixture on top. Bake the fish for about 12 minutes, or until done. (Take care not to overcook.) Serve warm.

## feta cornbread muffins

**RECIPE MAKES 9 MUFFINS TOTAL**
Canola oil cooking spray
²/₃ cup stone-ground, whole-grain yellow cornmeal
1 cup white whole-wheat flour
2 teaspoons baking powder
¹/₂ teaspoon unrefined sea salt
2 tablespoons raw honey
²/₃ cup unsweetened plain soy milk
¹/₄ cup extra virgin olive oil, plus more for dipping
2 cage-free organic omega-3 eggs, lightly beaten

1 cup frozen corn kernels
¹/₄ cup 2-percent low-fat organic cottage cheese
¹/₄ cup crumbled organic feta cheese

**Preheat** oven to 425 degrees F. Spray 9 muffin cups with cooking spray.

**In** a medium-size bowl, mix together the cornmeal, flour, baking powder, and salt. Make a well in the center of the mixture and add the honey, soy milk, ¹/₄ cup oil, and lightly beaten eggs; mix together until well blended. Stir in the frozen corn kernels. Mix in the cottage cheese and feta.

**Spoon** the batter into prepared muffin cups and bake for 18 minutes, or until a toothpick inserted in the middle of a muffin comes out clean. Run a knife around the edge of each muffin. Allow muffins to cool on a wire rack for 5 minutes before removing from the pan.

(NOTE: For the Thanksgiving Dinner version on page 254, eliminate the cottage cheese and feta cheese.)

## asparagus with sun-dried tomatoes

1 pound asparagus
¼ cup finely chopped sun-dried tomatoes packed in extra virgin olive oil (reserve the oil)
5 cloves garlic, crushed
2 tablespoons balsamic vinegar
Finely milled unrefined sea salt, to taste
Coarsely ground black pepper, to taste

**Preheat** oven to 425 degrees F.

**Trim** away the bottom ½ inch of each asparagus stalk. Arrange asparagus stalks on a baking sheet. Toss with tomatoes and garlic. Spread the asparagus out in a single layer. Drizzle with the vinegar and season with salt and pepper.

**Roast** asparagus for 10–12 minutes, or until crisp-tender. Serve warm.

# slow-cooker espresso brisket with fruit sauce and whole-wheat couscous and sautéed spinach

Serves: ▯▯▯▯

Prep time: 🕐

Complexity level: 🍎

## slow-cooker espresso brisket with fruit sauce

2¹/₂ pounds grass-fed beef brisket, trimmed of most of the fat
³/₄ cup dried pitted plums
³/₄ cup dried apricot halves
³/₄ cup white raisins
3 cloves garlic, chopped
1¹/₄ cups organic vegetable broth
³/₄ cup Merlot
1 teaspoon thyme
¹/₂ teaspoon unrefined sea salt
1 tablespoon finely ground espresso
1 teaspoon chili powder
¹/₄ teaspoon freshly ground black pepper
2 tablespoons white whole-wheat flour

**Cut** the brisket in half and place in a 5- or 6-quart slow cooker. Top with plums, apricots, raisins, and garlic.

**In** a separate bowl, whisk together the rest of the ingredients. Pour the liquid over the fruit and meat. Cover and cook over low heat for 5–6 hours.

**Allow** brisket to cool 10–15 minutes before serving. Serve brisket and stewed fruits over whole wheat couscous. Pour the extra sauce from the slow cooker on top of the brisket. Serve with a side of Sautéed Spinach (see page 157).

## whole-wheat couscous

1¹/₂ cups organic chicken broth (such as Pacific Natural Foods brand "Organic Free-Range Chicken Broth)
1 tablespoon extra-virgin olive oil
1¹/₂ cups whole-wheat couscous (such as Fantastic Foods brand)
4 scallions, thinly sliced
Salt, to taste
White pepper, to taste

**Bring** the chicken broth and oil to a boil in a medium saucepan. Place the couscous in a large glass or ceramic mixing bowl. Carefully pour the boiling liquid over the couscous and cover the mixing bowl with aluminum foil. Let couscous stand for 5 minutes. Fluff with a fork. Toss in the scallions and season with salt and white pepper.

## sautéed spinach—page 157

# crunchy salmon burgers with kicked-up bean and vegetable salad

Serves: | | | |
Prep time:
Complexity level:

## crunchy salmon burgers

1 cup oat bran cereal or corn flakes
2 tablespoons extra virgin olive oil, divided
1/2 cup diced onion
1/2 cup diced red bell pepper
2 tablespoons white whole-wheat flour
2 tablespoons lemon juice
1 teaspoon Worcestershire sauce
1 (14-ounce) can wild Alaska pink salmon, drained
Unrefined sea salt, to taste
Cayenne pepper, to taste
1/4 cup chopped parsley
1/4 cup freshly grated Parmesan cheese

**Preheat** oven to 400 degrees F. Lightly oil a baking sheet. Set aside.

**Place** cereal in a blender; pulse into fine crumbs. Divide and set aside.

**Heat** 1 tablespoon oil in a medium size skillet over medium-high heat. Add onion and sauté for 2–3 minutes. Add bell pepper and sauté an additional 2 minutes. Stir in flour and cook for 1 minute. Add lemon juice, Worcestershire sauce, salmon, and half the cereal crumbs. Mix well, breaking salmon up. Season with salt and cayenne pepper. Form mixture into 4 burgers. Set aside.

**To** the remaining cereal crumbs, add parsley, Parmesan cheese, and remaining oil. Coat each side of burgers in the cereal mixture. Place on baking sheet and bake for 20 minutes. Serve warm.

## kicked-up bean and vegetable salad

2 tablespoons extra virgin olive oil
2 large shallots, minced
2 tablespoons peeled and grated fresh ginger
2 tablespoons minced garlic
2 (15-ounce) cans 3-bean salad, rinsed and drained
2 cups frozen corn kernels, thawed
2 teaspoons honey
2 tablespoons apple cider vinegar
Unrefined sea salt, to taste

**Heat** oil in a medium-size skillet over medium-high heat; add shallots, ginger, and garlic. Sauté 2–3 minutes, until shallots are soft. Remove skillet from heat. Add the 3-bean salad and thawed corn kernels; toss to coat with the oil and shallots. Transfer to a serving bowl.

**In** a small bowl, whisk together the honey and vinegar. Pour over the beans and gently toss to coat. Season with salt. Serve chilled or at room temperature.

# slow-cooker chicken cacciatore and three reds salad

Serves: ⏐ ⏐ ⏐ ⏐

Prep time: ⏰
Complexity level: 🍎🍎

## slow-cooker chicken cacciatore

2 large Spanish onions, chopped
$1/2$ teaspoon unrefined sea salt, plus more to taste
$1/4$ teaspoon white pepper, plus more to taste
3 tablespoons extra virgin olive oil, divided
3 pounds boneless, skinless, free-range organic chicken breasts, lightly pounded
5 cloves garlic, chopped
1 large red bell pepper, chopped
$1/4$ cup white whole-wheat flour
2 teaspoons paprika
$1/2$ cup dry Chardonnay
$1/4$ cup free-range organic chicken broth
1 (14-ounce) can diced tomatoes, drained
$1/4$ cup chopped fresh basil
1 teaspoon oregano
3 tablespoons drained capers
$1/2$ pound baby bella mushrooms, thickly sliced

**Place** the onion in the bottom of a 5- or 6-quart slow cooker and season lightly with salt and pepper. Add 1 tablespoon oil and toss with onion to coat. Arrange chicken breasts on top of the onion.

**In** a medium-size bowl, mix together the remaining 2 tablespoons oil, garlic, bell pepper, flour, paprika, Chardonnay, chicken broth, tomatoes, basil, oregano, and capers. Pour the mixture on top of the chicken. Arrange the mushrooms on top.

**Cover** and cook the chicken on high for 4–5 hours. Allow chicken to cool for 15 minutes before serving. Serve alone or over steamed brown rice. (We often take a shortcut and buy premade steamed brown rice from our local Chinese restaurant.)

# three reds salad

3 small red onions, cut in half and sliced
   ¼ inch thick
¼ cup plus 2 tablespoons balsamic
   vinegar, divided
¼ cup extra virgin olive oil
1 teaspoon coarse unrefined sea salt,
   divided
1 teaspoon freshly ground black pepper,
   divided
1 tablespoon minced shallots
3 cloves garlic, minced
2 teaspoons Dijon mustard
1 teaspoon raw honey
¼ cup good-quality red wine vinegar
½ cup flax oil (such as Barlean's)
2 small heads red-leaf lettuce, washed,
   spun dry, and torn into pieces

**Preheat** the oven to 400 degrees F.

**Arrange** onions on a baking sheet and toss with ¼ cup balsamic vinegar, olive oil, ½ teaspoon salt, and ½ teaspoon pepper. Roast the onions for 18–20 minutes, or until just barely soft. Remove from the oven and toss with remaining vinegar. Set aside and cool to room temperature.

**While** onions are cooling, prepare the vinaigrette in a small bowl by whisking together the shallots, garlic, mustard, honey, red wine vinegar, flax oil, and remaining salt and pepper. Whisk until ingredients are well blended and emulsified.

**To** assemble the salad, place the red leaf lettuce in a large serving bowl and arrange the cooled balsamic onions on top. Pour vinaigrette to taste onto the lettuce leaves and gently toss to coat. Serve the remaining vinaigrette in a small dish at the table. (Note: you should have plenty of vinaigrette left over; this can be stored in a covered container in the refrigerator for 2–3 days.)

# barbecue tofu cutlets and southern-style cheese- and polenta-stuffed green peppers

Serves: | | | |

Prep time: 🍎

Complexity level: 🍎 🍎

## barbecue tofu cutlets

### BARBECUE SAUCE
½ cup ketchup
2 tablespoons good-quality soy sauce
1 tablespoon Dijon mustard
2 teaspoons raw honey
3 tablespoons chopped canned chipotle peppers in adobo sauce (available in the ethnic section of your supermarket)
1 teaspoon chili powder
1 teaspoon extra virgin olive oil

In a small bowl, make the barbecue sauce by mixing all ingredients together. Pour the sauce into a large ziplock bag (or pour ¾ cup of your favorite all-natural barbecue sauce into the bag). Set bag with sauce aside.

### TOFU
2 (14-ounce) blocks extra-firm tofu, drained and patted dry with paper towels
¾ cup white whole-wheat flour
¼ teaspoon unrefined sea salt
¼ teaspoon freshly ground black pepper
¾ cup wheat germ
2 tablespoons extra virgin olive oil, divided

Cut each tofu block into 4 rectangular blocks. (Take extra care to dry the tofu as much as possible. Press the excess water out of the tofu with paper towels or a clean kitchen towel.) Carefully place the tofu cutlets in the ziplock bag with the sauce and seal. Marinate the tofu cutlets at room temperature for 15–20 minutes, or refrigerate for up 8 hours.

When ready to start cooking, remove the tofu cutlets from the marinade and pour the barbecue sauce into a shallow bowl. Season flour with salt and pepper. Place seasoned flour on a large dinner plate. Place wheat germ on another large dinner plate.

One by one, dredge the tofu cutlets in the flour, then lightly dip them in the barbecue sauce, and then dredge them in the wheat germ. Set the tofu cutlets on a clean plate or tray.

In a large nonstick skillet, heat 1 table-spoon oil over medium-high heat. When the oil is very hot and slightly shimmering, add ½ of the cutlets (4 cutlets in total) to the skillet and cook, turning once, until brown and crisp, about 1 minute each side. Drain tofu cutlets on paper towels. Repeat process with remaining oil and tofu cutlets. Allow cutlets to cool for 5 minutes before serving. Serve warm.

# southern-style, cheese- and polenta-stuffed green peppers

4 large green bell peppers
2 tablespoons plus 2 teaspoons
  extra virgin olive oil, divided
¾ teaspoon unrefined sea salt, plus more
  to taste
3 cloves garlic, minced
½ onion, finely chopped
½ cup chopped roasted red peppers from
  a jar, drained and patted dry with paper
  towels
3 cups water
1 cup polenta cornmeal
2 pinches cayenne pepper, plus more to
  taste
1 cup frozen corn kernels
1½ cups shredded low-fat organic
  cheddar cheese

**Preheat** oven to 425 degrees F.

**Cut** bell peppers in half lengthwise and remove the seeds (leave the stem ends on). Massage the peppers, inside and out, with 1 tablespoon oil. Season peppers lightly with salt. Place peppers cut-side up on an oiled baking sheet and roast in oven for approximately 15 minutes, or just until tender.

**Meanwhile,** heat 2 teaspoons oil in a large nonstick skillet over medium-high heat; add the garlic and onion, and sauté 3–4 minutes, or until onion is tender. Add the red peppers and sauté 2–3 additional minutes. Remove the skillet from heat and set onion and red pepper mixture aside.

**In** a heavy saucepan, bring the water and ¾ teaspoon salt to a boil over medium-high heat. Gradually stir in the polenta. Reduce the heat and simmer gently, stirring frequently, until mixture is very thick, about 15 minutes. Stir in the cayenne pepper, corn kernels, remaining tablespoon oil, and 1 cup of the shredded cheese. Fold the onion and red pepper mixture into the polenta; stir to combine. Remove the saucepan from the heat.

**Fill** the green pepper halves with the polenta mixture. Sprinkle the tops with the remaining ½ cup shredded cheese. Return the peppers to the oven and roast for 5–10 additional minutes, until the cheese is melted. Remove the peppers from the oven and allow to cool 10 minutes before serving. Serve warm.

# open-faced vegetarian reuben with sauerkraut

**Serves:** | | | |

**Prep time:** ⏰

**Complexity level:** 🍎🍎

1 tablespoon plus 2 teaspoons extra virgin olive oil, divided
½ red onion, chopped
Unrefined sea salt, to taste
1 large fennel bulb, cleaned, cut, and chopped (reserve trimmed tops)
1 Granny Smith apple, chopped
2 teaspoons grass-fed organic butter
¼ teaspoon white pepper
¼ teaspoon cardamom
1 teaspoon brown sugar
½ cup apple cider
1 (27-ounce) can shredded sauerkraut, rinsed well with water and drained
1 (14-ounce) package extra-firm tofu, drained, patted dry with paper towels, and cut into 8 thin rectangular cutlets
1 cage-free organic omega-3 egg, lightly beaten
½ cup white whole-wheat flour
4 slices whole-grain rye or pumpernickel bread, toasted
2 tomatoes, thinly sliced
4 ounces organic Swiss cheese, thinly sliced

**Heat** 1 tablespoon oil in a large heavy saucepan over medium heat. Add the onion and cook for several minutes, until onion is softened. Season lightly with salt. Add the fennel and cook for 4–5 minutes. Add the apple, butter, pepper, cardamom, and brown sugar; cook for about 2–3 minutes, or until apple softens. Pour in the apple cider and add the drained sauerkraut, mixing all ingredients together. Cover and cook for 5 minutes. Uncover, stir, and cook for an additional 5–7 minutes. Remove sauerkraut from the heat and set aside to cool.

**While** sauerkraut is cooling, season all sides of the tofu cutlets with salt and pepper. Immerse the tofu cutlets in the beaten egg and then dredge both sides in the flour.

**Pour** 1 teaspoon oil in a large nonstick skillet, tilt the pan to coat with oil. Heat the oil to medium-high. When oil is hot, add half of the tofu cutlets to the pan and sear for 2–3 minutes on each side, until lightly golden. Repeat the process with the remaining oil and tofu.

**Assemble** the open-faced sandwiches on a baking sheet. Arrange the toasted bread slices an inch apart. Place 2 tofu cutlets on each slice, then top the tofu with about ¼ cup of the sauerkraut, layer the tomato slices on top of the sauerkraut, and place the cheese on top. Broil the sandwiches for 3 to 5 minutes, or until cheese melts. Serve warm with a side of the remaining sauerkraut. (There will be plenty of sauerkraut remaining for ample side dish servings.)

# red pesto-roasted tofu with spinach and pecan fettuccine

•••••••••••••••••••••••••••••••••••••••••••••••••••••••••••••

Serves: | | | |

Prep time: 🕐

Complexity level: 🍎 🍎

## red pesto-roasted tofu

Extra virgin olive oil cooking spray

1 (12-ounce) jar roasted red peppers, rinsed, drained, and patted dry

1 tablespoon extra virgin olive oil

1/4 cup shredded Asiago cheese

1/4 cup shelled, dry-roasted, salted pistachios

1/3 cup low-fat organic ricotta cheese

1 teaspoon brown sugar

1/8 teaspoon unrefined sea salt

1/2 teaspoon paprika

1/4 teaspoon cayenne pepper

3 (8-ounce) packages cubed tofu, drained and patted dry with paper towels

**Preheat** oven to 400 degrees F.

**Spray** an 8 x 8-inch baking dish with cooking spray.

**Combine** the red peppers, oil, cheese, pistachios, ricotta, brown sugar, salt, paprika, and cayenne pepper in a blender; process until smooth and creamy. Set pesto aside until ready to use. (Note: pesto can be made up to 3 days in advance and stored in a covered container in the refrigerator.)

**Spread** the tofu cubes in the bottom of the baking dish; pour the pesto on top and toss to coat. Bake the tofu for 20 minutes. Remove tofu from the oven and set aside until ready to use.

## spinach and pecan fettuccine

3 tablespoons extra virgin olive oil, divided

6 or 7 cloves garlic, chopped

1 (10-ounce) package frozen chopped spinach

Unrefined sea salt, to taste

3 cups cooked sprouted whole-grain fettuccine

1 1/2 cups shredded carrots

1/2 cup chopped pecans

**Heat** 2 tablespoons oil in a large skillet over medium-high heat; add the garlic and sauté for 1–2 minutes. Add the frozen chopped spinach and sauté until spinach is cooked through and liquid evaporates. Season with salt.

**Add** the cooked fettuccine and remaining tablespoon of oil to the skillet. Mix the pasta to thoroughly incorporate with the spinach. Mix in the carrots and pecans. Cook for 3–4 minutes, or until ingredients are heated through.

**To** serve, plate the fettuccine on four individual plates; top each portion with the red pesto–roasted tofu. Serve warm.

# baked cobia (or sea bass) with citrus-tahini sauce and tuscan panzanella

Serves: | | | |

Prep time: 🕐

Complexity level: 🍎 🍎

## baked cobia with citrus-tahini sauce

¼ cup plus 2 tablespoons tahini (sesame seed butter)

Juice from 1 whole orange

Juice from 1 whole lemon

½ teaspoon Dijon mustard

1½ pounds cobia fillets, skinned, rinsed, and patted dry (Note: if you can't get cobia, any firm-fleshed mild white fish will do, including mahi mahi and sea bass)

Unrefined sea salt, to taste

Pepper, to taste

2 teaspoons extra virgin olive oil

**Preheat** the oven to 450 degrees F and position the rack in the center of the oven.

**Prepare** the citrus-tahini sauce in a small bowl by whisking together the tahini, orange juice, lemon juice, and mustard. Set sauce aside.

**Season** the fish on both sides with salt and pepper.

**Pour** oil in a large ovenproof skillet and tilt the skillet to evenly distribute the oil; heat to medium-high heat. When oil is hot, add the fish fillets and sear 1½ minutes on each side. Remove the skillet from the heat and pour the citrus-tahini sauce evenly on top of the fish. Place the skillet in the oven and cook the fish for 7–10 minutes (rotating the pan midway to ensure even cooking), until fish is cooked through and easily flakes with a fork. Allow fish to sit several minutes before serving. Serve warm.

# tuscan panzanella

2 tablespoons extra virgin olive oil
6 slices whole-grain spelt bread, torn into
   bite-size pieces, crusts removed
1/4 teaspoon unrefined sea salt, plus
   more to taste
2 tablespoons red wine vinegar
1/4 cup flax oil (such as Barlean's)
2 teaspoons minced garlic
1/4 teaspoon Dijon mustard
1/4 teaspoon coarsely ground black
   pepper
4 large ripe tomatoes, chopped into
   1/2-inch pieces
1 large ball fresh mozzarella (about 4
   ounces), chopped into 1/2-inch pieces
1 cup pitted olives marinated in extra
   virgin olive oil (from a jar or deli bar),
   coarsely chopped
3/4 cup coarsely chopped fresh basil
   leaves
1/2 red onion, thinly sliced

**Preheat** oven to 350 degrees F.

**Pour** the oil into a large nonstick skillet and heat to medium-high. When the oil is hot, add the bread pieces and season lightly with salt to taste. Toast the bread stovetop, tossing frequently until nicely browned, about 5–8 minutes. Set bread cubes aside.

**In** a small dish, whisk together the vinegar, flax oil, garlic, mustard, and measured salt and pepper. Set vinaigrette aside.

**In** a large serving bowl, add the tomatoes, mozzarella, olives, basil, and onion. Gently toss the ingredients together. Add the toasted bread cubes to the bowl and toss well. Drizzle the vinaigrette over the bread and vegetables and gently toss the salad. Allow the salad to sit 10–15 minutes before serving. Serve at room temperature.

# grilled halibut with vegetable condiment and mediterranean millet tabouleh

• • • • • • • • • • • • • • • • • • • • • • • • • • • • • • • • • • • • • •

Serves: | | | |
Prep time: 🍎
Complexity level: 🍎 🍎

## grilled halibut

Extra virgin olive oil
2 pounds halibut steaks
Paprika, to taste
Freshly ground black pepper, to taste
Unrefined sea salt, to taste

**Brush** the halibut with oil on both sides. Season with paprika, pepper, and salt. Let the halibut sit as grill is prepared. (If using a charcoal grill, make sure the flames have died down and the coals are glowing before cooking the fish.) Sear the steaks on both sides and then move them to the edge of the grill to finish cooking. Top each fish with Vegetable Condiment and serve.

## vegetable condiment

¼ cup extra virgin olive oil
3 flat anchovies, mashed
4 cloves garlic, chopped
1 large Spanish onion, thinly sliced
1 red bell pepper, sliced
1 (14.5 ounce) can diced tomatoes
¾ cup halved pitted Kalamata olives or
   other brine-cured black olives
¼ teaspoon unrefined sea salt
¼ teaspoon black pepper
1 teaspoon savory spice
¼ cup chopped sun-dried tomatoes,
   packed in extra virgin olive oil and
   drained
1 tablespoon balsamic vinegar

**Pour** the oil in a large heavy saucepan; heat to medium-high. Add anchovies and garlic; sauté 30 seconds. Add onion, red bell pepper, tomatoes, and olives. Season with salt, black pepper, and savory. Cook for 5 minutes.

**Meanwhile,** place sun-dried tomatoes and balsamic vinegar in a blender; process until well blended. Add sun-dried tomato "paste" to the saucepan and stir to incorporate. Cook for an additional 10 minutes over medium-high. Cover and refrigerate until serving time. (Note: Condiment can be served chilled, room temperature, or warm.)

# mediterranean millet tabouleh

1¹/₄ cups millet
3 cups water
¹/₄ teaspoon unrefined sea salt
¹/₄ red onion, finely chopped
1 red bell pepper, finely chopped
2 cloves garlic, minced
¹/₄ cup chopped parsley
¹/₄ cup chopped cilantro
3 tablespoons flax oil (such as Barlean's)
1 tablespoon extra virgin olive oil
Juice from 2 whole limes
¹/₄ teaspoon cayenne pepper
Unrefined sea salt, to taste
1 large or 2 small firm Hass avocados, chopped into ¹/₄-inch cubes

**Rinse** millet and drain in a strainer. Bring water and salt to a boil in a medium-size saucepan; add millet, reduce heat, cover, and simmer for about 20–25 minutes, stirring occasionally, or until all water has been absorbed. (Note: you can also cook millet in a rice cooker.) Turn off heat and let millet stand, covered, for 5 minutes. Transfer millet to a medium-size serving bowl and fluff with a fork.

**In** another bowl, toss together the onion, bell pepper, garlic, parsley, cilantro, flax oil, olive oil, lime juice, cayenne pepper, and salt. Add vegetable mixture to the millet and toss to mix all ingredients. Gently fold in the avocado. Serve at room temperature.

# company is coming

········································

## flavor-forward menus for effortless entertaining

**In today's rush-rush** world, so many people rarely cook for their own families, much less company. This really is too bad, because we always find we have so much more fun hanging out in our own home entertaining friends and family than we ever do going out to eat. At home, you can make the meal as upscale or as casual as you like. But whatever your personal style, rest assured, you don't need to make the "Company is Coming" meal an all-day production. The meals in this chapter aren't even necessarily more elaborate or time consuming than the "Weeknight Dinners" meals from the last chapter, but they each have a distinct style—some fancy, some relaxed and informal—with a noticeable edge that distinguishes them from home-style "everyday" meals. And of course, each meal is based on healthy "whole foods," because there is certainly no need to compromise your good eating habits just because you are entertaining.

# fillet of flounder with nutty millet pilaf and haricots verts in tomatoes

• • • • • • • • • • • • • • • • • • • • • • • • • • • • • • • • • • • • • • • • • • • • • • • •

Serves: | | | |

Prep time: 🍎

Complexity level: 🍎 🍎

## fillet of flounder

**4 tablespoons extra virgin olive oil, divided**
**3 celery stalks, diced**
**1 leek stalk, diced**
**3 carrots, peeled and diced**
**Unrefined sea salt, to taste**
**White pepper, to taste**
**1 tablespoon mascarpone cheese**
**Juice from 1 whole lemon**
**2 pounds fillets of flounder**
**2 ripe tomatoes, sliced**
**1 tablespoon chopped fresh tarragon**

**Preheat** oven to 450 degrees F.

**Place** 4 squares (12 x 12 inches each) of cooking parchment or aluminum foil on a work surface.

**Heat** 2 tablespoons oil in a medium skillet to medium-high and sauté celery, leek, and carrots for about 5 minutes, or until tender. Season vegetables with salt and pepper.

**In** a small bowl, whisk the remaining 2 tablespoons oil with the mascarpone cheese until mixture is emulsified. Add the lemon juice to the oil mixture and stir to combine.

**On** each of the parchment or aluminum foil squares, layer ¼ of the ingredients in the following order: sautéed vegetables, flounder, salt and pepper, tomato slices, a drizzle of the olive oil–mascarpone mixture, and tarragon. Fold the packets securely, tucking the edges under, and place on a baking sheet. Bake for 20 minutes. Slit packages before serving, or allow guests to open their own.

## nutty millet pilaf

**Extra virgin olive oil cooking spray**
**4 tablespoons extra virgin olive oil**
**4 scallions, chopped**
**2 cloves garlic, minced**
**½ pound fresh button mushrooms, wiped, trimmed, and sliced**
**Unrefined sea salt, to taste**
**Coarsely ground black pepper, to taste**
**1½ cups dried millet**
**½ teaspoon dried thyme**
**1½ cups finely chopped pecans**
**3 cups organic vegetable broth (such as Pacific Natural Foods brand)**

**Preheat** oven to 400 degrees F.

**Spray** an 8 x 8-inch 2-quart casserole with cooking spray.

**Heat** oil in a medium skillet over medium-high heat; add the scallions, garlic, and mushrooms, and sauté for 4–5 minutes, or until mushrooms are just softened. Season with salt and pepper. Add the millet and stir until all the grains are coated with oil. Season with thyme. Stir in the pecans.

**Transfer** the millet-pecan mixture into the prepared casserole. Bring vegetable broth to a boil and pour over the grains. Cover and bake for 1 hour, or until all of the liquid is absorbed and the grains are soft. Serve warm or at room temperature. (Note: The pilaf can be made up to 24 hours in advance, stored in a covered container in the refrigerator, and reheated, uncovered, in a 350-degree F oven for 10 minutes before serving.)

# haricots verts in tomatoes

2$^1$/$_2$–3 cups water
$^1$/$_2$ teaspoon unrefined sea salt
12 ounces haricots verts, trimmed
1 tablespoon extra virgin olive oil
1 shallot, finely chopped
Unrefined sea salt, to taste
Freshly ground pepper, to taste
$^1$/$_4$ cup flax oil (such as Barlean's)
2 tablespoons lemon juice
1 teaspoon Dijon mustard
2 cloves garlic, crushed
4 beefsteak tomatoes

**Bring** a medium saucepan of salted water to a boil. Add the haricots verts and cook just until tender, about 2 minutes. Transfer haricots verts with a slotted spoon to an ice bath. Drain.

**Heat** oil in a large skillet to medium-high. Add the shallot and cook for 45 seconds. Add the drained haricots verts, salt, and pepper; cook, stirring, for 3 minutes, or until haricots verts are crisp-tender. Remove skillet from heat and set aside.

**In** a small bowl, whisk together the flax oil, lemon juice, mustard, garlic, and salt and pepper to taste.

**Slice** the top and bottom off each tomato. Remove the pulp with an apple corer to create hollow cylinders. Place as many steamed green beans as will fit into each of the 4 tomatoes. Arrange tomatoes on serving plates. Drizzle 1 teaspoon of the vinaigrette over each tomato. Serve at room temperature.

# n-gingered sea
## ....ops and edamame succotash

Serves: | | | |

Prep time: 🕐
Complexity level: 🍎 🍎

## edamame succotash

2 teaspoons grass-fed organic butter
1 tablespoon extra virgin olive oil
3 cloves garlic, minced
1 medium shallot, diced
1/2 medium red onion, diced
Unrefined sea salt, to taste
Cayenne pepper, to taste
2 cups frozen corn kernels
1 tablespoon freshly minced fresh ginger
1/2 cup organic chicken broth
1/2 cup 2-percent organic milk
2 cups frozen edamame beans

**Heat** butter and oil in a medium-size saucepan. When the butter has melted, add the garlic and sauté 30 seconds. Add shallot and sauté an additional 45 seconds. Add onion and season with salt and cayenne pepper. Sauté until onion is tender. Add the corn and ginger, and cook 1–2 minutes.

**Pour** the chicken broth and milk into the saucepan and simmer ingredients for 5 minutes. Remove from heat and allow corn to cool for 5–10 minutes.

**Transfer** half of the corn and liquid broth to a food processor or blender and purée for 30 seconds, or until ingredients are blended but not completely smooth. Pour the purée back into the saucepan and bring to a simmer. Add the edamame beans and cook over medium heat for 3–4 minutes. Cover and keep warm until ready to serve. To serve, ladle succotash into a soup bowl and top with Lemon-gingered Sea Scallops.

# lemon-gingered sea scallops

1/4 cup stone-ground corn flour
1/2 teaspoon unrefined sea salt
1/2 teaspoon ground ginger
2 pounds large sea scallops, rinsed and
    patted dry with paper towels
1/2 cup 2-percent organic milk
2 tablespoons extra virgin olive oil
1 teaspoon grass-fed organic butter
1 teaspoon minced garlic
1 teaspoon grated ginger
Juice from 1 whole lemon
1 tablespoon soy sauce

**Mix** together the corn flour, salt, and ground ginger. Set mixture aside.

**Dip** scallops in milk. Lightly dust scallops with corn flour mixture.

**Heat** the oil in a large skillet to medium-high; add the scallops and cook, turning once, until lightly browned on each side, about 2 minutes per side. Remove scallops from skillet and set aside.

**Add** the butter to the hot skillet and remove skillet from the heat (the butter should immediately begin to melt); add the garlic and ginger to the melted butter and stir, away from the heat, for 30 seconds. Add the lemon juice and soy sauce to the skillet. Place the skillet back on a medium-high heat stovetop and add the scallops back to the pan. Toss the scallops in the ginger mixture and heat through for about 30 seconds. Serve warm scallops over the Edamame Succotash.

# asian-style ahi tuna burgers with wasabi-lime mayonnaise and sesame slaw

Serves: | | | |

Prep time: ⏰

Complexity level: 🍎🍎

## ahi tuna burgers with wasabi-lime mayonnaise

3 tablespoons good-quality soy sauce
2–3 cloves garlic, crushed
1 (2-inch) piece fresh gingerroot, grated
1 teaspoon expeller-pressed sesame oil,
    plus more for brushing
1 red bell pepper, finely diced
3 scallions, finely diced
2 teaspoons coarsely ground black pepper
1 pound fresh tuna steaks
1/3 cup canola oil mayonnaise
1/2 teaspoon wasabi powder
1 tablespoon fresh lime juice
2 teaspoons brown sugar
Expeller-pressed sesame oil
4 sprouted whole-grain buns

**In** a large mixing bowl, combine the soy sauce, garlic, gingerroot, oil, bell pepper, scallions, and pepper. Set aside. Cut the tuna into chunks, add them to a food processor, and pulse a few times to break up the pieces until they are the consistency of ground beef. (Note: do not overprocess the tuna.) Add the tuna to the mixing bowl and mix the ingredients together with your hands; form the mixture into four 1 1/2-inch patties and chill in the refrigerator for 30 minutes.

**In** a small bowl, whisk together the mayonnaise, wasabi, lime juice, and brown sugar. Set aside.

**Heat** a large heavy skillet over moderately high heat or fire up the grill. Brush each tuna patty lightly with sesame oil. Cook the patties for 2 minutes per side for rare or 3–4 minutes for medium-rare.

**While** the patties are cooking, open up the rolls, lightly brush with sesame oil, and lightly toast them under the broiler for a few minutes. Transfer the patties to the toasted buns and top with the wasabi-lime mayonnaise.

## sesame slaw

1 tablespoon good-quality soy sauce
1 (2-inch) piece fresh gingerroot, grated
1 tablespoon expeller-pressed sesame oil
1 teaspoon coarsely ground black pepper
1 tablespoon fresh lime juice
2 tablespoons all-natural peanut butter
2 tablespoons plum sauce
2 tablespoons rice wine vinegar

1 (10-ounce) package coleslaw mix
1 tablespoon toasted sesame seeds

**In** a large serving bowl, whisk together the soy sauce, gingerroot, oil, pepper, lime juice, peanut butter, plum sauce, and vinegar. Add the coleslaw mix and sesame seeds, and toss to coat. Serve slaw as a side dish.

# shrimp kabobs with vodka-lime marinade and curried butternut squash soup

Serves: | | | |

Prep time: 🕐

Complexity level: 🍎 🍎

## shrimp kabobs with vodka-lime marinade

Juice from 3¹/₂ limes

2 tablespoons plus 1 teaspoon extra virgin olive oil

2 tablespoons vodka (the alcohol will cook away)

¹/₄ teaspoon unrefined sea salt

¹/₄ teaspoon paprika

¹/₄ teaspoon ground cinnamon

¹/₄ teaspoon cayenne pepper

1¹/₄ pounds large peeled shrimp (16–20 count)

Wooden skewers (soaked in water for about 30 minutes)

**In** a large ziplock plastic bag, combine lime juice, oil, vodka, salt, paprika, cinnamon, and pepper. Add the shrimp to the bag and marinate for 10 minutes (no longer!).

**Heat** grill to high.

**Remove** shrimp from the plastic bag and reserve the marinade. Place shrimp on the wooden skewers and grill, basting frequently with the reserved marinade, until shrimp turns pink, about 2 minutes per side.

## curried butternut squash soup

1 tablespoon extra virgin coconut oil (such as Barlean's)

1 Spanish onion, chopped

4 cloves garlic, chopped

1 cup crushed canned tomatoes

2 cups organic vegetable broth

1 (12-ounce) package frozen butternut squash, thawed

¹/₃ cup coconut milk

¹/₄ cup all-natural peanut butter

2 teaspoons curry powder

¹/₄ teaspoon cayenne pepper

Unrefined sea salt, to taste

**Heat** the oil in a large pot over medium heat. Add the onion and garlic, and sauté

for about 5 minutes, or until onion is tender.

**Add** the tomatoes, broth, butternut squash, and coconut milk; bring to a boil. Reduce heat and cook uncovered for 15 minutes. Stir in the peanut butter, curry powder, cayenne pepper, and salt. Remove the pot from the heat and allow to cool.

**Pour** the cooled soup into a food processor or blender and purée until smooth and creamy, about 1 minute. Pour the soup back into the pot and reheat before serving.

# lime-cooked tilapia and corn on the cob with parsley and paprika butter and spinach salad with artichokes and gorgonzola

•••••••••••••••••••••••••••••••••••••••••••••••••••••••

Serves: | | | |

Prep time: ⏰

Complexity level: 🍎 🍎

## lime-cooked tilapia

2 tablespoons extra virgin olive oil, divided
8–10 cloves garlic, thinly sliced
Unrefined sea salt, to taste
1¹/₂ pounds tilapia fillets
Cayenne pepper, to taste
2 tablespoons canned chopped green chiles (located in ethnic section of your supermarket)
¹/₂ cup freshly squeezed lime juice
1 cup cherry tomatoes
1¹/₂ cups chopped fresh cilantro

**Combine** 1 tablespoon oil with the garlic in a small heavy saucepan over medium-low heat. Cook, stirring frequently, until the garlic is almost browned, about 5 minutes. Season lightly with salt and set aside.

**Season** the tilapia fillets on both sides with salt and just a bit of cayenne pepper. (Go easy on the cayenne or your mouth will be on fire!)

**Heat** the remaining tablespoon oil in a large nonstick skillet over medium-high heat. Add the fish and cook for 2 minutes. Add the chiles, all but 2 table-spoons of the lime juice, and the cherry tomatoes. Cook for another 2 minutes, turn the fish once, and cook until fish is cooked through. Transfer fish and cherry tomatoes to a serving platter.

**Add** the cilantro and the remaining 2 tablespoons of lime juice to the hot skillet; stir the cilantro until it just begins to wilt. Top fish with the cilantro, pan juice, and fried garlic. Serve at once.

# corn on the cob with parsley and paprika butter

4 ears corn, in their husks
2 teaspoons salted grass-fed organic
  butter, slightly softened
2 teaspoons flax oil (such as Barlean's)
2 tablespoons dried parsley flakes
3 teaspoons paprika
Unrefined sea salt, to taste
2 fresh lemons, quartered

**Heat** grill to medium. Peel back the husks of the corn without removing them. Remove the silk and re-cover the corn with the husk. Soak the corn in a large bowl of cold water for 15 minutes.

Remove the corn from the water and shake off excess.

**Place** the corn on the grill, close the cover, and grill for 15 to 20 minutes.

**Meanwhile,** prepare the parsley and paprika butter by combining the butter, oil, parsley flakes, and paprika in a small bowl. Set aside until ready to use.

**Unwrap** the corn and brush with the parsley and paprika butter. Sprinkle with a little salt and freshly squeezed lemon juice. Serve warm.

# spinach salad with artichokes and gorgonzola

Extra virgin olive oil cooking spray
2 (9-ounce) packages frozen artichokes
2–3 teaspoons extra virgin olive oil
Unrefined sea salt, to taste
Freshly ground black pepper, to taste
2 tablespoons flax oil (such as Barlean's)
2 tablespoons canola oil mayonnaise
1 teaspoon crushed garlic
2 tablespoons red wine vinegar
Juice from 1 whole lemon
1 teaspoon raw honey
7 cups baby spinach leaves
1/2 cup crumbled Gorgonzola cheese
1/2 cup chopped walnuts
1/2 medium red onion, diced

**Preheat** oven to 450 degrees F.

**Spray** a baking sheet with cooking spray. Spread out the frozen artichokes on the baking sheet. Drizzle artichokes with 2–3 teaspoons of olive oil and season with salt and pepper. Roast artichokes for 20–25 minutes. Remove from oven and set aside to cool.

**Combine** the flax oil, mayonnaise, garlic, vinegar, lemon juice, and honey in the bottom of a large salad bowl. Whisk ingredients with a fork until emulsified. Add the spinach, cooled artichokes, Gorgonzola, walnuts, and red onion; toss to combine. Season with salt and pepper, and serve.

# cumin-crusted chicken breasts with white bean and orange sauce and red cabbage with mangos

· · · · · · · · · · · · · · · · · · · · · · · · · · · · · · · · · · · · · · · · · · · · · · · · · ·

Serves: | | | |

Prep time: 🕐

Complexity level: 🍎 🍎

## cumin-crusted chicken breasts

1 tablespoon cumin, plus more for seasoning

1/4 cup lime juice

3 tablespoons extra virgin olive oil, divided

2 tablespoons raw honey

1/4 teaspoon unrefined sea salt, plus more for seasoning

1/4 teaspoon pepper

2 pounds boneless, skinless, free-range organic chicken breasts, lightly pounded

5 scallions, chopped

**Whisk** together 1 tablespoon cumin, lime juice, 2 tablespoons oil, honey, 1/4 teaspoon salt, and pepper. Pour the marinade into a large ziplock bag, add the chicken breasts, and marinate for 1 hour in the refrigerator.

**Preheat** oven to 400 degrees F.

**Remove** chicken breasts from the marinade and wipe off any excess. Season chicken liberally with cumin and salt to taste on both sides. Heat the remaining tablespoon of oil in a large ovenproof skillet over medium-high heat. Place chicken in the pan and sear for 3–4 minutes on each side, or until golden brown but not cooked through.

**Spread** some of the White Bean and Orange Sauce on top of each chicken breast and place the skillet in the oven. Bake chicken for 8–12 minutes, depending on thickness of the breast, or until cooked through and no longer pink. Sprinkle scallions on top of chicken and serve warm with extra sauce on the side.

# white bean and orange sauce

2 tablespoons extra virgin olive oil
1/4 cup finely chopped shallots
1 (15.5-ounce) can white soybeans, rinsed
  and drained
2–3 tablespoons orange juice concentrate
2 tablespoons mascarpone cheese
1 teaspoon cayenne pepper
Unrefined sea salt, to taste

**In** a small saucepan, heat the oil over medium-high heat. Add the shallots and sauté for 4–5 minutes, or until tender and soft. Add the soybeans and cook 2–3 minutes.

**Transfer** the shallots and soybeans to a blender or food processor. Add the orange juice concentrate, mascarpone cheese, cayenne pepper, and salt to taste. Process until mixture is smooth and creamy. Set sauce aside. (Note: Sauce can be prepared one day in advance.)

# red cabbage with mangos

2 tablespoons extra virgin olive oil
1 1/2 cups finely chopped red onion
1 head of red cabbage, chopped
5 tablespoons balsamic vinegar
1/2 teaspoon unrefined sea salt
2/3 cup white raisins
2 cups chopped fresh mangos
Black pepper, to taste

**Heat** the oil in a large deep skillet (or wok) over medium-high heat. Add the onion and sauté for 5–6 minutes, or until soft. Add the cabbage and stir so that it is completely coated in oil. Reduce the heat to medium-low, stir in the vinegar, and cover the skillet. Continue cooking, stirring occasionally, for about 10 minutes, or until cabbage is rather wilted.

**Turn** the heat to low, stir in the salt and raisins. Cover and continue to cook, stirring occasionally, for about 20 minutes, or until cabbage is very tender.

**Stir** in the mangos and season with pepper. Serve hot or warm.

# chicken cutlets with sweet pea purée and garlicky oven-roasted vegetables and potatoes

· · · · · · · · · · · · · · · · · · · · · · · · · · · · · · · · · · · · · · · · · · · ·

Serves: ⏐⏐⏐⏐

Prep time: 🕐
Complexity level: 🍎

## chicken cutlets with sweet pea purée

1 (9-ounce) package frozen petite peas
¼ cup whipped organic cream cheese
2 tablespoons raw honey
Juice from ½ lemon
4 cloves garlic, minced
¼ cup fresh mint leaves
2 tablespoons Chardonnay
Unrefined sea salt, to taste
1½ pounds thinly sliced, boneless, skinless, free-range organic chicken breasts (also called cutlets)
White pepper, to taste
2 tablespoons extra virgin olive oil, divided

**Place** the frozen peas in a micro-wave-safe dish and heat for 3 minutes, or until thawed and barely warm.

**In** a food processor or blender, add the peas, cream cheese, honey, lemon juice, garlic, mint, Chardonnay, and salt. Process until the mixture is smooth and creamy. Set purée aside.

**Pat** chicken dry and sprinkle all over with salt and pepper. Heat 1 tablespoon oil in a 12-inch heavy skillet over moderately high heat until hot but not smoking. Sauté the chicken in 2 or 3 batches, turning over once, until golden and just cooked through, about 2 minutes per batch. Add remaining oil when necessary to keep chicken from sticking or burning.

**Transfer** chicken to serving plates and drizzle with Sweet Pea Purée. Serve purée on the side in a gravy boat.

# garlicky oven-roasted vegetables and potatoes

6 medium red-skinned potatoes,
 quartered
Unrefined sea salt, to taste
Coarsely ground black pepper, to taste
Paprika, to taste
3–4 tablespoons extra virgin olive oil,
 divided
2 red bell peppers, chopped into bite-size
 pieces
2 zucchini, chopped into 1/2-inch chunks
1 red onion, cut into bite-size pieces
1 head of garlic, each clove peeled and
 coarsely chopped

**Preheat** the oven to 400 degrees F.

**Place** the potatoes on a roasting pan lined with aluminum foil. Season the potatoes with salt, pepper, and paprika, and toss the potatoes with 1 tablespoon oil. Roast the potatoes for 20 minutes, tossing once.

**Place** the bell peppers, zucchini, red onion, and garlic on a second roasting pan lined with aluminum foil. Toss the vegetables with the remaining 2 or 3 tablespoons oil and season with salt. Place the vegetables in the oven next to the pan with the potatoes, and roast the vegetables and potatoes for 40 minutes.

**Remove** the potatoes and vegetables from the oven and allow to cool several minutes. Toss the potatoes and vegetables together lightly, season with a bit more salt, and serve at once.

# cod with hummus and olive tapenade and tomato gorgonzola soup and leeks à la grecque

Serves: | | | |

Prep time: ⏰

Complexity level: 🍎 🍎 🍎

## cod with hummus and olive tapenade

¾ cup Spanish green olives marinated in extra virgin olive oil and garlic (or look for fresh olives from your supermarket olive bar)

2 teaspoons capers

1 tablespoon plus 1 teaspoon flax oil (such as Barlean's)

3 cloves garlic, coarsely chopped

1 tablespoon balsamic vinegar

2 tablespoons chopped fresh basil

1½ pounds cod fillets

Unrefined sea salt, to taste

¼ cup prepared hummus

¼ teaspoon Dijon mustard

2 tablespoons canola oil mayonnaise

**Preheat** broiler. In a food processor, combine the olives, capers, flax oil, garlic, vinegar, and basil; pulse several times until ingredients are well combined but olives are still somewhat chunky. Set tapenade aside.

**Pat** cod dry with paper towels and season both sides with salt. In a small bowl, whisk together the hummus, mustard, and mayonnaise. Brush hummus mixture on top of cod. Place fillets in a broiler pan and broil 6–8 inches from heat for 8 to 10 minutes, or until cooked through. It is unnecessary to turn the fish—the heat of the pan will cook the bottom side.

**Remove** cod from the pan and spoon the olive tapenade on top. Serve at once.

## tomato-gorgonzola soup with croutons

4 tablespoons extra virgin olive oil, divided

1 Spanish onion, chopped

2 cloves garlic, minced

¼ teaspoon unrefined sea salt, plus more to taste

Freshly ground black pepper, to taste

1 (28-ounce) can whole peeled tomatoes

¼ cup chopped fresh basil

1 tablespoon brown sugar

½ cup plus 2 tablespoons crumbled Gorgonzola, divided

½ cup low-fat organic plain yogurt or kefir

3 slices sprouted whole-grain bread (such as Food for Life brand), crusts removed, cut into small cubes

**Heat** 2 tablespoons oil in a large saucepan to medium-high; add the onion and garlic, and sauté for 4–5 minutes, or until onion begins to caramelize. Season onion with salt and pepper to taste. Add the tomatoes, basil, brown sugar, and measured salt. Simmer for 15 minutes.

**Add** ½ cup of the Gorgonzola to the tomato soup and stir until well blended, about 2 minutes. Remove soup from the heat and allow liquid to cool for 4–5 minutes. Mix in the yogurt.

**Working** in small batches, transfer the tomato soup to a food processor or blender and purée until the entire batch of soup is smooth and creamy. Pour the puréed soup back into the saucepan and heat over medium-low heat.

**Preheat** oven to 400 degrees F.

**While** soup is reheating, prepare the croutons by tossing the bread cubes with the remaining 2 tablespoons oil, remaining 2 tablespoons Gorgonzola, and salt to taste in a skillet. Toast over moderate heat, stirring frequently until bread cubes are golden brown and cheese has melted on top of the croutons. Lightly oil a baking sheet and place the croutons on top. Bake the croutons at 400 degrees F for 5–8 minutes, or until toasted. Set toasted croutons on a paper towel and cool for several minutes.

**Serve** soup warm with crispy croutons scattered on top.

## leeks à la grecque

**4–5 cups water**
**½ teaspoon unrefined sea salt**
**3 stalks fat leeks, cleaned and sliced into 2-inch pieces**
**¾ cup organic vegetable broth**
**¾ cup dry white wine (Chardonnay is ideal)**
**2 tablespoons extra virgin olive oil**
**Juice from 1 whole lemon**
**1 sprig parsley**
**½ teaspoon dried tarragon**
**Coarse black pepper, to taste**
**Unrefined sea salt, to taste**

**Bring** a large stainless-steel saucepan of salted water to a boil. Add the leeks and boil over medium heat for 3 minutes. Drain.

**Return** leeks to the saucepan and add the remaining ingredients. Cover, reduce heat, and simmer for 10 minutes. Uncover the saucepan and cook for an additional 5 minutes.

**Remove** from heat and allow to cool to room temperature. To serve, scoop the leeks out of the saucepan and spoon a few tablespoons of the cooled liquid on top.

# shrimp and scallops with linguine and artichoke, tomato, and olive sauce

••••••••••••••••••••••••••••••••••••••••••••••••••••••

**Serves:** ❙❙❙❙

**Prep time:** ⏲

**Complexity level:** 🍎 🍎

## artichoke, tomato, and olive sauce

1 (9-ounce) package frozen artichokes
1 tablespoon plus 1 teaspoon extra virgin
  olive oil, divided
Unrefined sea salt, to taste
1 (15-ounce) can tomato sauce
$^1/_2$ cup dry white wine
1 (4-ounce) can chopped black olives
$^1/_4$ cup prepared hummus
$^1/_2$ teaspoon dried oregano
1 teaspoon garlic powder
Freshly ground black pepper, to taste
8 ounces fresh button mushrooms, sliced
$^1/_4$ cup chopped oil-packed sun-dried
  tomatoes
2–3 cloves garlic

**Preheat** oven to 400 degrees F. Arrange artichokes on a large baking sheet, drizzle with 1 teaspoon oil, and season with salt. Roast the artichokes for 30 minutes. Remove from oven and allow to cool. Coarsely chop artichokes.

**In** a medium bowl, mix together the tomato sauce, wine, olives, hummus, oregano, and garlic powder. Season with salt and pepper. Set sauce aside.

**Heat** the remaining tablespoon oil in the skillet over medium-high heat; add the mushrooms, tomatoes, and garlic. Sauté, stirring, for 4–5 minutes, or until mushrooms are soft. Add the artichokes and cook 1 minute. Add the tomato sauce mixture and stir to combine. Lower the heat to simmer and cook, uncovered, stirring occasionally, for 15 minutes.

# shrimp and scallops with linguine

8 ounces sprouted whole-grain linguine
2 tablespoons extra virgin olive oil
1 pound (30-count) shrimp, peeled and
  deveined
1 pound (20–30 count) scallops
3 cloves garlic, chopped
$1/4$ cup chopped fresh basil
$1/4$ cup freshly grated Parmesan cheese

**Cook** the linguine al dente according to package directions. Drain. Transfer linguine to a very large serving bowl. Set aside.

**Heat** the oil in a large heavy skillet over medium-high heat; add shrimp, scallops, and garlic, and cook, stirring, until shrimp are opaque and scallops are cooked through, about 3–4 minutes. Stir in the basil and cook for an additional 30 seconds. Add the Artichoke, Tomato and Olive Sauce (recipe on facing page) to the skillet with the seafood and stir to coat the seafood in the sauce.

**Pour** the warm seafood and sauce mixture over the pasta. Toss ingredients together gently. Sprinkle with Parmesan cheese and serve.

# moroccan burgers with balsamic beets and oranges

Serves: | | | |

Prep time: 🕐

Complexity level: 🍎 🍎

## moroccan burgers

Extra virgin olive oil

1 pound extra-lean grass-fed ground beef
or ground ostrich

¹/₄ cup crushed pine nuts

2 teaspoons cinnamon

12 dried apricots, finely chopped

4 cloves garlic, crushed

2 teaspoons cumin

¹/₂ teaspoon cayenne pepper

¹/₄ cup finely chopped red onion

Unrefined sea salt, to taste

2 tablespoons wheat germ

1 cage-free organic omega-3 egg

1 teaspoon Dijon mustard, plus more for
garnish

4 sprouted whole-grain buns

1 avocado, sliced

**Prepare** a grill or oil a large nonstick skillet with a bit of olive oil.

**In** a large mixing bowl, add the beef (or ostrich), pine nuts, cinnamon, apricots, garlic, cumin, cayenne pepper, onion, salt, wheat germ, egg, and 1 teaspoon mustard; mix all ingredients by hand. Divide the mixture into 4 equal patties and place them on a large plate. Refrigerate for 10 minutes.

**Cook** the patties on the grill or over medium-high heat in a stovetop skillet for about 4 minutes per side, or until desired doneness.

**While** the burgers are cooking, open up the buns, lightly brush with oil, and toast them under the broiler for 30–45 seconds.

**When** burgers are done, place them on the toasted buns and serve with mustard and avocado.

# balsamic beets and oranges

2 bunches fresh beets, about 5–6
   medium-size beet bulbs
2 oranges, chopped
2–3 cloves garlic, crushed
2 tablespoons balsamic vinegar
3 tablespoons flax oil (such as Barlean's)
2 teaspoons raw honey
1 teaspoon Dijon mustard
$1/2$ teaspoon cumin
Unrefined sea salt, to taste
Coarsely ground black pepper, to taste
3 tablespoons parsley

**Preheat** oven to 400 degrees F.

**Wrap** whole beet bulbs individually in aluminum foil and bake in the oven for about 30–40 minutes, or until tender when pierced with a fork. When beets are done cooking, cut them into bite-size pieces.

**Place** the beet chunks in a large mixing bowl and add the oranges and garlic; toss gently.

**In** a small bowl, whisk together the vinegar, oil, honey, mustard, and cumin. Pour the vinaigrette over the beets and oranges. Season with salt and pepper, and toss gently. Let beet salad sit for 15 minutes before serving. Mix in the parsley just before serving. (Note: This recipe can be made up to one day in advance.)

# bean and cashew burgers cilantro aioli and chipotle-cauliflower soup

**Serves:** ▮▮▮ ▮▮▮▮

**Prep time:** ⏰

**Complexity level:** 🍎 🍎 🍎

## pinto bean and cashew burgers

2 (14.5-ounce) cans pinto beans, rinsed
   and drained
1 teaspoon ground cumin
2 teaspoons chili powder
1 teaspoon paprika
½ cup shredded carrots
¼ cup wheat germ
½ cup chopped cilantro
½ teaspoon coarse unrefined sea salt
1 tablespoon lime juice
2 splashes Tabasco or other hot sauce
2 tablespoons plus 1 teaspoon extra virgin
   olive oil, divided
½ cup cashews
Stone-ground whole-grain cornmeal, for
   dusting
4 sprouted whole-grain buns
4 beefsteak tomatoes, sliced thick

**Roughly** mash the beans in a large bowl with a potato masher. Add the cumin, chili powder, paprika, carrots, wheat germ, cilantro, salt, lime juice, Tabasco, and 1 teaspoon oil; mix thoroughly. Set aside.

**Transfer** the cashews to a food processor and process into "crumbs." Add the cashew crumbs to the bean mixture and mix well.

**Form** the bean mixture into 6 (½-inch-thick) burgers. Lightly dust both sides of the burgers with cornmeal.

**Heat** 1 tablespoon oil in a large skillet over medium heat; cook half of the burgers for 3–4 minutes on each side (or until they form a crust). Repeat with the second batch.

**Top** each burger with the Cilantro Aioli and serve on a toasted bun with thick slices of beefsteak tomatoes.

# cilantro aioli

1/2 cup canola oil mayonnaise
3/4 cup chopped cilantro
2 tablespoons flax oil (such as Barlean's)
6 cloves garlic
2 teaspoons lime juice

**Combine** all ingredients in a food processor and purée until smooth and creamy. Cover and chill before serving. (Note: Cilantro Aioli can be prepared one day in advance.)

# chipotle-cauliflower soup

1 tablespoon extra virgin olive oil
1 tablespoon plus 2 teaspoons grass-fed organic butter
3 cloves garlic, chopped
2 chipotle peppers in adobo sauce, chopped
1 large onion, chopped
Coarse unrefined sea salt, to taste
1 1/2 pounds cauliflower, coarsely chopped
3 cups organic vegetable broth
1 cup unsweetened plain soy milk
1/2 cup prepared hummus

**Heat** the oil and butter in a soup pot over medium-high heat; add the garlic, peppers, and onion, and sauté for 2–3 minutes, until translucent. Lightly season with salt.

**Stir** in the cauliflower and cook for 2–3 additional minutes. Season again with salt to taste. Add the broth and soy milk; bring liquid to a simmer and cook until the vegetables are tender, about 8–10 minutes. Stir in the hummus. Remove the pot from the heat and set aside to cool.

**Once** the soup has cooled, work in small batches to purée the ingredients in a blender until silky smooth. (Note: Hot liquid can burst out of blenders, not only creating a mess but also potentially burning bystanders. Be sure the soup is cool before you purée it.)

**Soup** can be served warm, room temperature, or chilled.

# mahi mahi and tomato-avocado salsa with garbanzo bean and basil bisque

**Serves:** | | | |

**Prep time:**

**Complexity level:**

## mahi mahi and tomato-avocado salsa

2 yellow beefsteak tomatoes, cored and halved
2 red beefsteak tomatoes, cored and halved
1 small red onion, peeled and quartered
2 tablespoons extra virgin olive oil, plus more for the fish
Fine unrefined sea salt, to taste
1/4 cup chopped fresh basil
2 tablespoons lime juice, plus more for the fish
3 cloves garlic, crushed
2 tablespoons flax oil (such as Barlean's)
2 Hass avocados, coarsely chopped
Hot sauce, to taste
Coarsely ground black pepper, to taste
4 (5–6 ounce) mahi mahi fillets

**Heat** the grill to medium.

**Place** the tomatoes and onion in a bowl and toss with the measured olive oil and salt. Place the vegetables on the grill and cook for 5–10 minutes, or until lightly charred. Remove the vegetables from the grill and allow to cool.

**Roughly** chop the cooled tomatoes and onion, and place in a large nonreactive bowl. Add the basil, measured lime juice, garlic, flax oil, avocados, and hot sauce. Lightly toss the salsa and season with pepper. Set the salsa aside until the fish is done.

**Squeeze** lime juice on both sides of the mahi mahi and brush with olive oil. Season with salt and pepper. Grill the mahi mahi 3–4 minutes on each side for medium doneness. (Do not overcook; mahi mahi has a tendency to dry out.) Serve fish with salsa.

# garbanzo bean and basil bisque

1 cup toasted wheat germ
4 cups organic vegetable broth
2 cups water
2 tablespoons extra virgin olive oil
1 onion, chopped
3 cloves garlic, minced
Fine-grain unrefined sea salt, to taste
Cayenne pepper, to taste
1/4 cup diced sun-dried tomatoes packed
  in oil, patted dry with a paper towel
1 (10-ounce) package frozen butternut
  squash, thawed
1 (14.5-ounce) can garbanzo beans,
  drained and rinsed
1/2 cup coarsely chopped fresh basil

**Combine** the wheat germ, vegetable broth, and water in a heavy soup pot and slowly bring to a simmer over medium heat. Remove the pot from the heat and cover to keep warm.

**Meanwhile,** heat the oil in a large skillet to medium-high; add the onion, garlic, salt, and cayenne pepper. Sauté the onion for 5–6 minutes, or until soft. Stir in the sun-dried tomatoes and cook for an additional minute. Add the butternut squash and garbanzo beans, and gently stir.

**Add** the bean mixture to the liquid and stir well. Add the basil. Allow the liquid to cool to room temperature.

**When** the liquid is at room temperature, ladle 2–3 cups of the soup at a time into a blender; process each batch until smooth and creamy. Transfer the puréed soup into another soup pot. Continue processing the soup in small batches until the entire batch is puréed. Warm the soup over medium heat and serve.

# pork tenderloins with spicy fruit chutney and butternut squash with cranberries, ginger, and orange

Serves: ||||

Prep time: ⏰

Complexity level: 🍎🍎

## spicy fruit chutney

1 tablespoon extra virgin olive oil
1 cup chopped Spanish onion
1 tablespoon grated peeled ginger
4 cloves garlic, minced
1/4 cup canned crushed pineapple (no sugar added)
1/2 cup orange juice
1 cup raisins
1 cup golden raisins
2 tablespoons balsamic vinegar
1 tablespoon raw honey
1 tablespoon Dijon mustard
1/2 cup all-natural cherry preserves
1/4 teaspoon unrefined sea salt

**Heat** oil in a medium saucepan over medium-high heat. Add the onion, ginger, and garlic, and sauté for 4 minutes. Stir in the pineapple, orange juice, raisins, vinegar, and honey; bring mixture to a boil and simmer for approximately 15 minutes, or until most of the liquid is absorbed. Remove the chutney from the heat and stir in the mustard, preserves, and salt. Let chutney sit while preparing pork.

## pork tenderloins

1 1/4-pounds grass-fed pork tenderloin, trimmed and cut into 8 (1-inch-thick) slices
Unrefined sea salt, to taste
White pepper, to taste
1 tablespoon extra virgin olive oil
1/2 cup Riesling wine

**Season** the pork tenderloins with salt and pepper.

**Pour** the oil into a large nonstick skillet and swirl the pan to coat with the oil. Heat the oil over medium-high heat. Add the pork and cook approximately 5–6 minutes per side, or until pork is done. Transfer to a platter and set aside.

**Add** the wine to the skillet, scraping pan to loosen browned bits, and cook for 2 minutes. Add the prepared chutney and cook for 2 minutes. Serve Spicy Fruit Chutney on top of pork tenderloins.

# butternut squash with cranberries, ginger, and orange

Extra virgin olive oil cooking spray
3$^1/_2$ pounds butternut squash (about
   4$^1/_2$ cups), peeled, seeded, and cut Into
   $^1/_2$-inch cubes
2 teaspoons grass-fed organic butter,
   melted
2 tablespoons orange juice concentrate,
   thawed
2 teaspoons freshly grated ginger, divided
2 tablespoons extra virgin olive oil,
   divided
2 tablespoons brown sugar, divided
1 tablespoon orange zest
1 teaspoon raw honey
$^3/_4$ cup fresh cranberries
Unrefined sea salt, to taste
Freshly ground coarse black pepper, to
   taste
$^1/_2$ cup whole-wheat panko crumbs
Juice from $^1/_2$ lemon

**Preheat** oven to 400 degrees F.

**Spray** an 8 x 8-inch casserole with cooking spray. Add the butternut squash. In a small bowl, whisk together the butter, orange juice concentrate, 1 teaspoon grated ginger, 1 tablespoon oil, 1 tablespoon brown sugar, orange zest, and honey; pour liquid over the squash and toss to coat. Add the cranberries and gently toss. Season with salt and black pepper; gently toss ingredients together.

**In** a small bowl, mix together the panko crumbs, remaining teaspoon of grated ginger, remaining tablespoon of oil, and remaining tablespoon of brown sugar. Sprinkle the seasoned crumb mixture on top of the squash. Drizzle lemon juice on top.

**Roast** for 45–50 minutes, or until butternut squash cubes are soft. Allow squash to sit for 10–15 minutes before serving. Serve warm.

# lamb chops with orange-dijon marinade and vegetable gratin

Serves: | | | | | |

Prep time: ⏰
Complexity level: 🍎🍎🍎

## orange-dijon marinade

1/4 cup orange marmalade
2 tablespoons thawed frozen orange juice
  concentrate
3 tablespoons Dijon mustard
1/4 cup extra virgin olive oil
6 cloves garlic, crushed
2 teaspoons freshly chopped ginger
1 teaspoon dried rosemary
1/4 teaspoon dried oregano

**In** a large measuring cup, whisk together the marmalade, orange juice concentrate, mustard, and oil. Mix in the garlic, ginger, rosemary, and oregano. Transfer marinade to a large ziplock bag. Add lamb chops to the bag and seal the top. Marinate chops in the refrigerator for 1 to 3 hours, turning occasionally.

## lamb chops

8 well-trimmed grass-fed lamb loin chops
  (about 1 1/2 inches thick)
Unrefined sea salt, to taste
Freshly ground black pepper, to taste

**Preheat** a grill, grill pan, or barbecue to very hot. Shake the excess marinade from the chops and season chops with salt and pepper. Place chops on the grill and cook 4–5 minutes a side for medium-rare, or slightly longer for more well-done. Transfer to a warm platter and serve.

# vegetable gratin

**Extra virgin olive oil cooking spray**
**1 pound zucchini, ends trimmed, sliced crosswise into ¹/₄-inch-thick slices**
**1 pound yellow summer squash, ends trimmed, sliced crosswise into ¹/₄-inch-thick slices**
**2 teaspoons unrefined sea salt, divided, plus more to taste**
**4 large ripe tomatoes, sliced ¹/₄ inch thick**
**5 tablespoons extra virgin olive oil**
**2 Spanish onions, halved lengthwise and thinly sliced**
**³/₄ teaspoon freshly ground black pepper, divided**
**6 medium cloves garlic, minced, divided**
**2 tablespoons freshly minced tarragon, divided**
**2 slices sprouted whole-grain bread, torn into pieces**
**1 cup freshly grated Parmesan cheese**

**Set** oven rack to upper-middle position and heat oven to 400 degrees F. Spray a 13 x 9 inch baking dish with cooking spray. Set aside.

**Place** zucchini and squash slices in a large bowl. Toss with 1 teaspoon salt. Transfer to a colander set over a large bowl and let stand for about 45 minutes, or until vegetables release a little more than 2 tablespoons of liquid. Arrange slices on triple-layer paper towels. Firmly press each slice to remove as much liquid as possible.

**Place** tomato slices in a single layer on double-layer of paper towels and sprinkle evenly with ¹/₂ teaspoon salt; let sit 30 minutes. Place second double-layer of paper towels on top of tomatoes and press firmly to dry tomatoes.

**Heat** 1 tablespoon oil in a large nonstick skillet over medium heat. Add onions, remaining ¹/₂ teaspoon salt and ¹/₄ teaspoon pepper; cook, stirring occasionally, until onions are softened, about 20 minutes. Set aside.

**Combine** half of the garlic, 2 tablespoons oil, remaining ¹/₂ teaspoon pepper, and 1 tablespoon tarragon in a medium bowl.

**Place** zucchini and squash in a large bowl. Toss with half of the garlic-tarragon mixture. Arrange on the bottom of the prepared baking dish. Arrange onions in an even layer over the squash. Slightly overlap tomato slices in a single layer on top of the onions. Spoon the remaining garlic-tarragon mixture evenly over the tomatoes. Bake, uncovered, for 40 to 45 minutes.

**Place** bread in a food processor and pulse into fine crumbs. Add remaining oil, garlic, tarragon, and Parmesan cheese, and season with salt. Set crumb topping aside.

**Remove** baking dish from the oven and increase heat to 450 degrees F. Sprinkle bread crumb topping evenly on top of tomatoes. Bake gratin about 10 minutes, or until crumb topping is golden brown. Remove baking dish from the oven, carefully drain any excess liquid into the sink (there shouldn't be much), and let sit for 15 minutes. Serve at room temperature.

# leg of lamb with pistachio-parsley crust and bean and arugula salad and balsamic pears with gorgonzola

• • • • • • • • • • • • • • • • • • • • • • • • • • • • • • • • • • • • • • • • • • • • •

Serves: ║║║║

Prep time: ⏰

Complexity level: 🍎🍎🍎

## leg of lamb with pistachio-parsley crust

1 cup dry-roasted salted pistachios
3 tablespoons extra virgin olive oil
1 tablespoon lemon juice
½ cup whole-wheat panko crumbs
3 cloves garlic
¼ cup chopped fresh parsley
5-pound grass-fed leg of lamb, visible fat
   and bone removed
Unrefined sea salt, to taste
Ground pepper, to taste

**Preheat** oven to 400 degrees F.

**Place** pistachios, oil, lemon juice, panko crumbs, garlic, and parsley in a food processor and process until well blended. Set crumb mixture aside.

**Season** lamb with salt and pepper. Place lamb in a roasting pan or a large cast-iron skillet. Pat pistachio-parsley crumbs all over the lamb. Gently tie the lamb with kitchen string. Roast lamb for 20 minutes; then reduce heat to 350 degrees F and roast for an additional 10–12 minutes per pound.

**Remove** lamb from the oven anywhere from 130 to 135 degrees F for medium rare. Lamb should never be cooked until well done or it will be too dry. Let stand for 15–20 minutes before carving. Cut away the kitchen string and slice with a sharp carving knife into ½-inch-thick slices against the grain of the meat.

# bean and arugula salad

2 tablespoons extra virgin olive oil
1 shallot, diced
3 cloves garlic, chopped
$^1/_2$ cup diced carrots
$^1/_2$ cup diced celery
Unrefined sea salt, to taste
Paprika, to taste
White pepper, to taste
$^1/_2$ cup chopped sun-dried tomatoes
    marinated in extra virgin olive oil,
    drained
2 tablespoons balsamic vinegar
2 (14.5-ounce) cans cannellini beans,
    rinsed and drained
3 ounces arugula leaves, torn into bite-
    size pieces
1 tablespoon flax oil (such as Barlean's)
$^3/_4$ cup chopped pecans

**Heat** oil in a medium skillet to medium-high; add shallot and garlic, and cook 2 minutes. Add carrots and celery, and cook an additional 3–4 minutes, or until vegetables are tender. Season with salt, paprika, and pepper. Remove skillet from heat and stir in tomatoes and vinegar.

**Transfer** vegetables to a large salad bowl. Add beans and gently toss. Add arugula and flax oil, and gently toss again. Mix in the pecans. Let salad sit for 10–15 minutes before serving. Serve at room temperature.

# balsamic pears with gorgonzola

2 Bosc pears, washed, dried, and cut in
    half lengthwise (keep the skins on)
2 teaspoons extra virgin olive oil
2 teaspoons balsamic vinegar
Finely ground unrefined sea salt, to taste
Freshly ground black pepper, to taste
$^1/_4$ cup crumbled Gorgonzola cheese

**Preheat** oven to 350 degrees F.

**Toss** the pears with oil, vinegar, salt, and pepper. Lay the pears on a baking dish with the cut-side up. Roast pears for 15 minutes. Remove from the oven, top each pear half with Gorgonzola cheese, return pears to the oven, and roast for 5 more minutes, or until just tender but not mushy.

**Allow** pears to cool 5 minutes before serving. Serve warm.

# mussels and shrimp in coconut-lime broth and thai-style salad with peanuts and mandarin oranges

Serves: | | | |

Prep time: 

Complexity level: 

## mussels and shrimp in coconut-lime broth

2 pounds fresh mussels
1 tablespoon extra virgin coconut oil
  (such as Barlean's)
2 tablespoons extra virgin olive oil
5 cloves garlic, finely sliced
2 tablespoons peeled and finely sliced
  ginger
1 or 2 green chile peppers (depending on
  your heat preference), seeded and finely
  chopped
2 red bell peppers, finely chopped
1 red onion, finely chopped
Unrefined sea salt, to taste
1 (14-ounce) can coconut milk
3 cups organic vegetable broth
Juice from 2 limes
Orange peel from 1 orange
2 lemongrass stalks (each about 4 inches
  long), outer leaves discarded, stalks
  sliced down the middle and bruised
  with the back of a knife
3 scallions, chopped
20 large shrimp (about 1 pound), peeled
  and deveined
1/4 cup chopped fresh cilantro

**Scrub** the mussels under cold running water, removing any barnacles and beards. Discard any opened mussels or those that have broken or damaged shells. Drain mussels in a colander and set aside.

**Heat** oils in a very large saucepan over medium-high heat. When the oil is hot, add the garlic, ginger, chile peppers, bell peppers, and onion. Reduce heat to medium and sauté vegetables for 4–5 minutes, or until onion is softened. Season vegetables with salt.

**Add** the coconut milk, vegetable broth, lime juice, orange peel, and lemongrass stalks to the saucepan, and raise the heat to medium-high. Once the liquid just starts to boil, add the mussels and scallions, cover, and cook 2–4 minutes, or until mussels are open. Discard any mussels that remain closed.

**Toss** in the shrimp, cover, and cook for 1½ minutes, or until shrimp is done. Add the cilantro.

**To** serve, ladle the mussels and shrimp with the broth and vegetables into deep-dish soup bowls. (Note: For a heartier meal, you can serve the mussels and shrimp over soba noodles tossed in toasted sesame oil and soy sauce, or serve toasted spelt bread on the side for dipping into the broth.)

# thai-style salad with peanuts and mandarin oranges

1 head Boston lettuce, washed, dried, and torn into bite-size pieces
½ cup chopped fresh mint
½ cup chopped fresh cilantro
1 red bell pepper, finely chopped
1 cucumber, peeled, seeded, and finely chopped
½ red onion, finely chopped
1 (15-ounce) can whole baby corn, drained, chopped, and patted dry with paper towels
1 (11-ounce) can mandarin oranges, drained and patted dry with paper towels
1 (8-ounce) can chopped water chestnuts, drained and patted dry with paper towels
Unrefined sea salt, to taste
¼ cup toasted sesame oil
1 tablespoon raw honey
2 teaspoons rice wine vinegar
1 tablespoon good-quality soy sauce
Juice from 1 lime
1 teaspoon crushed red pepper flakes
1½ cups finely chopped dry-roasted peanuts

**In** a large serving bowl, add the lettuce, mint, cilantro, bell pepper, cucumber, onion, corn, oranges, and water chestnuts. Gently toss all ingredients. Season salad with salt and lightly toss once more.

**In** a cup, whisk together the sesame oil, honey, vinegar, soy sauce, lime juice, and red pepper flakes. Pour the vinaigrette over the salad and toss to coat. Let salad sit for 4–5 minutes. Sprinkle the peanuts on top of the salad and toss again. Serve salad at room temperature.

# grouper with carrot-ginger-cashew purée and spinach gratin cups

•••••••••••••••••••••••••••••••••••••••••••••••••••••

**Serves:** | | | |

**Prep time:**

**Complexity level:**

## grouper with carrot-ginger-cashew purée

3/4 pound baby carrots
3 tablespoons extra virgin olive oil, divided
1 teaspoon unrefined sea salt, plus more to taste
1/2 cup cashews
1 tablespoon freshly minced ginger
2 teaspoons raw honey
3 tablespoons coconut milk
3 tablespoons 2-percent organic milk
Juice from 2 limes
4 (6-ounce) grouper fillets
Extra virgin olive oil cooking spray

**Preheat** oven to 400 degrees F.

**Place** carrots on a foil-lined baking sheet and toss with 1 tablespoon oil and salt to taste. Roast the carrots for 40 minutes, or until very tender. Remove from the oven and allow to cool for 10 minutes.

**Place** the cooled carrots in a food processor or blender and add 1 tablespoon oil, cashews, ginger, honey, coconut milk, milk, and salt to taste. Process until mixture is smooth and creamy. Set purée aside.

**Lower** oven temperature to 375 degrees F.

**Prepare** the marinade in a ziplock bag by adding the lime juice, remaining tablespoon of oil, and 1 teaspoon salt. Place the grouper fillets in the bag and marinate for 10 minutes.

**Remove** the fillets from the marinade and shake off any excess liquid. Season the fillets with salt to taste. Spray the bottom of a 9 x 13-inch glass baking dish with cooking spray. Place the fillets in the dish and spread a thick layer of the carrot purée on top of each fillet. Sprinkle a little more salt on top of the carrot purée. Bake the fish for about 12 minutes, or until it is flaky. Remove fish from the oven and prepare the broiler. Place fish back in the oven on the top shelf and broil for 30–45 seconds, or until carrot purée is just slightly charred. Serve at once.

# spinach gratin cups

Extra virgin olive oil cooking spray
4 cups water
$1/2$ teaspoon salt
$1/2$ chopped onion
10 ounces fresh baby spinach leaves
4 cloves garlic, minced
2 cage-free organic omega-3 eggs, lightly
   beaten
$1/4$ cup 2-percent organic milk
1 tablespoon grass-fed organic butter,
   melted
$1/4$ teaspoon nutmeg
Salt, to taste
White pepper, to taste
$1/4$ cup Parmesan cheese, divided
$1/4$ cup whole-wheat panko crumbs (such
   as Ian's brand: www.iansnaturalfoods
   .com)
2 teaspoons extra virgin olive oil

**Preheat** the oven to 450 degrees F.

**Spray** 4 ($1/2$-cup) ramekins with cooking spray.

**Bring** a large pot of salted water to a boil. Add the onion and cook for 1 minute. Add the spinach to the pot and cook for an additional minute, or until wilted. Drain thoroughly in a colander and allow the spinach and onion to cool a bit. Chop the spinach and put it and the onion in a large bowl. Add in the garlic, eggs, milk, butter, nutmeg, salt, pepper, and $1/2$ of the Parmesan cheese. Mix well. Divide the spinach mixture among the 4 prepared ramekins.

**In** a small bowl, mix together the remaining Parmesan cheese, panko crumbs, and oil. Sprinkle the panko-cheese crumbs on top of the spinach mixture.

**Transfer** the ramekins to a large shallow baking dish and pour hot water into the baking dish so that it goes halfway up the ramekins. Bake for 20–25 minutes, or until mixture is set and topping is golden. Serve warm.

# joe riti's italian flatbread pizza with sautéed broccoli raab, ricotta, and tomatoes

Serves: |||| ||||

Prep time: 🕛

Complexity level: 🍎🍎🍎🍎

## marinara

¹/₄ cup extra virgin olive oil
8 cloves garlic, chopped
1 (29-ounce) can tomato sauce
1 (29-ounce) can crushed tomatoes
1 tablespoon tomato paste
2 teaspoons granulated garlic
¹/₂ teaspoon oregano
¹/₂ teaspoon unrefined sea salt
¹/₂ teaspoon pepper
¹/₂ cup chopped Italian parsley

**Heat** oil in a medium saucepan to medium-high. Add garlic and sauté 2–3 minutes. Add remaining ingredients and lower heat to a simmer. Simmer for 45 minutes to 2 hours. Set sauce aside to cool.

## sautéed broccoli raab

3 tablespoons extra virgin olive oil
8 cloves garlic, chopped
1 bunch broccoli raab, rinsed and stems removed
¹/₄ cup water
Granulated garlic, to taste
Unrefined sea salt, to taste
Crushed red pepper, to taste

**Heat** oil in a large skillet to medium-high; add the garlic and sauté for 30–45 seconds. Add broccoli raab and lightly toss to coat. Turn heat to medium-low and cook broccoli raab for 10–12 minutes. (It should start to wilt down.) Add the water and let broccoli raab steam for an additional 3–4 minutes, or until water evaporates. Season broccoli raab generously with granulated garlic, salt, and red pepper. Set broccoli raab aside.

# joe riti's italian flatbread pizza

1 cup lukewarm water (110 degrees F)
2 packages active dry yeast
2 tablespoons sugar
1 teaspoon raw honey
3¹/₂ cups white whole-wheat flour, plus
   more as needed
1 teaspoon unrefined sea salt
3 tablespoons extra virgin olive oil
3 cups prepared Marinara, plus more
   to taste
5 ounces fresh mozzarella balls, torn into
   bite-size pieces
1 cup low-fat organic ricotta cheese
2 beefsteak tomatoes, sliced paper-thin
1 bunch Sautéed Broccoli Raab
³/₄ cup thin strips of roasted red peppers
   from a jar, marinated in extra virgin
   olive oil, drained, and patted dry
¹/₄ cup freshly grated Parmesan cheese
Oregano, to taste
Granulated garlic, to taste

**For** the dough, place the lukewarm water in a medium-size bowl and add the yeast, sugar, and honey; stir to dissolve. In a separate large bowl, mix together the flour and salt. Make a well in the center of the bowl and pour in the liquid mixture. Add the oil and whisk ingredients together with a fork, working toward the outside of the well. Using your hands to mix the ingredients, add a little more flour as needed to make a soft but manageable dough. Gather the dough into a ball and knead for 8–10 minutes on a lightly floured work board. Place the dough in a medium-size bowl

and cover with plastic wrap. Let dough rise in a warm place for 30–60 minutes, or until dough has doubled in size. (To speed up the dough-rising process, place the dough in an extra warm place, such as near a heated oven.) Once the dough has doubled in size, use a knife to cut it in half and sprinkle about ¹/₈ cup flour onto two separate work boards. Place each dough half on one of the boards. Punch each dough half down with your fist and use a rolling pin to flatten.

**Preheat** oven to 400 degrees F.

**Lightly** oil two 12-inch pizza pans. Place the dough on each of the pizza pans and use your fingers to gently stretch the dough to fit the pans. Bake dough for 5 minutes.

**Remove** pizza crust from oven and assemble pizza by spreading about 1¹/₂ cups of marinara over each pizza crust (you should have plenty of Marinara left over!). Divide the torn mozzarella pieces on top of the marinara and gently spread the ricotta on top. Arrange the tomato slices on top of the ricotta and add some of the Sautéed Broccoli Raab on top of the tomatoes. (Serve remaining broccoli raab as a side dish.) Arrange the red pepper strips on top. Sprinkle pizza with Parmesan cheese, oregano, and granulated garlic. Bake pizza for about 15–18 minutes, or until crust is crisp. Let pizza cool for 10 minutes, slice, and serve.

# making it an occasion

## healthier recipes for special days and holidays

**Special days** and holidays are notorious occasions for igniting out-of-control splurging, probably because party fare and celebration-worthy food often favor taste over health. But, who says you can't have your cake, waistline, and good health too? Whether it's Super Bowl Sunday or Thanksgiving, you can still indulge in fabulous foods without sacrificing health. This chapter was created to show you just how easy it is to still eat the whole foods way—everyday and every occasion of the year. So there are no more excuses!

# super bowl party

Here, we've assembled touch-down-worthy all-American party food that goes way beyond the usual (snore) chips and dips. We've kept in line with the spirit of traditional football game grub, including **standby favorites** like wings and brownies; we've just punched things up a few notches in the taste and nutrition departments. So, whether your friends are after good taste, healthy food, or both, this **super spread** is sure to bowl the gang over on the day of the big game.

## on the menu

**chile-studded cheesy polenta bread**

**seven-layer taco bean dip**

**buffalo-style chicken "wings" with blue cheese dip**

**beef and dark beer chili with tomatoes**

**reese swirl brownies**

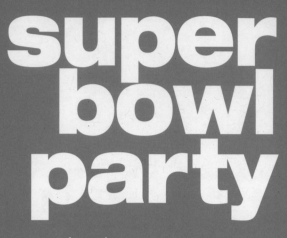

# chile-studded cheesy polenta bread

Serves: |||| ||||

Prep time: ⏰

Complexity level: 🍎 🍎

Extra virgin olive oil cooking spray
1/3 cup slivered almonds
3 cage-free organic omega-3 eggs, separated
2 egg yolks (from cage-free organic omega-3 eggs)
1/3 cup extra virgin olive oil
1/4 cup honey
2 (4-ounce) cans chopped green chiles, divided
1/2 cup white whole-wheat flour
1 cup stone-ground cornmeal
1/2 teaspoon unrefined sea salt
1 1/2 teaspoons baking powder
2 tablespoons canola oil mayonnaise
3/4 cup shredded low-fat organic cheddar cheese

**Preheat** oven to 350 degrees F. Coat two 9-inch round cake pans with cooking spray. Set pans aside.

**Place** the almonds in a food processor and pulse into fine crumbs. Set almond crumbs aside.

**Using** an electric mixer, beat the 3 egg whites until they are stiff but not dry.

**In** a separate bowl, use the electric mixer to mix the oil with the honey; add in the 5 egg yolks and mix thoroughly. Fold in one can chopped green chiles.

**In** a separate bowl, mix together the flour, cornmeal, salt, and baking powder.

**Using** a spatula, incorporate the flour-cornmeal mixture and almond crumbs with the egg yolk mixture. Mix until all ingredients are well-blended. Fold in the egg whites, moving the spatula delicately to incorporate them while maintaining the airiness they contribute to the batter.

**Divide** the batter between the 2 prepared cake pans. Bake for 12–13 minutes, or until a toothpick inserted in the middle comes out clean. Remove the pans from the oven and allow polenta bread to cool on a wire rack for at least 10 minutes.

**While** polenta bread is cooling, mix the mayonnaise, 2 tablespoons of chopped green chiles (from second can), and shredded cheese together in a medium-size mixing bowl.

**Carefully** remove the polenta breads from their pans. Place one layer of the polenta bread, bottom-side up, on a microwave-safe platter. Spread the cheese mixture on top of the polenta bread. Place the second layer of polenta bread on top of the cheese mixture. To serve; microwave the polenta bread for 2–3 minutes, or until cheese melts. Cut the polenta bread into triangular pieces and serve warm.

# seven-layer taco bean dip

Serves: | | | |  | | | |

Prep time: 🕐
Complexity level: 🍎 🍎

1 tablespoon extra virgin olive oil
3 cloves garlic, mashed
1 (16-ounce) can fat-free refried pinto
   beans
1 tablespoon all-natural taco seasoning
2 Hass avocados
1/4 cup finely chopped red onion
1 tablespoon lime juice
2 tablespoons chopped cilantro
Unrefined sea salt, to taste
1/4 cup low-fat organic sour cream
1/4 cup silken tofu, drained
2 tablespoons canola oil mayonnaise
2 tablespoons prepared hummus
1 1/2 cups pico de gallo (from deli section
   of your supermarket)
1/2 cup chopped green onions
1/2 head iceberg lettuce, shredded
1 (3.8-ounce) can sliced black olives,
   drained
1 1/2 cups shredded low-fat organic
   cheddar cheese or Mexican cheese
   blend
1 bag all-natural black bean chips

**Heat** oil in a large skillet over
medium-high; add garlic and sauté for
1–2 minutes. Add pinto beans, mashing
to incorporate beans with the garlic and
oil. Mix in the taco seasoning. Cook for
2–3 minutes. Spread bean mixture on
the bottom of an 8 x 8-inch serving dish.

**In** a separate bowl, mash avocados.
Mix in the red onion, lime juice, and
cilantro. Season with salt to taste.
Spread mixture on top of the beans.

**In** a blender, process the sour cream,
tofu, mayonnaise, and hummus until
smooth and creamy. Spread mixture on
top of the avocado mixture.

**Spread** the pico de gallo on top of
the sour cream mixture.

**Sprinkle** green onions on top of the
pico de gallo.

**Spread** the shredded lettuce on top
of the green onions.

**Scatter** the black olives on top of the
green lettuce.

**Sprinkle** shredded cheddar cheese
on top of the olives.

**Cover** bean dip with plastic wrap
and refrigerate for up to 24 hours
before serving. Allow dip to sit at room
temperature for 1 hour before serving.
Serve dip with chips.

# buffalo-style chicken "wings" with blue cheese dip

••••••••••••••••••••••••••••••••••••••••••••••••••••••••••••••••••

**Serves:** 🥄🥄🥄🥄🥄 🥄🥄🥄🥄🥄

**Prep time:** ⏰
**Complexity level:** 🍎🍎

3 tablespoons full-fat organic plain
   yogurt
3 tablespoons puréed chipotle peppers in
   adobo sauce, divided
1 teaspoon Dijon mustard
3 tablespoons plus 1 teaspoon apple
   cider vinegar, divided
Unrefined sea salt, to taste
1$1/2$ pounds boneless, organic, free-range
   chicken tenderloins
$1/2$ cup whole-milk organic cottage
   cheese
2 tablespoons canola oil mayonnaise
$1/2$ cup Danish blue cheese
$1/2$ teaspoon Worcestershire sauce
2 tablespoons minced shallots
$1/2$ cup white whole-wheat flour
$1/2$ cup whole-grain corn flour
Paprika, to taste
Cayenne pepper, to taste
2 tablespoons extra virgin olive oil,
   divided
1 teaspoon grass-fed organic butter,
   melted
Celery sticks, for garnish
Carrot sticks, for garnish

**Combine** yogurt, 1 tablespoon chipotle purée, mustard, 2 tablespoons vinegar, and salt in a ziplock bag. Add the chicken and toss to coat. Refrigerate chicken and marinate for 1–2 hours.

**While** the chicken marinates, combine cottage cheese, mayonnaise, blue cheese, Worcestershire sauce, 1 tablespoon chipotle purée, and 1 teaspoon apple cider vinegar in a food processor or blender; process until smooth and creamy. Stir in the shallots. Transfer dip to a small bowl, cover, and refrigerate until serving time.

**In** a shallow bowl, combine the whole-wheat flour with the corn flour. Remove the chicken from the marinade. Season chicken with salt, paprika, and cayenne pepper to taste. (Go easy on the cayenne!) Dredge the chicken in the flour mixture to evenly coat both sides.

**Heat** 1 tablespoon of oil in a large nonstick skillet over medium-high heat. When the oil is hot, add half of the chicken and cook until golden brown on each side and cooked through, about 3–4 minutes per side. Transfer chicken to a serving platter. Repeat with remaining half of the chicken.

**Whisk** together the remaining tablespoon of chipotle purée, 1 tablespoon of vinegar, and the melted butter. Drizzle sauce over chicken. Place chicken "wings" on a platter with carrot and celery sticks and a bowl of blue cheese dip. Serve at once.

# beef and dark beer chili with tomatoes

Serves:
Prep time:
Complexity level:

4 tablespoons extra virgin olive oil
1 large Spanish onion, chopped
4 cloves garlic, minced
1/2 teaspoon unrefined sea salt, plus more to taste
1 pound lean grass-fed ground beef or ground ostrich
3 tablespoons white whole-wheat flour
1 (8-ounce) package tempeh, crumbled
3/4 cup yellow raisins
2 (14.5-ounce) cans diced fire-roasted tomatoes with juices
2 (14.5-ounce) cans pinto beans, rinsed and drained
2 packed tablespoons chopped canned chipotle peppers (seeds removed) in adobo sauce
3 tablespoons chili powder
1 teaspoon cumin
2 teaspoons paprika
1/4 teaspoon cayenne pepper
1/4 cup canned pumpkin
1 (12-ounce) jar roasted red peppers marinated in oil, drained and patted dry
1 (12-ounce) bottle dark beer
1 1/2 cups shredded low-fat organic extra-sharp cheddar cheese
6 scallions, finely chopped

**Heat** the oil in a large nonstick skillet over medium-high heat; add onion and garlic, and sauté 5–6 minutes, until onions are soft. Season the onion and garlic lightly with salt to taste. Add the ground beef (or ostrich) and sauté, breaking it up with a spoon, until the meat is no longer pink, about 5 minutes. Add the flour and stir until well blended. Stir in the crumbled tempeh. Season again with salt to taste.

**Transfer** the onion, meat, and tempeh mixture to a 5- or 6-quart slow cooker. Stir in the raisins, tomatoes, pinto beans, and chipotle peppers.

**Place** the chili powder, cumin, paprika, cayenne pepper, pumpkin, red peppers, and beer in a blender and purée until smooth. Add the beer purée to the slow cooker. Place the cover on the slow cooker and cook the chili on low heat for 5–6 hours. Allow the chili to cool 15 minutes before serving. Season with salt. To serve, ladle the chili into deep bowls and top with shredded cheese and scallions.

# reese swirl brownies

● ● ● ● ● ● ● ● ● ● ● ● ● ● ● ● ● ● ● ● ● ● ● ● ● ● ● ● ● ● ● ● ● ● ● ● ● ● ● ● ● ● ● ● ● ●

**Serves:** ⫯⫯⫯⫯⫯ ⫯⫯⫯⫯

**Prep time:** 🕐
**Complexity level:** 🍎

Canola oil cooking spray
1/3 cup plus 2 tablespoons all-natural
    creamy peanut butter, divided
1/3 cup 1-percent low-fat organic milk
1/3 cup plus 3 tablespoons brown sugar,
    divided
1 banana
1 cage-free organic omega-3 egg
3 tablespoons high-oleic canola oil
1 tablespoon grass-fed organic butter,
    softened
1/4 cup water
1/4 cup high-quality unsweetened cocoa
1 teaspoon pure vanilla extract
1/2 cup mini dark chocolate chips (60
    percent cocoa)
1 1/4 cups white whole-wheat flour
1/2 teaspoon baking powder
1/2 teaspoon unrefined sea salt
1/4 cup coarsely chopped peanuts
2 tablespoons cream cheese
2 tablespoons water

**Preheat** oven to 350 degrees F. Spray an 8 x 8-inch baking dish with cooking spray.

**In** a blender, add 1/3 cup peanut butter, milk, 1/3 cup plus 2 tablespoons brown sugar, banana, egg, oil, butter, water, cocoa, and vanilla extract; purée until smooth and creamy. Pour mixture into a medium-size bowl.

**Place** chocolate chips in a small microwave-safe dish and microwave on high for 1 minute. Using a fork, mix the softened chocolate until smooth and creamy; add to peanut butter mixture. Use a fork to blend all ingredients together.

**In** a separate bowl, mix the flour, baking powder, and salt together. Add the dry ingredients to the wet ingredients. Mix thoroughly. Stir in the peanuts. Pour the mixture into the prepared baking dish.

**In** a small bowl, combine the remaining 2 tablespoons peanut butter, 1 tablespoon brown sugar, cream cheese, and water; whisk ingredients together until smooth and creamy. Drop the peanut butter–cream cheese mixture by tablespoonfuls onto the top of the brownie batter; use a knife to swirl the peanut butter–cream cheese mixture for a marble effect.

**Bake** brownies for 35 minutes. Remove from oven and cool for 5 minutes before slicing. (Note: Brownies can be made up to 2 days in advance and stored in a covered container in the refrigerator. Just before serving, microwave for 1 minute.)

# valentine's day

You know what they say about men, food, stomachs, and their hearts. Andy can vouch for the men, and he agrees—a **delicious** meal can do wonders to spark passionate interest from almost any man. Here we've put together a **romantically heart-healthy** "steak-house-style" Valentine's **menu** any guy we know will appreciate. And, just in case you're wondering, we include serving suggestions for four people on this menu, not because we invite other couples to our house for Valentine's dinner but because this meal **makes a great dinner** for general entertaining.

## on the menu

**arugula salad with garlic-infused lemon vinaigrette**

**twice-baked potatoes**

**cabernet filet mignon with gourmet mushrooms**

**red raspberry cake with mascarpone frosting**

# arugula salad with garlic-infused lemon vinaigrette

Serves: ▯▯▯▯

Prep time:

Complexity level:

8 cups trimmed arugula leaves

1 (12–14 ounce) can hearts of palm packed in water, drained, rinsed with cold water, patted dry, and sliced lengthwise

1/4 cup extra virgin olive oil

2 cloves garlic, smashed

1/3 cup fresh lemon juice

1/4 teaspoon unrefined sea salt, plus more to taste

1/8 teaspoon coarsely ground black pepper, plus more to taste

1/4 teaspoon sugar

1/4 cup freshly grated Parmesan cheese

1/4 cup finely chopped pecans

**Divide** the arugula leaves evenly onto four salad plates and nestle the hearts of palm on top of the arugula. Set salad plates aside.

**Heat** oil and garlic in a small saucepan over medium-high heat; simmer the garlic in the oil for about 1½ minutes, taking care not to let the garlic brown. Remove the garlic from the saucepan and discard; pour the oil into a small bowl.

**Wipe** the saucepan clean with a paper towel and return to the heat; add the lemon juice and simmer for about 30 seconds. Pour the lemon juice into the bowl with the warm oil. Whisk in the salt, pepper, and sugar.

**Drizzle** the vinaigrette over the arugula leaves and sprinkle the cheese and pecans on top. Serve at once.

# twice-baked potatoes

Serves: | | | |

Prep time: ⏰
Complexity level: 🍎🍎

2 Idaho baking potatoes (about 8 ounces each)
¹/₄ cup plus 2 tablespoons ready-made hummus (look for hummus made with extra virgin olive oil in the deli section of your supermarket)
3 tablespoons low-fat organic ricotta cheese
3 tablespoons minced sun-dried tomatoes, packed in oil (use kitchen shears to mince the tomatoes)
2 tablespoons chopped parsley
Unrefined sea salt, to taste
Coarsely ground black pepper, to taste
¹/₄ cup freshly grated Parmesan cheese

**Preheat** oven to 400 degrees F. Use a fork to poke holes all over each potato; bake potatoes on an upper oven rack for 1 hour. Remove potatoes from the oven, but leave the oven on.

**As** soon as the potatoes are cool enough to handle, slice them in half lengthwise and gently scoop out the centers, taking extra care not to tear the shell. Add the potato centers to a large bowl and mix in the hummus, ricotta cheese, tomatoes, parsley, salt, and pepper. Mash ingredients together with a potato masher until potatoes are lump-free and mostly smooth.

**Scoop** the seasoned potatoes back into their shells and sprinkle the Parmesan cheese on top of each potato. Place the potatoes on a baking dish lined with aluminum foil and bake at 400 degrees F for another 15 minutes. Remove from oven and cover lightly with aluminum foil until serving time.

# cabernet filet mignon with gourmet mushrooms

Serves: | | | |

Prep time: ⏰
Complexity level: 🍎

4 (5–6 ounce) 1-inch-thick grass-fed filet mignon steaks, trimmed of all visible fat (kitchen shears make snipping fat a snap)

4 teaspoons extra virgin olive oil, plus more for coating steaks

Coarsely ground unrefined sea salt, to taste

Coarsely ground fresh black pepper, to taste

1/2 cup cabernet wine (can substitute any dry red wine)

1 teaspoon grass-fed organic butter

3 cloves garlic, minced

8 ounces gourmet blend of sliced mushrooms (baby bella, shiitake, and oyster)

**Bring** steaks to room temperature before cooking. Coat steaks lightly with oil and season both sides of the meat with salt and pepper (press the pepper in with your hands).

**Heat** 1 teaspoon oil in a heavy skillet (a cast-iron frying pan would be best) to medium-high. Tilt the pan, swirl the oil over the bottom, and then sear the steaks, moving them with tongs a little so they don't stick to the bottom, for about 5–6 minutes per side (well-done steaks will need to cook longer). When the steaks are crusty-charred and done to your liking, remove from the pan and cover loosely with aluminum foil.

**Add** the wine to the skillet and bring to a boil, scraping any pieces of steak off the bottom of the pan and stirring them into the emerging sauce. Let the liquid boil until reduced to approximately 1/3 cup. Remove pan from heat. Add the butter and mix it in by swirling the pan. Transfer sauce to a small bowl.

**Wipe** the skillet with a paper towel and pour in the remaining 3 teaspoons oil, heat to medium-high and add the garlic; sauté the garlic for about 30 seconds and then add the mushrooms. Sauté the mushrooms for several minutes, until just wilted. Season lightly with salt and pepper to taste.

**To** serve, place each steak on individual plates, top with mushrooms, and pour the sauce over the steaks just before serving.

# red raspberry cake with mascarpone frosting

Serves: 🥄🥄🥄🥄 🥄🥄🥄🥄

Prep time: ⏰

Complexity level: 🍎🍎🍎

Canola oil cooking spray
1½ cups white whole-wheat flour
1 teaspoon baking powder
1 teaspoon aluminum-free baking soda
1 teaspoon unrefined sea salt
¼ cup unsweetened plain soy milk (we recommend Silk brand)
¼ cup orange juice concentrate
½ cup plus 2 tablespoons water
1 teaspoon pure lemon extract
4 tablespoons extra virgin coconut oil (such as Barlean's)
½ cup brown sugar
2 cage-free organic omega-3 eggs
3½ cups fresh raspberries, divided
5 tablespoons confectioners' sugar, divided
⅓ cup mascarpone cheese
¼ cup organic Neufchâtel cream cheese
1 tablespoon lemon juice

**Position** rack in center of oven and preheat to 400 degrees F. Spray a 9½-inch-square aluminum cake pan with cooking spray. Line the bottom of the pan with wax paper and spray the wax paper with cooking spray.

**Sift** the flour, baking powder, baking soda, and salt together in a medium-size bowl. In a small bowl, whisk together the soy milk, orange juice concentrate, water, and lemon extract.

Pour the wet ingredients into the bowl with the dry ingredients and mix well.

**Using** a hand-held mixer, beat the coconut oil and sugar together in a medium-size bowl. Add the eggs one at a time, beating well after each addition. Add the egg mixture to the batter and stir to combine.

**Transfer** the batter to the prepared pan. Sprinkle the cake with 2½ cups of raspberries. Bake until top is gently set, about 20 minutes. Reduce oven temperature to 375 degrees F. Sprinkle the top of the cake with 2 tablespoons of confectioners' sugar. Continue baking until tester inserted into the center of cake comes out clean, about 15 minutes. Cool in pan on rack. Run a sharp knife around the edges of the pan to loosen the cake. Cool cake to room temperature and then invert and remove the wax paper from the bottom. Turn the cake over again so that the raspberries are showing on top and transfer cake to a serving platter.

**In** a small bowl, whisk together the mascarpone cheese, cream cheese, 3 tablespoons confectioners' sugar, and lemon juice. Lightly spread a thin layer of frosting on top of the cake. Cut the cake and serve with fresh raspberries on the side.

# st. patrick's day

Our "special days and holidays" section wouldn't be complete without a traditional **Irish feast** to celebrate St. Patrick's Day. Ivy gained an appreciation for Irish culture while attending college in London and rooming with Mirsada, who is now one of her best friends. A true Irish girl at heart, Mirsada made frequent weekend trips to visit her **family and friends** in Ireland and came back to London reporting how almost everything was better on the Emerald Isle. Everything except for the fact that the land of saints and scholars has never been particularly well known for being the land of light and nutritious cuisine. For this holiday meal, we were able to **healthfully** adapt authentic **Irish recipes** while still keeping that stick-to-your-ribs homey appeal. We hope Mirsada approves.

## on the menu

cottage pie

creamy irish-style cabbage soup

irish whiskey apple and oatmeal crisp with spiked whipped cream

# cottage pie

●●●●●●●●●●●●●●●●●●●●●●●●●●●●●●●●●●●●●●●●●●●●●●●●●●●●●●

**Serves:** ⵎ ⵎ

**Prep time:** ⏰
**Complexity level:** 🍎 🍎

2 pounds russet (baking) potatoes, cubed
   with skins on
2 tablespoons organic Neufchâtel cream
   cheese
2 tablespoons plus 1 teaspoon extra
   virgin olive oil, divided
1 cage-free organic omega-3 egg yolk
1/2 cup plus 1/3 cup organic vegetable
   broth, divided
1/2 teaspoon unrefined sea salt, plus
   more to taste
Freshly ground black pepper, to taste
1 medium leek stalk, sliced into 1/2-inch-
   thick pieces
2 tablespoons white whole-wheat flour
1/3 cup dry white wine
2 teaspoons Worcestershire sauce
1 tablespoon tomato paste
4 cloves garlic, minced
1 1/4 pounds lean grass-fed ground beef
1 carrot, peeled and minced
2 teaspoons fresh thyme
1 cup frozen petite peas
Paprika, to taste
Fresh parsley, for garnish

**Bring** a large pot of salted water to a boil; carefully add potatoes and boil for 15 minutes, or until tender. Drain potatoes and transfer to a large bowl. In a separate small bowl, whisk together the cream cheese, 1 tablespoon oil, egg yolk, and 1/2 cup of vegetable broth. Add the liquid mixture to the potatoes and mash the potatoes with a potato masher until creamy.

Season potatoes with 1/2 teaspoon salt and pepper to taste. Set potatoes aside.

**Working** in small batches, place the sliced leek rounds into a food processor or mini Cuisinart and pulse to shred. Set aside the shredded leeks.

**In** a small saucepan, heat 1 tablespoon oil over medium-high heat; whisk in the flour and stir for 30 seconds. Add the remaining 1/3 cup vegetable broth, wine, Worcestershire sauce, and tomato paste. Cook sauce for 1 minute to thicken. Place a lid on the sauce to keep warm and set aside.

**In** a large skillet, heat the remaining 1 teaspoon oil over medium-high heat. Add garlic and sauté for 30 seconds. Add the beef, crumble, and cook for 3–4 minutes. Season beef with salt and pepper to taste. Add the carrot and leek, and cook for 5 minutes, stirring frequently. Stir in the fresh thyme and peas. Add the sauce to the meat and stir to combine.

**Preheat** the broiler.

**Spread** the meat mixture evenly in an 8 x 8-inch baking dish. Spoon the potatoes over the meat and smooth with the back of a spoon. Sprinkle paprika and salt on top of the potatoes. Brush potatoes lightly with oil. Broil 6–8 inches from the heat for about 5 minutes, or until potatoes are lightly browned. Remove pie from the oven and let sit for 10 minutes before serving. Garnish with parsley and serve.

# creamy irish-style cabbage soup

• • • • • • • • • • • • • • • • • • • • • • • • • • • • • • • • • • • • • • • • • • • • • • • • • • • •

Serves: |||  |||

Prep time: ⏰
Complexity level: 🍎 🍎

1 (2-pound) cabbage, cored and
    quartered
2 tablespoons extra virgin olive oil
1 medium onion, finely chopped
Unrefined sea salt, to taste
2 tablespoons white whole-wheat flour
1/2 teaspoon nutmeg
1 cup frozen cauliflower florets, thawed
2 cups 2-percent low-fat organic milk
2 cups free-range organic chicken broth
1 teaspoon white pepper
2 tablespoons finely chopped parsley

**Bring** a large pot of salted water to a boil. Place the cabbage in a large bowl. Pour enough boiling water over the cabbage to cover it. Let cabbage stand in the water for 5 minutes. Drain well and pat dry with paper towels. Cut cabbage into thin slices.

**Heat** the oil in a large heavy skillet over medium-high heat. Add the onion and sauté until translucent, about 10 minutes. Season onion with salt to taste. Stir in the flour and nutmeg, and cook for 2 minutes. Add the cauliflower and cook for an additional 1 minute. Gradually add the milk and chicken broth. Bring liquid to a boil. Reduce heat and simmer for 20 minutes, stirring often. Stir in white pepper. Set soup aside to cool.

**Purée** the soup in batches in a blender or food processor until smooth. Return soup to saucepan and adjust seasoning. Bring soup to a simmer, ladle into bowls, and sprinkle with fresh parsley.

# irish whiskey apple and oatmeal crisp with spiked whipped cream

•••••••••••••••••••••••••••••••••••••••••••••••••••

**Serves:** 🥄🥄🥄 🥄🥄🥄

**Prep time:** ⏰
**Complexity level:** 🍎

Canola oil cooking spray
1 teaspoon plus 2 tablespoons grass-fed organic butter, divided
4 tablespoons plus 1 teaspoon Irish whiskey, divided
3 firm Granny Smith apples, cored and sliced into thin rounds (keep the skins on)
1 teaspoon cinnamon
1/2 teaspoon cardamom
1/4 cup plus 2 tablespoons brown sugar, divided
Pinch of unrefined sea salt
1 cup chopped walnuts, divided
1/2 cup old-fashioned oats
1 tablespoon white whole-wheat flour
1/4 cup wheat germ
1/4 cup ground flaxseed (such as Barlean's)
1/2 cup heavy organic whipping cream

**Preheat** oven to 350 degrees F. Spray an 8-inch round by 2-inch-deep glass baking dish with cooking spray.

**Place** 1 teaspoon of the butter in a small microwave-safe dish. Melt in microwave for 30 seconds. Stir in 3 tablespoons of Irish whiskey. Place the apples in a large bowl, add the butter-whiskey mixture and toss to coat. Add the cinnamon, cardamom, 1 tablespoon of sugar, and salt. Toss to coat apples in the sugar-spice mixture.

**Arrange** apples in a single layer on the bottom of the prepared pie dish. Top apples with 1/3 of the walnuts. Repeat layering until all apples and walnuts are in the pie dish.

**In** a medium-size bowl, combine 1/4 cup sugar, oats, flour, wheat germ, and flaxseed. Use your fingers to mix in the remaining 2 tablespoons of butter until ingredients are crumbly. Sprinkle oat mixture evenly over the top of the apples. Bake for 35–40 minutes.

**While** apple crisp is baking, whip the cream until it begins to form soft peaks. Add the remaining 1 tablespoon sugar and 1 tablespoon plus 1 teaspoon whiskey and beat until stiff peaks form. Cover and chill until needed.

**Cut** apple crisp and serve each portion with a dollop of whiskey cream.

# mother's day brunch

Winter is over, flowers are blooming, days are longer, **spring** is in the air, and Mother's Day is right around the corner. For us, it's simply not possible to separate Mother's Day and spring. Why not surprise mom with a fabulous spring-fling feast? By the way, this **elegant meal** could also serve double duty as Easter brunch.

## on the menu

**lamb chops with tangy horseradish sauce**

**bulgur and sweet pea pilaf with feta and mint**

**chardonnay-braised carrots and shallots**

**warm pistachio pudding**

# lamb chops with tangy horseradish sauce

Serves: | | | |

Prep time: 

Complexity level: 

2 tablespoons prepared hummus
1 tablespoon light sour cream
1 tablespoon lemon juice
1 tablespoon Dijon mustard
2 teaspoons prepared horseradish
8 grass-fed lamb loin chops (1 1/2- to
   2-inch-thick chops, about 3 pounds),
   trimmed of all visible fat
Coarse unrefined sea salt, to taste
Freshly ground black pepper, to taste

**Prepare** the horseradish sauce in a small bowl; whisk together the hummus, sour cream, lemon juice, mustard and horseradish. Set aside. Note: the horseradish sauce can be prepared up to 2 days in advance if refrigerated and stored in a covered container.

**Season** both sides of the chops with coarse salt and black pepper.

**Position** an oven rack 5–6 inches from the broiler and heat the broiler on high. Line the bottom of a broiler pan with foil and put the perforated top back on the pan. Arrange the chops on top of the pan. Broil the chops until one side is well-browned (about 8 minutes); turn the chops over with tongs and continue to broil until they are well-browned and the center is cooked to your liking (3–5 minutes more for medium-rare).

**Transfer** the lamb chops to a serving platter and top each with the horseradish sauce. Serve at once.

# bulgur and sweet pea pilaf with feta and mint

Serves: | | | |

Prep time:

Complexity level:

1 cup bulgur wheat
3 cups water
$1/2$ teaspoon unrefined sea salt, plus more
   to taste
$1^1/2$ cups thawed frozen petite sweet peas
3 tablespoons flax oil (such as Barlean's)
$1/2$ cup crumbled feta cheese
$1/4$ cup finely chopped walnuts
$1/4$ cup chopped fresh mint
Juice from $1/2$ lemon
Freshly ground black pepper, to taste

**Add** bulgur to salted water in a medium-size pot and bring to a boil, stirring constantly. Reduce heat, cover, and simmer for 12–15 minutes. Remove pot from the heat and allow bulgur to cool for several minutes. Drain liquid and set bulgur aside to cool.

**Transfer** the cooled bulgur to a large serving bowl; fluff with a fork and add the peas, flax oil, feta, walnuts, and mint. Gently toss all ingredients together. Squeeze the lemon juice over the bulgur pilaf and season with pepper Lightly toss all ingredients once again.

**The** bulgur pilaf can sit at room temperature for up to one hour before serving or can be stored in a covered container in the refrigerator for up to two days before serving. Note: the bulgur pilaf should be served at room temperature. Do not heat the pilaf or you will destroy the delicate essential fats in the flax oil.

# chardonnay-braised carrots and shallots

Serves: | | | |

Prep time: ⏰

Complexity level: 🍎

7 medium carrots (about 1¹/₂ pounds),
  peeled
2 tablespoons extra virgin olive oil
1 teaspoon grass-fed organic butter
4 shallots, thinly sliced
Unrefined sea salt, to taste
3 large cloves garlic, finely chopped
Pinch of cayenne pepper
¹/₄ cup Chardonnay
1 tablespoon chopped fresh parsley
2 tablespoons chopped fresh dill

**Cut** each carrot into thirds length-wise; then cut the carrots into long thin pieces.

**Heat** the oil and butter in a large heavy saucepan over medium heat; when the butter melts, add the shallots and season with salt. Cook the shallots, stirring occasionally, until softened and slightly browned, about 5 minutes. Remove the shallots from the saucepan with a slotted spoon and set them aside. Reserve the shallot-infused oil left in the pan.

**Add** the carrots to the saucepan with the seasoned oil and cook over medium heat for about 10 minutes, or until carrots are just tender. Season with salt to taste. Stir in the garlic, cayenne, shallots, and Chardonnay; cook for an additional 2–3 minutes, or until Chardonnay is mostly evaporated.

**Remove** the carrots from the heat and toss in the parsley and dill. Allow to cool for 10–15 minutes. Serve warm.

# warm pistachio pudding

Serves: | | | |

Prep time: ⏰

Complexity level: 🍎 🍎 🍎

Canola oil cooking spray
1/2 cup salted shelled pistachios
1/2 cup brown sugar
1 tablespoon cold grass-fed organic
   butter, cut into small pieces
2 tablespoons white whole-wheat flour
2 egg yolks, lightly beaten
1/4 cup lemon juice
1 cup unsweetened plain soy milk
4 egg whites

**Preheat** oven to 375 degrees F. Coat 4 (6-ounce) ceramic ramekins with cooking spray.

**Place** the pistachios, brown sugar, and butter in a food processor and process into fine crumbs. Transfer the crumbs to a medium-size mixing bowl. Reserve 2 tablespoons of the pistachio–brown sugar mixture for later use.

**Add** the flour to the bowl with the pistachio–brown sugar mixture; use your hands to thoroughly mix all of the ingredients. Add egg yolks, lemon juice, and soy milk; using a handheld mixer, mix until all ingredients are well combined.

**In** a clean, nonreactive, medium-size bowl, beat egg whites until stiff but not dry. Lightly fold the egg whites into the pistachio mixture.

**Pour** the pistachio mixture into the four prepared ramekins; place the ramekins in a 13 x 9-inch casserole and pour warm water around the sides, stopping once the water is halfway up the sides of the ramekins. Sprinkle the reserved 2 tablespoons pistachio–brown sugar mixture on top of the pistachio pudding mixture. Transfer the ramekins to the oven and bake for 25 minutes.

**Remove** the ramekins from the oven and allow the pudding to cool for 5–10 minutes before serving. Serve warm or at room temperature.

# the 4th of july

This festive, made-in-the-USA, fireworks-worthy feast is ideal for a laid-back hot summer holiday afternoon and is just the thing for pulling you out of a summer slump. We'll be frank: we're not exactly **enthusiasts** of the generic foods typically served at picnic parties, so we aimed to **punch up the flavor** in these recipes with a few gourmet twists and turns. We think we've still managed to preserve the All-American nostalgic picnic with **style and flair** for a celebration everyone can enjoy.

## on the menu

**picnic pasta salad with red peppers, chives, and goat cheese**

**grilled portobellos topped with avocado salad**

**california turkey burgers**

**strawberry-lemon chill cake**

# picnic pasta salad with red peppers, chives, and goat cheese

**Serves:** ||| |||

**Prep time:** 

**Complexity level:** 

1 tablespoon extra virgin olive oil
3 cloves garlic, minced
$^1/_2$ red onion, finely chopped
Unrefined sea salt, to taste
Coarsely ground black pepper, to taste
1$^1/_2$ cups frozen corn kernels
1 (12-ounce) jar fire-roasted red peppers, drained, rinsed, patted dry with paper towels, and chopped
2 cups cooked whole-wheat shell pasta
$^1/_4$ cup chopped chives
$^3/_4$ cup chopped marinated pitted green olives (if possible, look for olives marinated in garlic and extra virgin olive oil from your deli olive bar)
1 pint cherry tomatoes, cut in half
2 tablespoons flax oil (such as Barlean's)
2 teaspoons apple cider vinegar
1 teaspoon Dijon mustard
$^1/_4$ cup crumbled goat cheese

**Heat** olive oil in a large nonstick skillet over medium-high heat; add the garlic and onion, and sauté for 3–4 minutes, or until onion is softened. Season onion with salt and pepper to taste. Add frozen corn to the skillet and sauté for 2–3 minutes. Mix in the red peppers and cook for an additional 2 minutes. Remove the skillet from the heat.

**Transfer** the onion, corn, and red pepper mixture to a large serving bowl. Toss in the cooked pasta shells, chives, olives, and cherry tomatoes. Season to taste with salt and pepper.

**In** a small bowl, whisk together the oil, vinegar, and mustard. Pour the vinaigrette over the pasta salad and gently toss to mix. Stir in the crumbled goat cheese. Cover with plastic wrap and refrigerate until serving time. Note: Pasta salad can be made up to one day in advance.

# grilled portobellos topped with avocado salad

Serves: | | | |

Prep time: ⏲

Complexity level: 🍎🍎

8 portobello mushroom caps, wiped
  clean with a damp cloth
1/3–1/2 cup extra virgin olive oil, for
  liberal drizzling
Unrefined sea salt, to taste
Ground pepper, to taste
2 firm Hass avocados, finely chopped
1/2 cup finely chopped red onion
1 pound ball fresh mozzarella, finely
  chopped
1/2 cup finely chopped jarred roasted red
  peppers, drained
Juice from 1/2 lemon
1 tablespoon flax oil (such as Barlean's)

**Preheat** a grill or grill pan to medium-high. Drizzle the mushrooms with olive oil and season with salt and pepper. Grill mushrooms until fork-tender, about 3–4 minutes per side. Remove portobellos from grill and set aside.

**In** a large bowl, gently toss together the avocados, onion, mozzarella, and red peppers. Add the lemon juice and flax oil, and season with salt and pepper to taste.

**Pile** the avocado salad evenly on top of the mushroom caps. Serve at room temperature.

# california turkey burgers

Serves: ▮▮▮▮

Prep time: ⏰

Complexity level: 🍎🍎

1 tablespoon extra-virgin olive oil (or avocado oil)

¼ cup finely chopped red onion

½ Granny Smith apple, peeled and diced

1 pound extra-lean organic free-range turkey

3 tablespoons minced green olives (look for large Greek olives marinated in extra virgin olive oil; these are available from a supermarket olive bar)

2 tablespoons finely chopped cilantro

1 teaspoon Dijon mustard

3 tablespoons minced sun-dried tomatoes, packed in extra virgin olive oil

½ teaspoon unrefined sea salt, plus more to taste

2 large Hass avocados

3 cloves garlic, crushed

1 tablespoon lime juice

Pinch cayenne pepper

4 sprouted whole-grain buns, toasted

Thick tomato slices

**HEAT** oil in a small skillet over medium-high heat; add the onion and sauté 2–3 minutes. Add the apple and sauté for an additional 2 minutes.

**PLACE** the sautéed onions and apple in a large mixing bowl. Add ground turkey, olives, cilantro, mustard, tomatoes, and measured salt. Using clean hands, thoroughly mix ingredients together. Shape into 4½-inch-thick burgers. Place burgers on a large platter and refrigerate for 2 hours.

**SCOOP** the avocado pulp into a medium-size mixing bowl. Add garlic and lime juice. Mash ingredients together with the back of a fork. Season with salt and cayenne pepper. Set avocado butter aside.

**REMOVE** turkey burgers from the refrigerator and season with salt.

**LIGHTLY** oil a charcoal grill (or large skillet) and heat over medium-high. Add the burgers to the grill and cook for about 7 minutes each side, or until meat is cooked through and no longer pink. Let burgers sit for 5 minutes. Lightly toast the buns on the grill.

**SERVE** burgers with avocado butter and tomato slices.

# strawberry-lemon chill cake

• • • • • • • • • • • • • • • • • • • • • • • • • • • • • • • • • • • • • • • • • • • • • • •

Serves: ╷╷╷╷ ╷╷╷╷ ╷╷╷╷

Prep time: ⏰
Complexity level: 🍎🍎🍎

### CAKE
Canola oil cooking spray
3 cups all-natural strawberry organic
   ice cream
³/₄ cup confectioners' sugar
¹/₂ cup unsweetened plain soy milk
¹/₂ cup banana purée baby food
¹/₃ cup high-oleic or high-heat canola oil
2 cage-free organic omega-3 eggs
2 tablespoons lemon juice
1 teaspoon pure lemon extract
2 cups white whole-wheat flour
³/₄ cup all-natural strawberry preserves,
   divided
2 teaspoons baking powder
¹/₄ teaspoon unrefined sea salt
1 pint fresh strawberries, sliced in half
   lengthwise (leave the green stems on)
   and drained on paper towels

### FROSTING
1 (8-ounce) package Neufchâtel cream
   cheese
¹/₃ cup all-natural strawberry preserves
¹/₃ cup confectioners' sugar

**Preheat** oven to 350 degrees F. Coat two 9-inch round cake pans with cooking spray.

**Line** a third 9-inch round cake pan with plastic wrap. Spread the ice cream in the pan, cover with plastic wrap, and freeze for 3–4 hours, or until ice cream is firm.

**Add** the sugar, soy milk, banana purée, oil, eggs, lemon juice, and lemon extract to a large bowl; beat on medium speed for 2 minutes. Mix in the flour, ¼ cup of strawberry preserves, baking powder, and salt.

**Divide** the batter between the 2 coated cake pans. Bake for approximately 18–22 minutes, or until a knife inserted in the middle of each cake comes out clean. Set cakes on a wire rack and allow to cool for 10 minutes. Carefully remove the cakes from their pans and wrap with plastic wrap. Freeze cakes for 2 hours, or until slightly frozen.

**While** cakes are freezing, prepare frosting by beating together the cream cheese, strawberry preserves, and sugar. Cover frosting and refrigerate.

**To** assemble cake, place one cake layer bottom-side up on a cake pedestal. Spread cake with ¼ cup strawberry preserves. Remove ice cream layer from freezer; remove plastic wrap. Place ice cream layer bottom-side up on top of cake layer. Spread ice cream layer with the remaining ¼ cup strawberry preserves. Top ice cream with remaining cake layer. Spread frosting over the top and sides of cake. Decorate the outer perimeter of the cake with sliced strawberries (green stems facing outward). Freeze the cake until ready to serve. Let cake stand at room temperature for 10 minutes before slicing.

# thanksgiving day

Thanksgiving dinner is the culinary occasion of the year. However, preparing a full Thanksgiving dinner can also spark a nervous breakdown for those at high risk, notably **frazzled moms** with little ones in tow. No one would argue that cooking Thanksgiving dinner is a major undertaking. To save you stress and headache, we've created a simple to prepare yet **tastefully stunning menu.** We've also added a few interesting flavor twists to update what many would consider the most traditional holiday meal. Of course, we've kept your waistline in mind too, since holiday time is no excuse for derailing your healthy diet habits.

## on the menu

**creamy butternut squash and apple soup**

**rosemary-orange perfect roast turkey**

**cornbread and wild rice stuffing with sage and white raisins**

**pumpkin-walnut torte with cream cheese frosting**

# creamy butternut squash and apple soup

**Serves:** |||| ||||

**Prep time:** 🕐

**Complexity level:** 🍎 🍎

2 tablespoons extra virgin olive oil
1 large red onion, chopped
2 cloves garlic, crushed
1 tablespoon freshly grated ginger
4 cups diced Granny Smith apple (keep the skins on)
4 cups prepared organic vegetable broth
1/4 teaspoon cinnamon
1/4 teaspoon ground nutmeg
1/4 teaspoon cardamom
12 ounces frozen butternut squash, thawed
2 cups organic grass-fed 2 percent low-fat milk, divided
1–2 tablespoons brown sugar
Unrefined sea salt, to taste
White pepper, to taste

**Heat** the oil in a large soup pot. Add the onion, garlic, and ginger, and sauté over medium-low heat until golden, 8–10 minutes.

**Add** the apples, broth, and spices. Bring to a simmer, then cover and simmer gently until the apples are soft, about 10 minutes.

**In** a food processor, purée the thawed squash with 1/2 cup of milk until completely smooth. Transfer to a bowl.

**Transfer** the apple-onion mixture to the food processor and purée. Return mixture to the soup pot and add the squash purée; stir together. Add the remaining milk, using a bit more if the purée is too thick.

**Bring** the soup to a gentle simmer, then cook over low heat until well heated through, 5–10 minutes. Add the sugar and season with salt and white pepper to taste. Serve at once, or let the soup stand off the heat for 1–2 hours, then heat through as needed before serving.

# turkey talk

Your first decision regarding the Thanksgiving dinner preparation will be selecting between a frozen or fresh turkey. A fresh bird is more expensive, but this is a once-a-year occasion, so we think the splurge is well worth it. We prefer free-range, kosher, organic turkey. The koshering process, which involves soaking the meat in brine and then rubbing it with coarse salt (hence, "kosher salt"), accounts for what many consider the superior flavor, texture, and juiciness of kosher turkey. The second decision is how much turkey to buy. If you are buying a whole turkey, a good rule of thumb is 1 pound per person. We love leftovers so we always buy what some might consider to be an obscene amount of turkey (we use an 18-pound turkey in this particular recipe). The next thing you'll have to do is figure out just how long to cook your turkey. If you are buying an 18-pound turkey, you can follow our cooking recommendations in the recipe that follows. However, if you decide to buy a smaller (or bigger) turkey, you can use the chart below. Finally, while basting is not necessary, it does promote even browning. For the record, we only baste our turkey once during the roasting process.

| weight of bird | roasting time (unstuffed) |
| --- | --- |
| 10–18 pounds | 2$\frac{1}{4}$ to 3 hours |
| 15–22 pounds | 3 to 3$\frac{1}{2}$ hours |
| 22–24 pounds | 3$\frac{1}{2}$ to 4 hours |

Finally, let's chat a bit about doneness. The best test for doneness is the temperature of the meat, not the color of the skin. The turkey is done when the thigh meat reaches an internal temperature of 165 degrees F. The "turkey police" will tell you to cook the turkey to 175 or 180 degrees F, but this temperature inevitably results in a dry turkey. If you think about it, once you remove the turkey from the oven and cover it with a foil tent, it's going to continue to heat—and cook—the meat. So, to avoid dreadfully dry turkey meat, be sure to remove the turkey once the temperature reaches 165 degrees F. Begin testing for doneness 30 minutes before the total roasting time is reached. When the turkey is done, remove from the oven and allow turkey to sit for about 20 minutes before carving.

# rosemary-orange perfect roast turkey

**Serves:**

**Prep time:**
**Complexity level:**

1 (18–22 pound) whole, fresh, free-range, kosher organic turkey
4 tablespoons extra virgin olive oil, divided
1 teaspoon unrefined sea salt, plus more to taste
Ground black pepper, to taste
Extra virgin olive oil cooking spray
1/3 cup chopped fresh rosemary
3 tablespoons grated orange zest
1 tablespoon grated lemon zest
1 teaspoon grass-fed organic butter, melted
1 1/4 cups fresh orange juice, divided
1/8 teaspoon pure lemon extract
3 tablespoons raw honey, divided
1 red onion, cut into eight large chunks
1 fennel bulb, chopped, reserving 1/2 cup chopped fennel fronds
1 orange, peeled and chopped
2 tablespoons white whole-wheat flour
2 tablespoons mascarpone cheese

**Preheat** oven to 325 degrees F. Adjust oven rack to lowest position. Remove and discard giblets and neck from turkey. Remove and discard any plastic or metal trussing device holding the drumsticks. Rinse turkey with cool water and pat dry with paper towels. Set the turkey breast-side down; brush with 2 tablespoons oil and season with salt and pepper. Turn the turkey over, breast-side up, and brush with the remaining 2 tablespoons oil and season with salt and pepper. Place the turkey on the rack of a roasting pan coated with cooking spray.

**In** a small bowl, combine the rosemary, orange zest, lemon zest, butter, and 1 teaspoon salt. Starting at the neck cavity, loosen skin from breast and drumstick by inserting fingers, gently pushing between skin and meat. Rub the rosemary mixture under the loosened skin and inside the cavity.

**Combine** 1/4 cup orange juice, lemon extract, and 1 tablespoon honey; pour liquid over turkey. Place onion, fennel, fennel fronds, and orange inside body cavity.

**Insert** meat thermometer into meat part of thigh, making sure not to touch the bone. Roast turkey for approximately 3 hours, or until meat thermometer registers 165 degrees F. When the turkey is done, remove from the oven, cover with a foil tent, and allow to stand for about 20 minutes before carving.

**To** make the sauce, pour reserved pan drippings into a ziplock bag. Seal bag; snip off a small corner of the bag. Drain drippings into a medium saucepan, stopping before the fat layer reaches the opening; discard fat. You should have at least 1 cup of drippings (if not, add free-range organic turkey broth to make up the difference). Add remaining 1 cup orange juice, flour, mascarpone cheese, remaining 2 tablespoons honey, and salt to taste. Bring mixture to a boil while whisking ingredients together and stirring constantly. Boil for 1 minute. Reduce heat to a simmer and simmer for 4–5 minutes. Serve orange sauce with turkey.

# rnbread and wild rice stuffing with sage and white raisins

Serves: | | | | | | | |

Prep time: 🦃
Complexity level: 🍎 🍎 🍎

1 cup uncooked gourmet blend of wild and brown rice
2 1/2 cups organic vegetable broth, divided
3 tablespoons extra virgin olive oil
2 shallots, finely chopped
1 1/2 medium onions, chopped
4 cloves garlic, minced
Unrefined sea salt, to taste
2 stalks celery, chopped
1/2 cup white raisins
2 Granny Smith apples, chopped (leave the skins on)
9 whole-grain cornbread muffins, crumbled
1/2 teaspoon white pepper
2 tablespoons chopped fresh sage
2 cage-free organic omega-3 eggs
1/2 cup Chardonnay
2 tablespoons grass-fed organic butter, melted
3/4 cup chopped walnuts

**Combine** rice and 2 cups vegetable broth in a pot with a tight-fitting lid. Bring to a boil. Stir once. Cover with the lid. Reduce heat to simmer and cook 50 minutes. Remove from heat. Let stand in covered pot for 10 minutes. (Alternatively, you can cook rice in a rice cooker for 50 minutes; allow rice to sit covered for 10 minutes before removing.) Set cooked rice aside.

**Preheat** oven to 350 degrees F.

**Add** oil to a large skillet and heat over medium-high; add the shallots, onion, and garlic, and sauté until onions are soft, about 5 minutes. Season with salt.

**Add** the celery, raisins, and apples to the skillet and cook for about 4 minutes, until apples soften. Season again with salt.

**In** a large bowl, toss together the vegetables and apples with the rice and cornbread muffins. Add the pepper and sage. Season with salt.

**Lightly** beat the eggs; whisk in the Chardonnay, melted butter, and remaining 1/2 cup of vegetable broth. Add the liquid to the stuffing, a little at a time, until the stuffing is moist but not soggy. (If you prefer a very "wet" stuffing, you can add a little more vegetable broth.) Mix in the chopped walnuts.

**Transfer** the cornbread and rice stuffing to two 8 x 8-inch casserole dishes. Cover and bake for 45 minutes. Remove cover and bake for an additional 15 minutes. Allow stuffing to cool 10–15 minutes. Serve warm.

**(NOTE: See feta cheese version of the cornbread recipe on page 170.)**

# pumpkin-walnut torte with cream cheese frosting

• • • • • • • • • • • • • • • • • • • • • • • • • • • • • • • • • • • • • • • • • • • • • • • • • • •

**Serves:** ⎮⎮⎮⎮ ⎮⎮⎮⎮

**Prep time:** ⏰
**Complexity level:** 🍎 🍎

Canola oil cooking spray
³/₄ cup walnut crumbs, divided (see
　directions for processing below)
¹/₄ cup plus 2 tablespoons white whole-
　wheat flour
1 teaspoon baking powder
1 teaspoon ground cinnamon
¹/₄ teaspoon ground cloves
¹/₄ teaspoon ground ginger
¹/₈ teaspoon allspice
5 cage-free organic omega-3 eggs,
　separated
³/₄ cup brown sugar, divided
1 cup solid-pack canned pumpkin
1 teaspoon pure vanilla extract
³/₄ cup organic Neufchâtel cream cheese
1 tablespoon lemon juice
¹/₄ cup powdered sugar
1 tablespoon organic sour cream

**Preheat** oven to 350 degrees F.
Spray a 9¹/₂-inch round springform pan
with cooking spray.

**Place** walnuts in a mini food processor and process into fine crumbs. Set
aside.

**In** a small bowl, combine the flour,
baking powder, cinnamon, cloves,

ginger, and allspice. In another bowl,
beat the egg whites until foamy; add 3
tablespoons of brown sugar and beat
until stiff peaks form. In a large bowl,
beat egg yolks with remaining sugar
until frothy, about 1 minute. Add the
pumpkin and vanilla extract, and beat
until well blended. Stir in flour mixture.
Fold in eggs whites and ¹/₂ cup of the
walnut crumbs.

**Pour** the pumpkin mixture into the
prepared pan. Bake for 45–50 minutes,
or until a knife inserted in the middle
comes out clean. Remove torte from
the oven and run a knife around the
edges. Release the springform pan and
allow torte to cool on a wire rack for 20
minutes.

**Meanwhile,** add the cream cheese,
lemon juice, powdered sugar, and sour
cream to a medium-size mixing bowl;
whip ingredients together with a hand
mixer for 2–3 minutes, or until well
blended. Use a cake spatula to frost the
top of the cooled torte with the cream
cheese frosting.

**Decorate** the edges of the torte with
the remaining walnut crumbs. Serve the
torte at room temperature.

# christmas day

A healthy holiday meal sounds, if not totally un-festive, a misnomer at the very least. If your family just can't get into the swing of eating a whole foods Christmas, then just don't mention it. The menu for this feast is **intriguing and indulgent.** The recipes and flavor combinations meld so pleasantly and harmoniously together, and there's enough **seductive richness** in each dish that we absolutely guarantee zero gripes from anyone, including those **family members** who go out of their way to eat unhealthy at every given opportunity. No one will complain come New Year's Day when they can **still fit into their preholiday jeans!**

## on the menu

**mixed baby greens salad with apples, blue cheese, and walnut vinaigrette**

**roasted potatoes with pistachio-parmesan crust**

**pork loin roast with spiced fruit infusion**

**braised fennel with crème fraîche**

**christmas cranberry bars with walnut crust**

# mixed baby greens salad with apples, blue cheese, and walnut vinaigrette

Serves: ∣∣∣ ∣∣∣

Prep time: ⏰
Complexity level: 🍎

## WALNUT VINAIGRETTE

1 tablespoon Dijon mustard
3 tablespoons balsamic vinegar
1 tablespoon fresh lemon juice
$1/2$ cup walnut oil
3 whole walnuts
$1/4$ teaspoon unrefined sea salt, plus more to taste
$1/4$ teaspoon freshly ground black pepper, plus more to taste

## MIXED BABY GREEN SALAD WITH APPLES AND BLUE CHEESE

5 cups mixed baby lettuces (such as red leaf, chicory, and butter)
$1/4$ cup roughly chopped fresh tarragon
6 ounces strong blue cheese, crumbled
1 cup coarsely chopped walnuts
1 Granny Smith apple, sliced (keep the skins on!)

## WALNUT VINAIGRETTE

**Place** all ingredients for the vinaigrette in the blender. Process for 1 minute, or until smooth and creamy.

## SALAD

**IN** a large salad bowl, combine the lettuces, tarragon, blue cheese, walnuts, and apple slices. Add just enough walnut vinaigrette to coat the leaves. (Note: You should have plenty of vinaigrette left over!) Season salad with salt and pepper to taste. Toss and serve.

# roasted potatoes with pistachio-parmesan crust

Serves: | | | | | |

Prep time: ⏰

Complexity level: 🍎🍎

3/4 cup shelled, dry-roasted salted pistachios

1/4 cup freshly grated Parmesan cheese

4 tablespoons extra virgin olive oil, divided

8 large Yukon gold potatoes, cut into bite-size chunks

Unrefined sea salt, to taste

Freshly ground black pepper, to taste

1/2 cup chopped parsley

**Preheat** oven to 400 degrees F.

**Place** the pistachios in a food processor and process into fine crumbs. Toss pistachio crumbs with the Parmesan cheese and 1 tablespoon oil. Set aside.

**Spread** the potatoes on an oiled baking sheet. Toss potatoes with remaining oil, salt, and pepper. Roast the potatoes for 30 minutes, remove them from the oven, and toss them again. Continue to roast the potatoes for another 20 minutes. Remove potatoes from the oven and toss thoroughly with the pistachio-Parmesan mixture. Return potatoes to the oven and roast for another 10 minutes. Sprinkle the parsley on top and toss potatoes. Serve warm.

# pork loin roast with spiced fruit infusion

Serves: | | | | | |

Prep time: ⏰

Complexity level: 🍎🍎🍎🍎

SPICED FRUIT INFUSION

1/3 cup bite-size pitted prunes

1/3 cup dried apricots

1/3 cup dried cherries

1/2 cup Riesling wine

1 tablespoon canola oil

3 cloves garlic, minced

2 teaspoons grated ginger

1/4 cup finely chopped shallots

1/4 cup cardamom

1/2 teaspoon Dijon mustard

2 tablespoons cherry preserves

### PORK LOIN ROAST

1 (3-pound) boneless grass-fed pork loin roast (roughly 2¹/₄ pounds trimmed), visible fat removed (ask the butcher)
Unrefined sea salt, to taste
White pepper, to taste
10–12 cloves garlic, split in half
2 tablespoons extra virgin olive oil,
2 oranges, sliced into rounds
Parsley, for garnish


### SPICED FRUIT INFUSION

**Place** the dried prunes, apricots, and cherries in a microwave-safe bowl; pour the wine over the fruit, cover with a paper towel, and microwave on high for 2 minutes. Drain wine and set the softened fruit aside.

**Heat** oil in a small skillet over medium heat. Add the garlic, ginger, and shallots, and cook 3–4 minutes, or until shallots soften. Add the softened fruit and cook for 1 minute. Stir in the cardamom, mustard, and cherry preserves, and cook for 1–2 more minutes. Remove the skillet from the heat and allow fruit to cool.

**Place** the cooled fruit infusion in a blender and process until well blended but still somewhat chunky. Note: fruit infusion can be made up to 3 days in advance and stored in the refrigerator in a sealed container.

### PORK LOIN ROAST

**Preheat** oven to 325 degrees F.

**Untie** the pork loin and cut lengthwise down the loin almost to, but not through, the bottom. Open the loin like a book. Season with salt and white pepper. Rub all sides with 1 tablespoon oil.

**Place** the loin cut-side up and spread the fruit infusion evenly over the exposed surfaces. Roll the loin jelly-roll style and secure with butcher's twine. Use a knife to make 7 or 8 slits on the top and sides of the loin; stuff each slit with a slice of garlic.

**Lightly** spread 1 tablespoon oil on the bottom of a medium or large cast-iron skillet and heat over medium-high heat. Sear loin in the skillet for 1 minute on each side. Lift the loin from the skillet and place the sliced oranges on the bottom. Scatter the remaining cloves of garlic on top of the orange slices. Drizzle the oranges and garlic with a tablespoon of oil. Place the loin on top of the orange slices. Transfer the loin to the oven and roast for approximately 20–25 minutes per pound. (Take care not to overcook the pork loin or it will be too dry.) Remove the loin roast from the oven and allow it to sit for 15–20 minutes (the pork will continue to cook while it sits).

**Carefully** lift the pork from the cast-iron skillet and slice. Squeeze the juice from the roasted oranges on top of the pork before serving. Garnish with fresh oranges and parsley.

# braised fennel with crème fraîche

• • • • • • • • • • • • • • • • • • • • • • • • • • • • • • • • • • • • • • • • • • •

Serves: ▮▮▮ ▮▮▮

Prep time: 🕐
Complexity level: 🍎 🍎 🍎

3 fennel bulbs
³/₄ cup 2-percent organic milk
1 tablespoon crème fraîche
1 tablespoon extra virgin olive oil
Paprika, to taste
Unrefined sea salt, to taste
White pepper, to taste
¹/₄ cup freshly grated Parmesan cheese
1 garlic clove, minced
1 slice toasted sprouted whole-grain
   bread, torn into bite-size pieces
1 teaspoon grass-fed organic butter
Extra virgin olive oil cooking spray

**Preheat** the oven to 400 degrees F.

**Quarter** the fennel bulbs length-wise. Core and slice the fennel into thin strips; then cut the strips into thirds. Reserve ½ cup of the feathery fronds.

**Place** the milk in a microwave-safe dish and heat on high for 1 minute; use a fork to whisk the crème fraîche and oil with the milk.

**Arrange** the fennel strips in a large sauté pan. Pour the milk mixture on top of the fennel and sprinkle with paprika, salt, and pepper. Bring the milk to a simmer over medium heat, reduce the heat to medium-low, cover partially, and simmer for 15 minutes. Turn the fennel over once while cooking. Uncover, raise the heat slightly, and cook until the milk is reduced to about 1 or 2 tablespoons, approximately 15 minutes more.

**Use** a blender or food processor to process the Parmesan, garlic, toast pieces, and butter into fine crumbs. Set crumbs aside.

**Spray** the bottom and sides of a 9 x 13-inch casserole with cooking spray. Use a spatula to transfer the fennel and its liquid to the baking dish, arranging the fennel in one direction. Top with the Parmesan-crumb mixture. Bake until golden on top, about 10–15 minutes. Remove fennel from the oven; chop the reserved feathery fronds and sprinkle over the top. Serve at once.

# christmas cranberry bars with walnut crust

Serves: | | | | | | | | | |

Prep time: ⏰

Complexity level: 🍎 🍎

High-oleic canola oil cooking spray
1/2 cup walnut crumbs (see directions below for how to process crumbs)
1¼ cups fresh cranberries
1¼ cup confectioners' sugar, divided
2 tablespoons softened grass-fed organic butter
2 tablespoons extra virgin coconut oil (such as Barlean's)
³/₄ cup white whole-wheat flour, divided
3 cage-free organic omega-3 eggs
¹/₂ teaspoon baking powder
¹/₂ teaspoon unrefined sea salt

**Preheat** oven to 350 degrees F. Spray an 8 x 8-inch baking pan with cooking spray.

**Place** the walnuts in a food processor; pulse to make fine crumbs and then set aside.

**Place** the cranberries in a microwave-safe dish and microwave on high for 2 minutes, or until berries are soft. Set aside.

**Beat** ¼ cup sugar, butter, and coconut oil on medium speed until creamy. Gradually add ½ cup flour and mix on low speed until the mixture is crumbly. Stir in the walnut crumbs.

**Press** the walnut crumb mixture into the bottom of the pan. Bake for 12 minutes, or until crust is just golden brown. Remove the baking pan from the oven and lightly spray the top of the crust with cooking spray. Set the pan on a wire rack to cool.

**Reduce** oven temperature to 325 degrees F.

**Add** the eggs to a medium-size mixing bowl and beat with a handheld mixer on medium speed until foamy. Add the remaining ½ cup sugar, ¼ cup flour, baking powder, and salt, and beat on medium speed until well blended. Add the cranberries and beat for 1 minute. (Mixture should be pinkish with chunks of cranberries interspersed throughout.)

**Pour** the cranberry mixture over the crust and bake until set, about 20–25 minutes. Remove the cranberries from the oven and cool on a wire rack.

**Run** the edge of a knife around the sides of the cranberry bars and cut them into 9 squares. Carefully lift the bars from the baking pan with a spatula. Arrange the bars on a serving platter and sprinkle with remaining confectioners' sugar. Serve at once. (Note: Bars can also be made up to 3 days in advance and stored in the refrigerator in a covered container.)

# a swanky soiree

## wine flight and taste of the world's appetizers

**While it's always fun** to entertain at home, the truth is the whole occasion can turn into project chaos if you have to prepare and serve a full spread for more than four or six people. In comparison to making dinner for a crowd, we've found themed appetizer parties to be a fun and relaxed way to entertain friends without stressing ourselves silly. We often set the theme and then prepare three or four appetizers and ask our friends to bring just one themed appetizer apiece. We also have fun combining our appetizer party with a blind wine tasting. For the wine tasting, ask your friends to bring their favorite wine in unmarked brown bags and whoever brings the "winning" wine wins a prize! To give you a few ideas, we've included some of our personal favorite, *economical*, and nationally available wines throughout this chapter. Cheers!

# passport to
## italy

Italian-themed parties are easy and fun, and since pretty much everyone loves Italian food, it's a safe way to go when planning a party. We've included three complementary appetizers, but feel free to add a classic Italian antipasto featuring items such as carpaccio, bruschetta, marinated anchovies, olives, and artichokes in oil.

## wine flight suggestions

Cecchi Chianti Classico (approximately $13)

Cesari Due Torri Pinot Grigio Delle Venezie (under $10)

Massanera Particolare Rosso Toscana (approximately $17)

## on the menu

**mini quinoa pizzas**

**sicilian-style crab cakes**

**bite-size spinach and mozzarella frittatas**

# mini quinoa pizzas

**Serves:** ❙❙❙❙

**Prep time:** 🕐

**Complexity level:** 🍎 🍎 🍎 🍎

1 cup uncooked quinoa
2 cups water
$1/2$ teaspoon salt, plus more to taste
$1/4$ teaspoon granulated garlic
2 cage-free organio omega-3 eggs, lightly
  beaten
$1/4$ cup stone-ground whole-grain corn flour
4–5 tablespoons extra virgin olive oil, divided
Extra virgin olive oil cooking spray
$3/4$ cups good-quality marinara sauce
$3/4$ cups freshly grated Parmesan cheese
4–5 fresh basil leaves, finely chopped

**Rinse** quinoa in a small strainer. Bring the measured water and $1/2$ teaspoon salt to a boil in a heavy medium saucepan. Stir quinoa into boiling water and return to a boil; then simmer, covered, until quinoa is dry and water is absorbed, about 20–30 minutes. Remove pot from heat and let stand, covered, for 5 minutes. Stir in the granulated garlic.

**Transfer** cooked quinoa to a large bowl and cool, stirring occasionally, 10 minutes. Season with salt to taste. Mix in the eggs, flour, and 2 tablespoons oil.

**Line** a baking sheet with plastic wrap and lightly spray with cooking spray. Lightly oil a $1/4$-cup dry-ingredient measuring cup. Pack quinoa into the cup. Unmold onto the baking sheet and lightly pat with a spatula to flatten the patty. Make 11 more cakes. Chill, uncovered, in the refrigerator for 15 to 20 minutes.

**Preheat** oven to 425 degrees F. Lightly oil a baking sheet.

**Heat** 1 tablespoon oil in a large nonstick skillet over medium-high heat until oil shimmers. Carefully add 3 or 4 quinoa cakes and cook for 3–4 minutes per side, turning once. Transfer quinoa cakes to the prepared baking sheet. Repeat process with remaining oil and quinoa cakes.

**Top** each quinoa cake with 1 tablespoon of the marinara and then 1 tablespoon of the Parmesan cheese. Transfer quinoa cakes to the oven and bake for 8–10 minutes, or until cheese melts. Lift quinoa cakes with a spatula and transfer to a serving platter. Top each quinoa cake with finely chopped basil leaves. Serve warm or at room temperature.

## 🍾 cecchi chianti classico

Italian food tends to pair well with medium-bodied red wine. High-quality Chianti can stand up to the finest wines in the world at a fraction of the cost. "Chianti Classico" is only slightly more expensive than plain "Chianti," yet the "Classico" designation tends to ensure a richer, fuller, more flavorful wine. This product is typical of the region. Its flavor can be described as subtle, dry, balanced, with some berry flavors.

# sicilian-style crab cakes

Serves: | | | |

Prep time: 🕐

Complexity level: 🍎 🍎 🍎

16 saltine-style whole-wheat crackers
$^{1}/_{2}$ cup fresh basil
3 tablespoons extra virgin olive oil, divided
2 shallots, minced
4 cloves garlic, minced
$^{1}/_{2}$ cup wheat germ
$^{1}/_{4}$ cup canola oil mayonnaise
2 tablespoons lemon juice
$^{1}/_{4}$ teaspoon cayenne pepper, or more to taste
1 teaspoon oregano
Unrefined sea salt, to taste
1 pound pasteurized jumbo lump crabmeat
2 cage-free organic omega-3 eggs, lightly beaten

**Preheat** oven to 400 degrees. Place the crackers and basil in a food processor or blender and blend together until the crackers are pulverized. Transfer the crumbs to a large mixing bowl.

**Heat** 1 tablespoon oil in a large non-stick skillet over medium-high heat; add the shallots and garlic, and sauté until soft. Transfer the softened shallots and garlic to the mixing bowl with the cracker crumbs. Set the skillet aside.

**Add** the wheat germ, mayonnaise, lemon juice, cayenne pepper, oregano, and salt to the mixing bowl; mix thoroughly (you may need to use your hands). Stir in the crabmeat. Add the eggs and mix until all ingredients are thoroughly combined.

**Using** your hands, form 10 crab cakes and arrange them on a large platter. (You can either cover and refrigerate the crab cakes for up to 2 hours or proceed to the next step.)

**Heat** 2 teaspoons oil in the skillet over medium-high heat; add 5 crab cakes, and cook for 3–4 minutes per side. Repeat the process with the second batch of crab cakes.

**Arrange** the crab cakes 1 inch apart on a large nonstick baking sheet. Bake for 7 minutes. Transfer the crab cakes to a large serving platter and serve warm.

## 🥂 cesari due torri pinot grigio delle venezie

While the Italian climate is best suited for red wine, Pinot Grigio has garnered quite a bit of popularity in the last few years. Pinot Grigio is a "drinking" wine, not a gourmet selection. The Due Torri product is crisp, dry, and fruity, and makes the perfect start to a fun Italian-themed party or any casual get-together.

# bite-size spinach and mozzarella frittatas

Serves: | | | |

Prep time: 🕰️

Complexity level: 🍎 🍎

1 tablespoon extra virgin olive oil
1/4 cup finely chopped shallots
4 cloves garlic, minced
1 (10-ounce) package frozen chopped spinach, thawed and patted as dry as possible with paper towels
5 cage-free organic omega-3 eggs
1/4 cup prepared hummus
1/4 cup coarsely chopped green olives
1/4 cup chopped sun-dried tomatoes marinated in extra virgin olive oil, drained, and patted dry with paper towels
1 teaspoon dried basil
1/2 teaspoon unrefined sea salt
1/4 teaspoon coarsely ground black pepper
Extra virgin olive oil cooking spray
5 ounces fresh mozzarella, cut into small teaspoon-size chunks

**Heat** oil in a medium-size skillet over medium-high heat; add the shallots and garlic, and sauté for 3–4 minutes, or until shallots are soft. Add the chopped spinach and sauté for 2–3 additional minutes. Set spinach mixture aside.

**In** a medium bowl, whisk the eggs and hummus together. Add the olives, tomatoes, basil, salt, and pepper, and mix thoroughly. Stir in the spinach mixture.

**Spray** 22 mini muffin cups with cooking spray. Place one small mozzarella chunk in the middle of each muffin cup. Spoon spinach and egg mixture on top of the mozzarella chunks. Bake for 12–15 minutes, or until eggs are set and custard is fluffy. Allow frittatas to cool for 5 minutes before transferring to a serving platter. Serve warm.

## 🥂 massanera particolare rosso toscana

Excellent affordable red wines created by blending numerous types of grapes, many times in nontraditional ways, are available from Italy's Tuscany region. This particular selection can be described as tangy, dry, and berry-flavored. Tuscan wines in general are moderately complex, fruit-forward wines at a fair price. They are great for guests who believe Cabernet Sauvignon tastes too strong, too alcoholic, too bitter, or too dry. These wines pair well with almost any food but are especially good with cheese and pasta dishes.

# thai bite night

Adventurous guests will be intrigued and impressed with this bold-flavored, exotic, Thai-style appetizer menu. Thai cuisine was originally influenced by the Eastern culture, thereby adopting its tendencies of harmoniously combining sweet, sour, bitter, spicy, and salty for a most titillating taste experience!

## wine flight suggestions

Covey Run Columbia Valley Riesling (under $10)
Rodney Strong Sonoma County Chardonnay (approximately $15)
Sterling Napa Valley Sauvignon Blanc (approximately $15)

## on the menu

corn fritters with red onion relish

southeast asian meatballs with red chile–lime dipping sauce

thai-style coconut-peanut pizza wedges with cilantro and feta

# corn fritters with red onion relish

**Serves:** | | | |

**Prep time:** ⏰

**Complexity level:** 🍎🍎🍎

## CORN FRITTERS
3 tablespoons toasted sesame oil, divided
1/2 cup finely diced red onion
1 red chile, seeded and finely chopped
2 cloves garlic, minced
2 teaspoons minced fresh ginger
1 teaspoon ground coriander
1 1/2 cups frozen corn, thawed
3 scallions, trimmed and finely sliced
1 cage-free organic omega-3 egg, lightly beaten
Unrefined sea salt, to taste
Black pepper, to taste
1/4 cup plus 2 tablespoons white whole-wheat flour
1 teaspoon baking powder
2 tablespoons finely chopped fresh cilantro

## ONION RELISH
1 tablespoon toasted sesame oil
1/3 cup chopped red onion
1/2 teaspoon crushed red pepper
3 cloves garlic, chopped
1 teaspoon chopped ginger
2 tablespoons plum sauce

## CORN FRITTERS
**Heat** 1 tablespoon oil in a skillet over medium-high; add onion and cook until softened. Add the chile, garlic, ginger, and coriander, and cook for 1 minute, stirring continuously.

**Place** corn in a mixing bowl and lightly crush with a potato masher. Add the cooked onion mixture, scallions, and egg. Season mixture with salt and pepper. Mix in the flour, baking powder, and cilantro.

**Heat** 1 tablespoon oil in a large nonstick skillet over medium-high heat; drop four 1/4-cup portions of the batter into the skillet, flatten each with the back of a spatula to form 1/2-inch-thick fritters. Fry for approximately 4 minutes per side, or until golden brown and crisp. Transfer fritters to a paper towel and gently blot excess oil. Repeat cooking process with remainder of the batter. (Batter should yield 8 corn fritters.)

**These** corn fritters are delicious right from the frying pan or at room temperature. To serve, place warm corn fritters on a serving platter with a small dish of Onion Relish on the side (recipe below).

## ONION RELISH
**Combine** relish ingredients in a mini food processor and process for 30–45 seconds, or until onion is almost puréed and ingredients are well combined. Transfer relish to a small serving dish.

## 🥂 covey run columbia valley riesling

Spicy Thai food pairs well with cool, fruity, slightly sweet, less complex wine. Affordable Riesling from Washington State is a perfect match. Riesling offers a delicious occasional alternative to Chardonnay, and is also loved by fans of White Zinfandel. The Covey Run Riesling is full of fruit flavor, semisweet, and an amazing value.

# southeast asian meatballs with red chile-lime dipping sauce

Serves: | | | |

Prep time: 🕐

Complexity level: 🍎 🍎

### SOUTHEAST ASIAN MEATBALLS
Extra virgin olive oil cooking spray
8 ounces lean ground grass-fed pork
1/4 red onion, minced
1 eggplant, peeled and finely diced (about 1 cup)
1 cage-free organic omega-3 egg
1/4 cup wheat germ
1/4 cup chopped scallions
2 tablespoons high-quality soy sauce
4 cloves garlic, minced
1 tablespoon minced fresh ginger
1 teaspoon Dijon mustard
2 teaspoons roasted red chile paste

### RED CHILE–LIME DIPPING SAUCE
1/4 cup tahini
Juice from 2 limes
1 tablespoon roasted red chile paste
1 tablespoon water
2 teaspoons raw honey

### SOUTHEAST ASIAN MEATBALLS
**Put** oven rack in middle position and preheat oven to 450 degrees F. Spray a baking sheet with cooking spray.

**In** a medium bowl, combine all of the meatball ingredients. Mix thoroughly with clean hands.

**Shape** the mixture into 12 small meatballs, about 2 tablespoons each. Bake meatballs for 10–12 minutes, or until cooked through. Transfer meatballs to a serving dish and serve with a small bowl of dipping sauce on the side.

### RED CHILE-LIME DIPPING SAUCE
**In** a small bowl, whisk all ingredients together until emulsified. Pour mixture into a serving dish.

## 🥂 rodney strong sonoma county chardonnay

California Chardonnay is the best in the world as far as we are concerned. This product offers a classic example of balanced, slightly fruit-forward, slightly creamy, full-bodied California Chardonnay flavor with minimal oak. It works well with Thai food. Kendall-Jackson California Vintner's Reserve Chardonnay, at about the same price, is also great if you desire more "bright" acidity and less of the mellow cream texture found in the Rodney Strong product.

# thai-style coconut-peanut pizza wedges with cilantro and feta

Serves: | | | |

Prep time: ⏰
Complexity level: 🍎

2 whole-wheat or oat bran pitas
Toasted sesame oil
1/2 cup all-natural creamy peanut butter
1/4 cup organic coconut milk
1 tablespoon brown sugar
1 tablespoon good-quality soy sauce
Juice from 1/2 lime
2 cloves garlic, chopped
2 teaspoons finely chopped fresh ginger
1 teaspoon crushed red pepper
1/4 cup plus 2 tablespoons unsalted finely
   chopped peanuts
1/4 cup finely chopped fresh cilantro
1/2 cup crumbled feta cheese

**Preheat** oven to 425 degrees F.

**Cut** each pita into 4 triangles; open each triangle so that there is a total of 16 thin triangle wedges. Place pita wedges on a baking sheet. Brush each pita lightly with oil. Lightly toast pita wedges for 2 minutes in the preheated oven. Remove pita wedges from oven and set aside.

**In** a blender, add the peanut butter, coconut milk, brown sugar, soy sauce, lime juice, garlic, ginger, and red pepper; process until smooth and creamy.

**Spread** a thin layer of the coconut-peanut butter mixture on top of each pita wedge. Top each pita with chopped peanuts, cilantro, and feta cheese. Bake pita wedges for 4–5 minutes, or until just crispy. Remove pita wedges from oven and place on a serving platter. Serve warm.

## 🥂 sterling napa valley sauvignon blanc

Sauvignon Blanc is also a good choice for pairing with hot and spicy Thai foods. When pairing with tangy Thai food, choose a bottle that is not too dry or too grassy flavored as many are. Sterling Sauvignon Blanc is more full-flavored and fruit-forward than most. This is a great all-around wine for getting any higher-end dinner party started.

# uptown all-american

No, your guests won't find cheese nips, macaroni salad, and baked beans at this American-themed get-together (unless they bring their own!), but they will find an interesting selection of mouthwatering foods they just might actually like better than their standby favorites. Additional foods to consider serving include beef sliders (made with grass-fed ground beef, if possible), crab-filled mushrooms, and simple chicken kabobs to dip in a sauce of your choice.

## wine flight suggestions

Morgan Santa Lucia Highlands Pinot Noir (approximately $25)
Mumm Napa Brut Prestige Napa Valley Sparkling Wine (approximately $18)
Benziger Family Winery Carneros Chardonnay (approximately $17)

## on the menu

### oysters rockefeller

### gorgonzola and walnut crostini

### crispy basil-crusted tofu nuggets with tomato walnut pesto

# oysters rockefeller

Serves: ❙❙❙❙

Prep time: ⏲

Complexity level: 🍎🍎

1/3 cup whole-wheat panko crumbs
2 tablespoons chopped fresh tarragon, divided
3 tablespoons freshly grated Parmesan cheese
Unrefined sea salt, to taste
Freshly ground black pepper, to taste
1 tablespoon grass-fed organic butter
2 tablespoons extra virgin olive oil
2 cloves garlic, minced
1/4 cup finely chopped shallots
1 (10-ounce) package frozen chopped spinach, thawed, drained, and patted dry with paper towels
3 tablespoons prepared hummus
2 tablespoons Chardonnay
1/4 cup water
1/4 teaspoon hot sauce
2 teaspoons mashed anchovies
Rock salt
2 dozen oysters on the half shell
Lemon wedges, for garnish

PREHEAT oven to 425 degrees.

IN a small bowl, mix together the panko crumbs, 1 tablespoon tarragon, Parmesan cheese, salt, and pepper. Set aside.

HEAT the butter and oil in a medium-size skillet over medium high. Once butter melts, add garlic and sauté 2 minutes. Transfer 1 tablespoon of the oil-butter mixture to the crumb mixture and mix thoroughly. Set crumb mixture aside.

ADD the shallots to the skillet with the garlic and cook for 2–3 minutes, or until shallots are soft. Add the spinach, hummus, Chardonnay, water, remaining tablespoon of tarragon, hot sauce, and mashed anchovies. Cook spinach mixture for 3–4 minutes, or until liquid evaporates. Season with salt and pepper to taste.

SPRINKLE a baking pan with rock salt (to stabilize the oysters). Arrange the oysters on top of the salt. Spoon 1 heaping teaspoon of the spinach mixture on top of each oyster, followed by a heaping teaspoon of the crumb mixture. Bake oysters for about 12 minutes, or until crumb topping is golden. Serve with lemon wedges.

## 🥂 morgan santa lucia highlands pinot noir

Pinot Noir is the grape of choice in France's Burgundy region. Its flavor is far more delicate than Cabernet Sauvignon yet often more complex.

The cost of good Pinot Noir can be high. Our selection is a "Wow!" wine that will surely impress. It's velvety smooth without any harsh flavors.

# gorgonzola and walnut crostini

**Serves:** 〡〡〡〡

**Prep time:** ⏲

**Complexity level:** 🍎

1/2 cup chopped walnuts
1/4 cup gorgonzola
2 tablespoons organic ricotta
1/4 cup chopped parsley
4 tablespoons extra virgin olive oil, divided
1 teaspoon raw honey
1 tablespoon plus 2 teaspoons lemon juice
3 tablespoons freshly grated Parmesan cheese
8 slices sprouted whole-grain bread, crusts removed, cut in half diagonally

**PREHEAT** oven to 400 degrees.

**USING** a mini food processor, process walnuts into fine crumbs. Add the gorgonzola, ricotta, parsley, 2 tablespoons of oil, honey, lemon juice and Parmesan cheese. Process ingredients until thoroughly blended. Set mixture aside.

**ARRANGE** the sixteen bread triangles on a cookie sheet. Brush bread with the remaining 2 tablespoons of oil. Toast bread for 10 minutes. Remove from oven. Spread toast with the gorgonzola-walnut mixture, return to oven and bake for an additional 3 minutes. Remove toasts from oven and serve warm or at room temperature.

## 🥂 mumm napa brut prestige napa valley sparkling wine

Sparkling wines add a touch of class to any get-together. Don't skimp on cost here. Production cost for these wines is fairly high so it is almost impossible to find decent sparkling wine for less than ten dollars a bottle. On the other hand, many California sparkling wines offer tastes as distinctive as French champagne for less than half the cost. The Mumm Napa Sparkling Wine is tart and full-bodied, and will impress the most discriminating uptown guest.

## 🥂 benziger family winery carneros chardonnay

This selection is a step above typical California Chardonnay. It's a delicious, well-balanced, fruit-forward wine without any significant oak-barrel flavor.

Your guests will appreciate this selection as being "outside the box" while still maintaining all of the attributes fine Chardonnay is known for. It's definitely uptown!

# crispy basil-crusted tofu nuggets with tomato-walnut pesto

Serves: | | | |

Prep time: 🕐

Complexity level: 🍎🍎🍎

## CRISPY BASIL-CRUSTED TOFU NUGGETS
- 1/4 cup wheat germ
- 2 pieces toasted sprouted whole-grain bread, broken into bite-size pieces
- 2 tablespoons freshly grated Parmesan cheese
- 3 cloves garlic, coarsely chopped
- 3 tablespoons chopped fresh basil
- Unrefined sea salt, to taste
- 2 tablespoons canola oil mayonnaise
- 1 cage-free organic omega-3 egg
- 1/4 cup prepared hummus
- 1 (14-ounce) package firm tofu, drained and patted dry with paper towels
- Extra-virgin olive oil cooking spray
- 1 tablespoon extra virgin olive oil

## TOMATO-WALNUT PESTO
- 1 cup loosely packed fresh basil leaves
- 1/2 cup walnuts
- 5 cloves garlic, coarsely chopped
- 2 tablespoons flax oil (such as Barlean's)
- 2 tablespoons lemon juice
- 1/4 cup Parmesan cheese
- 1/4 cup chopped sun-dried tomatoes marinated in extra virgin olive oil, drained of excess oil
- 1/2 teaspoon Dijon mustard
- 1/2 cup water

## CRISPY BASIL-CRUSTED TOFU NUGGETS

**IN** a food processor or blender, place the wheat germ, toasted bread pieces, Parmesan cheese, garlic, basil, and salt; process to make coarse bread crumbs. Set aside.

**IN** a wide shallow bowl, whisk together the mayonnaise, egg, and hummus.

**Gently** press the drained tofu with more paper towels (the drier the tofu, the better!). Cut the tofu into bite-size blocks and toss with salt to taste.

**DIP** the tofu pieces into the egg mixture and then roll them in the bread crumbs until the tofu is completely coated on all sides.

**SPRAY** a large nonstick skillet with cooking spray. When the skillet is hot, add the oil and tilt the skillet so the oil coats the surface. Add the tofu nuggets in a single layer (don't crowd the tofu in the pan!) and fry until golden brown on one side, about 2–3 minutes. Gently turn the tofu and cook 2–3 minutes more, until all sides are crisp and golden brown.

**INSERT** toothpicks into the center of each tofu nugget and artfully arrange the nuggets on a serving platter. Place the small bowl of tomato-walnut pesto on the platter and serve. (Note: Kids will gobble up the tofu nuggets if you serve them with ketchup instead of the tomato walnut pesto.)

## TOMATO-WALNUT PESTO

**Place** all of the ingredients in a food processor or blender and pulse until well blended.

# mexican fiesta

Whether your party includes mariachis or piñatas is up to you, but the sophisticated versions of these Mexican-style nibbles will surely please your south-of-the-border food-loving friends. Additional appetizers such as fresh pico de gallo purchased from your local deli (or homemade!) with stone-ground tortilla chips, guacamole, and veggie quesadillas are easy hassle-free additions to your Mexican fiesta.

## wine flight suggestions

Martin Codax Albarino Riax Baixas (approximately $13)
Rogue Chipotle Ale (under $5 per serving)
Sobon Estate Amador County Viognier (approximately $17)

## on the menu

**rotisserie chicken and black bean enchilada wedges with poblano pepper sauce**

**cherry tomatoes stuffed with mexican-style pesto and crab**

**spicy scallop ceviche with avocado and lime**

# rotisserie chicken and black bean enchilada wedges with poblano pepper sauce

Serves: | | | |

Prep time: 🕐
Complexity level: 🍎🍎🍎

2 poblano peppers, seeded and cut in
   half lengthwise
5 tablespoons extra virgin olive oil,
   divided
3 tablespoons canned pumpkin purée
1 tablespoon raw honey
1/4 teaspoon unrefined sea salt, plus
   more to taste
1/8 teaspoon cumin
Juice from 1 whole lime
2 tablespoons organic sour cream
2 cloves garlic, minced
1/2 red onion, finely chopped
1 (15-ounce) can black beans, drained
   and rinsed
8 ounces rotisserie chicken (white meat
   only, no skin), shredded
1 teaspoon chili powder
1 or 2 pinches cayenne pepper, to taste
1/2 cup chopped fresh cilantro
8 whole-wheat or sprouted whole-grain
   tortillas
Extra virgin olive oil cooking spray
3/4 cup shredded organic cheddar cheese

**Preheat** oven to 475 degrees.

**Place** poblano peppers, cut-side down, on a foil-lined baking sheet. Roast the peppers for 20 minutes, or until charred. Remove the peppers from the oven. When peppers are cool enough to handle, remove their outer skins.

**Place** the peppers in a blender, along with 3 tablespoons oil, pumpkin purée, honey, measured salt, cumin, lime juice, and sour cream; purée until sauce is smooth and creamy. Set aside.

**Pour** the remaining 2 tablespoons oil in a large nonstick skillet and heat over medium-high heat. Add the garlic and red onion, and sauté several minutes, or until onions are soft and tender. Stir in the black beans and shredded chicken. Season the mixture with chili powder and cayenne pepper. Stir in the cilantro. Remove skillet from heat and set aside.

**Lower** the oven heat to 350 degrees F.

**Spray** a medium-size nonstick skillet with cooking spray and heat over medium-high heat. Meanwhile, spread the black bean and chicken mixture onto one tortilla, spread a generous dollop of the poblano sauce on top, and sprinkle cheese on top of the sauce. Place another tortilla on top of the cheese to make an enchilada "sandwich." Place the tortilla on the heated skillet and put a small lid on top of the tortilla to press the tortilla together; cook for 3 minutes on each side. Remove enchilada from the heat and cut into 4 wedges. Place the wedges on a large baking sheet lined with aluminum foil. Top each wedge with a dollop of poblano sauce and a sprinkling of cheese.

**Repeat** with remaining ingredients.

**Bake** the enchilada wedges at 350 degrees F for 4–5 minutes, or until cheese melts. Arrange wedges on a serving platter and serve warm.

# cherry tomatoes stuffed with mexican-style pesto and crab

**Serves:** | | | |

**Prep time:** 🕐

**Complexity level:** 🍎 🍎

2 cups (1 pint) cherry tomatoes
2 cups packed cilantro
1/2 cup slivered almonds
1/4 cup chopped red onion
1/4 cup flax oil (such as Barlean's)
2 cloves garlic, minced
1/4 teaspoon cayenne pepper
1/4 cup plus 2 tablespoons Neufchâtel
   organic cream cheese
2 tablespoons lime juice
1/4 cup freshly grated Parmesan cheese
1 teaspoon raw honey
3 ounces drained jumbo lump crabmeat,
   chopped

**Cut** tops off cherry tomatoes and scoop out the pulp. Drain tomatoes upside down on paper towels while preparing the pesto.

**To** prepare the pesto, place the remaining ingredients (except the crabmeat) in a blender and process until smooth and creamy.

**Mix** the crab in with the pesto.

**Fill** the cherry tomatoes with the pesto-crab mixture; chill for at least one hour and serve. (Note: the pesto can be made up to 2 days in advance and stored in the refrigerator in a sealed container. If you are making the cilantro pesto in advance, add the crab at the end and stuff the tomatoes no more than 3 hours before serving.)

## 🥂 martin codax albarino riax baixas

Richer, bolder, drier, and more alcoholic than the German Riesling wines from which they descend, Albarino grapes deserve their place among the world's respected grape varietals. Serve Albarino wine to guests who are just starting to appreciate the world of fine wine. This selection pairs well with spicy Mexican foods, Thai food, Cuban food, or almost any warm-weather cuisine you can imagine.

# spicy scallop ceviche with avocado and lime

**Serves:** | | | |

**Prep time:**

**Complexity level:**

1/2 pound fresh large sea scallops, adductor muscle removed, sliced thin across grain
1 cup finely chopped red bell pepper
1 cup finely chopped firm Hass avocado
1/2 teaspoon cumin
1/4 teaspoon unrefined sea salt
3 tablespoons lime juice
1 teaspoon hot sauce, such as Tabasco
Pinch of cayenne pepper
3 tablespoons finely chopped cilantro, for garnish

**Put** scallops in a medium-size sterile serving bowl. Add the bell pepper, avocado, cumin, salt, lime juice, hot sauce, and cayenne pepper; gently toss all ingredients together. Cover and refrigerater for 2–4 hours. *(Note: If forgotten and left in refrigerator, scallops will overcook!)*

**Divide** ceviche into 4 martini glasses. Top with cilantro and serve chilled.

## rogue chipotle ale

Mexican food always pairs well with beer, so this is a fitting location to emphasize that many craft beers offer the same combination of complex flavor and lasting health benefits as do fine wines. While standard Corona with lime works just fine, this Rogue Chipotle Ale adds a subtle chipotle pepper flavor to the medium-bodied craft brew base.

## sobon estate amador county viognier

Viognier is a white grape varietal strong enough to stand up to hearty, heavy meals, yet it is sweet enough and bright enough to work with heavily seasoned South of the Border fare. This selection combines thick, almost buttery flavored with a spicy kick. It stands up to the heaviest meats and cheeses while still pairing well with fruits and salsa. It is another great choice for guests who are learning more about the world's finest wines.

# bonjour paris

In our opinion, a French-inspired themed appetizer party should serve attractively presented food with flair and a little pizzazz. The following recipes are certainly sophisticated and chic, but if you think your guests might want something a little heartier, you can always embellish the appetizer table with a bowl of fancy mixed nuts, whole grain crackers, fruit, cheese, mini quiche, and marinated olives.

## wine flight suggestions

Joseph Drouhin Macon-Villages (under $10)

Chateau Bellevue Bordeaux (approximately $13)

Sauvion Muscadet Sevre et Maine (approximately $10)

## on the menu

**french-style three-cheese and tarragon-baked stuffed mushrooms**

**french-style mini panini with fresh apples, brie, and basil**

**green pea blinis with black caviar and smoked salmon**

# french-style three-cheese and tarragon-baked stuffed mushrooms

**Serves:** | | | |

**Prep time:** ⏰

**Complexity level:** 🍎 🍎

18 large (1¹/₂- to 2-inch-wide) white
mushroom caps
3 tablespoons extra virgin olive oil,
divided
8 cloves garlic, minced or pressed
through a garlic press (about 3
tablespoons)
Unrefined sea salt, to taste
Ground black pepper, to taste
1 slice sprouted whole-grain bread,
toasted and broken into cubes
2 tablespoons wheat germ
Paprika, to taste
¹/₄ cup goat cheese
¹/₄ cup low-fat organic ricotta cheese
2 tablespoons mascarpone
2 tablespoons finely chopped fresh
tarragon

**Preheat** the oven to 450 degrees.
Line a baking sheet with foil.

**Toss** the mushroom caps with 2
tablespoons oil, 2 tablespoons garlic,
salt, and pepper. Lay the caps, gill-side-
down, on the prepared baking sheet.
Roast the mushrooms for 20 minutes.
Remove mushrooms from oven. Flip
them over once they are cool enough to
handle. Set aside.

**Place** the toasted bread cubes,
wheat germ, remaining tablespoon oil,
remaining tablespoon garlic, paprika,
salt, and pepper in a blender or food
processor; pulse mixture into fine
crumbs. Set crumbs aside.

**In** a small bowl, mix together the goat
cheese, ricotta, and mascarpone. Stir in
the fresh tarragon.

**Stuff** the mushrooms with the
cheese-tarragon mixture and sprinkle
the crumbs on top. Transfer the stuffed
mushrooms to the oven and bake for
6–7 minutes, or until the crumbs are
slightly browned and crisp. Serve warm.

## 🥂 joseph drouhin macon-villages

French cuisine can often be replicated
by the astute gourmet, yet understanding the subtleties of French wine
remains a challenge to all but the
most diligent connoisseur. Joseph

Drouhin Macon-Villages offers a
simple, bright, refreshing Chardonnay
with a more subtle grassy flavor not
commonly seen in California products.
The price is definitely fair.

# french-style mini panini with fresh apples, brie, and basil

Serves: | | |

Prep time: ⏰
Complexity level: 🍎🍎

1 Granny Smith apple (leave the skin on)
5 ounces Brie cheese
6 slices whole-grain spelt bread, crusts removed
1/4 cup all-natural apple butter (look for one made without high-fructose corn syrup)
1/4 cup fresh whole basil leaves
3 tablespoons extra virgin olive oil, divided

**Slice** the apple as thin as possible (use a mandolin slicer if you have one).

**Spread** Brie evenly over three of the bread slices. Spread apple butter over the remaining three slices of bread.

Arrange apple slices evenly over each of the three Brie-smothered bread slices and then sprinkle the evenly divided basil leaves over the apple slices. Place the apple butter–smothered bread slices on top of the apple and basil. There should be three sandwiches after this process. Use your hands to press and somewhat flatten the sandwiches.

**Pour** 1 tablespoon oil in a cast-iron skillet. Use a paper towel to evenly spread the oil around the skillet. Heat the skillet over medium-high heat. Add one sandwich to the skillet, place a small heavy pot or cast-iron skillet on the sandwich, and cook 2 minutes on each side, or until each side turns a golden brown; place sandwich on a cutting board. Repeat the process with the remaining two sandwiches.

**Cut** each sandwich into four equal squares. Serve immediately.

## 🍷 chateau bellevue bordeaux

Bordeaux red wines are the most collectible, most expensive, most cherished in the world. The flavor is powerful, deep, and velvety smooth. The price offered is phenomenal considering the quality. Bordeaux wine can be enjoyed with a broad variety of foods, although rich cheeses, creamy sauces, and hearty cuts of meat such as beef and dark meat turkey or chicken make optimal pairings. The 2005 wines are among the greatest vintages of all time for this region.

# green pea blinis with black caviar and smoked salmon

Serves: ❙❙❙❙

Prep time: ⏰

Complexity level: 🍎 🍎 🍎

¹/₄ cup frozen petite peas, thawed
2 tablespoons full-fat organic plain yogurt
¹/₄ cup 2-percent organic milk
2 tablespoons water
1 cage-free organic omega-3 egg, lightly beaten
¹/₄ cup white whole-wheat flour
1 teaspoon instant yeast
¹/₂ teaspoon raw honey
¹/₈ teaspoon unrefined sea salt
2 teaspoons grass-fed organic butter, divided
¹/₄ cup crème fraîche
8 ounces smoked salmon, sliced into thin strips
1 (3.5-ounce) jar black caviar, drained and lightly blotted dry with a paper towel
3 tablespoons minced red onion

**In** a blender, combine the peas, yogurt, milk, and water; process for 1 minute, or until smooth and creamy.

**Add** the egg to a medium-size mixing bowl. Whisk in the flour, yeast, honey, and salt. Mix in the puréed pea-mixture. Cover the bowl with a damp tea towel and let sit for 2 hours (or all day in the refrigerator).

**Preheat** oven to 250 degrees F and put in a large ovenproof plate.

**Melt** 1 teaspoon butter in a medium nonstick skillet over medium-high, tilt pan so the butter coats evenly. Drop batter into the skillet 1 tablespoon at a time. Cook blinis until edges are just lightly browned, about 2 minutes; flip with a spatula and cook for about another minute on the other side. Transfer blinis to the warmed plate, season lightly with salt, and keep warm in the oven while cooking the remainder of the batter. (Batter yields approximately 16 blinis.)

**To** serve, place a dollop of crème frâiche on each blini. Top blinis with smoked salmon strips, a small dollop of caviar, and minced onion. Serve warm.

## 🥂 sauvion muscadet sevre et maine

This is a distinctively French wine with flavor that is difficult to reproduce elsewhere. Vaguely reminiscent of Sauvignon Blanc, wines labeled "Muscadet Sevre et Maine" are produced along France's northern Atlantic coast and pair well with seafood, especially caviar, mussels, and oysters. The taste is light, crisp, and dry. This wine also pairs well with sweet and sour Chinese fare or spicy Thai delights.

# mid-east mini mezze

This cosmopolitan Middle Eastern mezze (which translates to appetizer or spread of small finger foods) menu is casually contemporary. It's also a celebration of the healthful and nutritional benefits of authentic Mediterranean cuisine. But rest assured, the mouthwatering ethnic fare and gastronomic journey of new tastes is sure to please even those guests not one bit interested in health!

## wine flight suggestions

Aquinas Napa Valley Merlot (approximately $14)

Sebastiani Sonoma County Chardonnay (approximately $14)

Montes Colchagua Valley Chile Malbec (under $10)

## on the menu

**falafel with tahini-lime dipping sauce**

**lemony white bean and brie hummus with toasted pitas**

**lebanese shish taouk (chicken skewers) with yogurt and red onion dip**

# falafel with tahini-lime dipping sauce

**Serves:** | | | |

**Prep time:** 🕐

**Complexity level:** 🍎 🍎

### FALAFEL
Extra virgin olive oil cooking spray

2 (15-ounce) cans chickpeas, rinsed and drained

3/4 cup chopped scallions (green only)

1/2 cup chopped parsley

4 cloves garlic, crushed

1/4 teaspoon cayenne pepper

2 teaspoons cumin

2 teaspoons paprika

1/2 teaspoon unrefined sea salt

1/2 teaspoon baking soda

2 teaspoons aluminum-free baking powder

1/4 cup wheat germ

2 cage-free organic omega-3 eggs, lightly beaten

3 tablespoons extra virgin olive oil

4 teaspoons lemon juice

6 stalks celery, cut into thin 4-inch-long strips, for garnish

### TAHINI-LIME DIPPING SAUCE
1/2 cup tahini

1/4 cup fresh lime juice

1/2 cup full-fat organic plain yogurt

4–6 cloves garlic, crushed

1/8 teaspoon unrefined sea salt, plus more to taste

2 teaspoons raw honey

### FALAFEL
**Preheat** oven to 350 degrees F. Spray a nonstick baking sheet with cooking spray.

**Place** chickpeas in a large bowl and roughly mash with a potato masher. Add the scallions, parsley, garlic, cayenne pepper, cumin, paprika, and salt, and mix until ingredients are well blended. Mix in the baking soda and baking powder. Add wheat germ and, using clean hands, mix well. Stir in the eggs, oil, and lemon juice. Let mixture stand 10 minutes.

**Divide** mixture into 18 equal portions (about 2 tablespoons per portion). Press each portion into a round patty and place on prepared baking dish. Bake for 10 minutes, or until lightly browned. Let cool 6–8 minutes. Serve falafel on a platter with Tahini-Lime Dipping Sauce and celery sticks.

### TAHINI-LIME DIPPING SAUCE
**Place** ingredients in a blender and process until smooth and creamy. Transfer sauce to a small dish and serve with falafel.

## 🥂 aquinas napa valley merlot

Merlot grapes delight alone or when mixed with other varietals to create Bordeaux or "Meritage" wines. This Aquinas selection is powerful with a drier, more complex fruit flavor than the Italian reds. Merlot pairs well with most foods and is a better match than Cabernet Sauvignon for spicy Middle Eastern cuisine.

# lemony white bean and brie hummus with toasted pitas

**Serves:** | | | |

**Prep time:** ⏰

**Complexity level:** 🍎

4 whole-wheat pita bread pockets
1/4 cup plus 2 tablespoons extra virgin
   olive oil, divided
Unrefined sea salt, to taste
Paprika, to taste
2 (15-ounce) cans white beans, rinsed and
   drained
Juice from 1 whole lemon
1/4 cup plus 2 tablespoons water
10 ounces Brie cheese

**Preheat** oven to 325 degrees F. Split each pita pocket in half; then cut each half into 4 triangles. Pour 2 tablespoons oil into a small bowl and then brush both sides of each triangle with the oil. Sprinkle with salt and paprika.

**Arrange** the triangles in a single layer on two cookie sheets. Bake for 8 minutes, or until triangles are lightly browned.

**In** a food processor or blender, combine the beans, 1/4 cup oil, lemon juice, and water; purée until smooth and creamy. Season with salt to taste.

**Remove** the rind from the Brie and cut the cheese into bite-size chunks. Place the Brie and bean purée in a microwave-safe bowl. Microwave at full power for 1 minute, until the cheese melts. Stir the mixture with a fork until well combined.

**Serve** the bean and Brie hummus in a bowl with the toasted pita chips surrounding it.

## 🥂 sebastiani sonoma county chardonnay

This powerful Chardonnay has a more woody oak flavor than most. This wine complements Middle East food and offers distinctive, sophisticated taste while remaining affordable. The Sebastiani brand offers a delicious Merlot and a dry Cabernet Sauvignon. Oaky Sebastiani Chardonnay is great with falafel, hummus, lamb, chicken, and other Middle Eastern delights.

## 🍷 montes colchagua valley chile malbec

Malbec is a red wine grape grown most commonly in Chile and Argentina. The taste is comparable to that of Shiraz with a subtle plum and berry flavor that complements most foods without overpowering them. A good choice for Middle Eastern fare, South American wines tend to offer good value.

# lebanese shish taouk (chicken skewers) with yogurt and red onion dip

**Serves:** ▮▮▮▮

**Prep time:** ⏰

**Complexity level:** 👹 👹

## LEBANESE SHISH TAOUK (CHICKEN SKEWERS)

Juice from 4 whole lemons
2 tablespoons extra virgin olive oil
8 cloves garlic, chopped
$1/2$ teaspoon cumin
$1/2$ teaspoon cayenne pepper
$1/2$ teaspoon paprika
2 teaspoons brown sugar
$1/2$ teaspoon unrefined sea salt
$1/2$ teaspoon pepper
$1/2$ cup shaved almonds
2 pounds boneless, skinless, free-range organic chicken breasts, cut into 1-inch cubes

## YOGURT AND RED ONION DIP

1 tablespoon extra virgin olive oil
$3/4$ cup minced red onion
3–4 cloves garlic, crushed (1 teaspoon)
1 teaspoon cumin
$1/2$ teaspoon cardamom
1 teaspoon cinnamon
$1/2$ teaspoon unrefined sea salt
$1/8$ teaspoon cayenne pepper
2 teaspoons sugar
2 tablespoons tahini
1 cup whole-milk Greek-style plain yogurt

## LEBANESE SHISH TAOUK (CHICKEN SKEWERS)

**Place** all ingredients except chicken in a mini food processor and process for 30–45 seconds, or until well blended.

Transfer spiced marinade to a ziplock bag and add the chicken cubes. Refrigerate and marinate for 2 to 24 hours.

**Remove** chicken from the marinade and thread onto metal skewers (about 5 pieces per skewer).

**Prepare** a fire in a charcoal grill or preheat a broiler.

**Place** the chicken skewers on an oiled grill rack or a broiler pan; grill or broil, turning once, about 4–5 minutes per side, or until no longer pink in the center when cut into with a knife.

**Transfer** the chicken skewers to a platter to cool. When cool enough to handle, remove the chicken from the skewers and thread onto decorative toothpicks. Place chicken on a serving platter and serve with Yogurt and Red Onion Dip (recipe below).

## YOGURT AND RED ONION DIP

**Heat** oil in a small skillet over medium-high heat; add onion and garlic, and cook for 4–5 minutes, or until soft. Reduce the heat to simmer and add the cumin, cardamom, cinnamon, salt, pepper, and sugar. Cook for 1 minute. Remove skillet from heat. Stir in the tahini. Add the yogurt to onion mixture and stir to combine. (Note: If you prefer a thinner consistency, add 1–2 tablespoons of water.)

**Transfer** the yogurt and onion mixture to a bowl and serve at room temperature along with the chicken.

# endnotes

## The Whole Food Edge

1 "The Effect of Vitamin E and Beta Carotene on the Incidence of Lung Cancer and Other Cancers in Male Smokers. The Alpha-Tocopherol, Beta Carotene Cancer Prevention Study Group," *New England Journal of Medicine* 330 (1994): 1029–35.

2 M. A. Pereira, et al., "Effects of a Low-Glycemic Load Diet on Resting Energy Expenditure and Heart Disease Risk Factors during Weight Loss," *Journal of the American Medical Association* 292 (2004): 2482–90.

## Nutritional Nuts and Bolts

1 D. R. Labarthe, "Dietary Fiber: Further Epidemiological Support for a High-Intake Dietary Pattern," *Circulation* 94 (1996): 2696–98. Recent findings from two long-term large-scale studies of men suggest that high-fiber intake can significantly lower the risk of heart attack. Men who ate the most fiber-rich foods (35 grams a day, on average) suffered one-third fewer heart attacks than those who had the lowest fiber intake (15 grams a day), according to a Finnish study of 21,903 male smokers aged 50 to 69. Findings from a U.S. study of 43,757 male health professionals suggest that those who ate more than 25 grams of fiber per day had a 36 percent lower risk of developing heart disease than those who consumed less than 15 grams daily. In the Finnish study, each 10 grams of fiber added to the diet decreased the risk of dying from heart disease by 17 percent; in the U.S. study, risk was decreased by 29 percent.

2 D. E. King, et al., "Effect of a High-Fiber Diet vs. a Fiber-Supplemented Diet on C-Reactive Protein Level," *Archives of Internal Medicine* 167 (2007): 502–6.

3 "Position of the American Dietetic Association: Phytochemicals and Functional Foods," *Journal of the American Dietetic Association* 95 (1995): 493–96.

4 M. J. Brown, et al., "Carotenoid Bioavailability Is Higher from Salads Ingested with Full-Fat Than with Fat-Reduced Salad Dressings as Measured with Electrochemical Detection," *American Journal of Clinical Nutrition* 80 (2004): 396–403.

5 J. W. Anderson, et al., "Meta-Analysis of the Effects of Soy Protein Intake on Serum Lipids," *New England Journal of Medicine* 333 (1995): 276–82.

6 S. Holt, et al., "A Satiety Index of Common Foods," *European Journal of Clinical Nutrition* 49 (1995): 675-90.

## The Flexitarian Lifestyle

1 J. E. Chavarro, et al., "Protein Intake and Ovulatory Infertility," *American Journal of Obstetrics and Gynecology* 198 (2008): 210.e1–7.

2 N. I. Lipoeto, et al., "Dietary Intake and the Risk of Coronary Heart Disease among the Coconut-Consuming Minangkabau in West

Sumatra, Indonesia," *Asia Pacific Journal of Clinical Nutrition* 13 (2004): 377–84.

**3** H. Kaunitz and C. S. Dayrit, "Coconut Oil Consumption and Coronary Heart Disease," *Philippine Journal of Internal Medicine* 30 (1992): 165–71.

**4** M. L. Kelly, et al., "Effect of Intake of Pasture on Concentrations of Conjugated Linoleic Acid in Milk of Lactating Cows," *Journal of Dairy Science* 81 (1998): 1630–36.

**5** U. Riserus, et al., "Treatment with Dietary Trans10cis12 Conjugated Linoleic Acid Causes Isomer-Specific Insulin Resistance in Obese Men with the Metabolic Syndrome," *Diabetes Care* 25 (2002): 1516–21.

**Fake and Phony**
**1** N. M. de Roos, et al, "Replacement of Dietary Saturated Fatty Acids by Trans Fatty Acids Lowers Serum HDL Cholesterol and Impairs Endothelial Function in Healthy Men and Women," *Arteriosclerosis Thrombosis Vascular Biology* 21 (2001): 1233–37.

**2** W. C. Willett, et al. "Intake of Trans Fatty Acids and Risk of Coronary Heart Disease among Women." *Lancet* 341 (1993): 581–85.

**3** J. E. Chavarro, et al., "Dietary Fatty Acid Intakes and the Risk of Ovulatory Infertility," *American Journal of Clinical Nutrition* 85 (2007): 231–37.

**4** A. P. Simopolous, "The Importance of the Ratio of Omega-6/Omega-3 Essential Fatty Acids," *Biomedicine and Pharmacotherapy* 56 (2002): 365–79; Daniel Yam, et al., "Diet and Disease—The Israeli Paradox: Possible Dangers of a High Omega-6 Polyunsaturated Fatty Acid Diet," *Israeli Journal of Medical Science* 32 (1996): 1134–43.

**Pure Indulgence**
**1** J. Baur, et al., "Resveratrol Improves Health and Increases Survival of Mice on a High-Calorie Diet," *Nature* 444 (2006): 337–42.

**2** R. C. Cabot, "The Relation of Alcohol to Arteriosclerosis," *Journal of the American Medical Association* 43 (1904): 774–75.

**3** D. Coate, "Moderate Drinking and Coronary Heart Disease Mortality: Evidence from NHANES I and NHANES I Follow-up," *American Journal of Public Health* 83 (1993): 888–90. The following studies support that moderate drinkers live longer than those who abstain: P. Boffetta and L. Garfinkel, "Alcohol Drinking and Mortality among Men Enrolled in an American Cancer Society Prospective Study," *Epidemiology* 1 (1990): 342–48; G. Maskarinec, et al., "Alcohol Intake, Body Weight, and Mortality in a Multiethnic Prospective Cohort," *Epidemiology* 9 (1998): 654–61; and J. M. Gaziano, et al., "Light-to-Moderate Alcohol Consumption and Mortality in the Physicians' Health Study Enrollment Cohort," *Journal of the American College of Cardiology* 35 (2000): 96–105.

**4** C. Maraldi, et al., "Impact of Inflammation on the Relationship among Alcohol Consumption, Mortality, and Cardiac Events: the Health, Aging, and Body Composition Study," *Archives of Internal Medicine* 166 (2006): 1490–97; and M. Trevisan, et al., "Drinking Patterns and Mortality: A Longitudinal Study"; J. M. Gaziano, et al., "A Prospective Cohort Study of Moderate Alcohol Consumption and Sudden Death in the Physicians' Health Study"; U. Keil, et al., "The Relation of Alcohol to Coronary Heart Disease and Total Mortality in a Beer Drinking Population in Southern Germany"; A. Waskiewicz, et al., "Alcohol Consumption and 11-Year Total and CVD Mortality among Men in Pol-MONICA Study"; D. E. Grobbee, et al., "Alcohol and Cardiovascular Risk in the Elderly." All studies were presented at the 4th International Conference on Preventive Cardiology, Montreal, Canada, June 29–July 3, 1997, and published in Abstracts from the 4th International Conference on Preventive Cardiology. *The Canadian Journal of Cardiology* 13 (June 1997), Supplement B.

**5** T. A. Pearson, "Alcohol and Heart Disease," *Circulation* 94 (1996): 3023–25 (for the American Heart Association); and H. Rodgers, et al., "Alcohol and Stroke: A Case-Control Study of Drinking Habits Past and Present," *Stroke* 24 (1993): 1473–77.

**6** L. Koppes, et al., "Moderate Alcohol Consumption Lowers the Risk of Type 2 Diabetes: A Meta-analysis of Prospective Observational Studies," *Diabetes Care* 28 (2005): 719–25; and M. Wei, et al., "Alcohol Intake and Incidence of Type 2 Diabetes in Men," *Diabetes Care* 23 (2000): 18–22.

**7** S. Cohen, et al., "Smoking, Alcohol Consumption and Susceptibility to the Common Cold," *American Journal of Public Health* 83 (1993): 1277–83.

**8** C. A. Camargo, et al., "Prospective Study of Moderate Alcohol Consumption and Risk of Peripheral Arterial Disease in U.S. Male Physicians," *Circulation* 95 (1997): 577–80.

**9** H. S. Kahn, et al., "Stable Behaviors Associated with Adults' 10-Year Change in Body Mass Index and Likelihood of Gain at the Waist," *American Journal of Public Health* 87 (1997): 747–54; A. M. Prentice, "Alcohol and Obesity," *International Journal of Obesity* 19 (1995): Suppl. 5, S44–50; S. Liu, et al., "A Prospective Study of Alcohol Intake and Change in Body Weight among U.S. Adults," *American Journal of Epidemiology* 140 (1994): 912–20; W. L. Hellerstedt, et al., "The Association between Alcohol Intake and Adiposity in the General Population," *American Journal of Epidemiology* 132 (1990): 594–611.

**10** R. C. Klesges, et al., "Effects of Alcohol Intake on Resting Energy Expenditure in Young Women Social Drinkers," *American Journal of Clinical Nutrition* 59 (1994): 805–9.

**11** G. Colditz, et al., "Alcohol Intake in Relation to Diet and Obesity in Women and Men," *American Journal of Clinical Nutrition* 54 (1991): 49–55.

**12** J. A. Vinson, "Polyphenols: Total Amounts in Foods and Beverages and U.S. Per Capita Consumption." Paper presented at 2005 American Chemical Society Meeting & Exposition, Washington, D.C.

**13** G. Hu, et al., "Coffee and Tea Consumption and the Risk of Parkinson's Disease," *Movement Disorders* 22 (2007): 2242–48; and J. L. Barranco Quintana, et al., "Alzheimer's Disease and Coffee: A Quantitative Review," *Neurological Research* 29 (2007): 91–95.

**14** M. F. Leitzmann, et al., "Coffee Intake Is Associated with Lower Risk of Symptomatic Gallstone Disease in Women," *Gastroenterology* 123 (2002): 1823–30.

**15** E. Salazar-Martinez, et al., "Coffee Consumption and Risk for Type 2 Diabetes," *Annals of Internal Medicine* 140 (2004): 1–8.

**16** I. Kawachi, et al., "A Prospective Study of Coffee Drinking and Suicide in Women," *Archives of Internal Medicine* 156 (1996): 521–25.

**17** N. Iwai, et al., "Relationship between Coffee and Green Tea Consumption and All-Cause Mortality in a Cohort of a Rural Japanese Population," *Journal of Epidemiology* 12 (2002): 191–98.

# resources

The products and brands listed are our favorites. More and more brands are appearing on the market every day, so ask about and check the Internet. You can also check our book Web site at **www.wholefoodsdietcookbook.com** for any updates on products.

## Broths, Organic Vegetable and Organic Free-Range Chicken
Look for Pacific Natural Foods (www.pacificfoods.com) and Imagine Foods (www.imaginefoods.com). Both brands are available in mainstream and natural foods stores.

## Chicken Sausage, All-Natural
Han's (www.hansallnatural.com) chicken sausages are much lower in saturated fat than regular sausages, and contain no artificial hormones, no nitrates, and no antibiotics.

## Cocoa, Good Quality Unsweetened
• Green and Black's Organic (www.greenandblacks.com)

• Ghirardelli (www.ghirardelli.com)

## Coconut Milk
Thai Kitchen (www.thaikitchen.com) canned coconut milk is available in mainstream supermarkets.

## Coconut Oil, Organic Extra virgin
Extra virgin coconut oil is an antioxidant- and phytochemical-rich alternative to using butter for many baking recipes. Barlean's (www.barleans.com) makes the best-tasting coconut oil we have found. It's available online and at many natural foods stores nationwide.

## Dairy and Eggs, Organic
In addition to natural foods stores, most mainstream supermarkets across the country now carry organic dairy and eggs. Widely available brands include

• Natural by Nature (www.natural-by-nature.com) has both organic and pasture-fed milk, cream, whipping cream, butter, sour cream, and ricotta cheese.

• Organic Valley (www.organicvalley.com). In addition to a wide selection of organic dairy products, Organic Valley also sells omega-3-rich eggs and two varieties of raw cheeses.

• Stonyfield Farms (www.stonyfieldfarms.com). Look for Stonyfield Farms plain yogurts.

## Dark Chocolate, Good-Quality
Endangered Species makes the best tasting, richest, and darkest chocolate we have found. It's available at Whole Foods Market and in many natural foods stores as well as online at www.chocolatebar.com.

## Drinks
Greens to Go (www.greenstogo.com) is a super-food drink powder that comes in handy travel packets, and it's the perfect way to spike your water bottle with nutrients! It contains zero added sugar, has a refreshingly delicious apple-melon flavor, and has more antioxidant power than one serving of bananas, broccoli, cantaloupe, tomatoes, lettuce, and carrots combined!

## Energy Bars and Snacks

Most snack or energy bars are loaded with sugars and oils, but the LÄRABAR (www.larabar.com) contains just dried fruit, nuts, and spices, and comes in an amazing assortment of flavors. These bars are everywhere.

Sahale Snacks (www.sahalesnacks.com) sticks to a simple idea: use only whole foods in their natural form, avoid artificial ingredients and add "culinary magic" to produce amazingly delicious and nutritious nut and dried fruit snack mixes. Sahale Snacks are like gourmet versions of trail mix!

## Flax Oil

Buy only flax oil that has been refrigerated and then keep it refrigerated. Purchase a high-quality flax oil to ensure freshness. We've come to rely exclusively on Barlean's brand (www.barleans.com) for consistently delicious oil. Barlean's is available at natural foods stores nationwide.

## Flaxseed, Ground

Barlean's (www.barleans.com) produces Forti-Flax, a freshly cold-milled, delicious, 100% organic, pesticide- and herbicide-free product. Forti-Flax is available at natural foods stores nationwide.

## Grass-Fed Meat, Poultry, Eggs, and Game

Many natural foods stores carry select grass-fed animal products. However, you can also find a good selection over the Internet. The following Web sites are very helpful:

- wwwbuffalohuntermeats.com

- www.eatwild.com

- www.grasslandandbeef.com (this is the Web site for U.S. Wellness Meats, the company we order all of our meat from—the meats are absolutely delicious!)
- www.nimanranch.com (this is a network of several hundred independent farmers and ranchers who raise traditional beef, lamb, and pork)

## Greek Yogurt

Greek yogurt is creamier than regular yogurt and is less likely to curdle when heated. Greek yogurt is also richer in protein than regular yogurt. The following Greek yogurt brands are widely available nationwide:

- Oikos Organic (www.oikosorganic.com). This brand is actually made by Stonyfield Farms.

- Fage (www.fageusa.com)

## Honey, Raw

Really Raw Honey (www.reallyrawhoney.com) is totally unprocessed honey. It still contains pollen, propolis, honeycomb, and live enzymes. Look for this brand in natural foods stores.

## Hummus, Prepared

Prepared hummus is used a lot in our recipes; one of the best-tasting brands we have found is made by Hannah (www.hannahfoods.net) and is available at Costco. Hannah also makes delicious and healthy bruschetta, tabouleh, and olive tapenade.

### Juice Plus +
The many healthful benefits of Juice Plus + have been demonstrated through numerous clinical research studies and published in peer-reviewed medical journals. We believe Juice Plus + is the next best thing to fresh fruits and vegetables. For more information, visit iLarsonJuicePlus.com.

### Kefir, Organic
Lifeway (www.lifeway.com) makes a delicious and widely available low-fat organic plain kefir, often used in place of yogurt.

### Marinara Sauces, Prepared
With so many tasty, healthy, widely available name-brand products to choose from, keep in mind the following guidelines:

- Avoid sauces that include meat in their ingredients list because the meats are usually high in saturated fat

- Avoid sauces made with any other type of oil other than extra virgin olive oil

- Avoid sauces that contain added sugars in the form of high-fructose corn syrup

Our favorite-tasting healthy brands include

- Rao's Homemade (www.raos.com)

- Gia Russa (www.giarussa.com)

- Amy's (www.amyskitchen.com)

### Mayonnaise, Canola Oil
Hellmann's (www.hellmanns.com) makes one of the best-tasting canola oil–based mayonnaises ever, and it's available practically everywhere! Whole Foods Market also makes a delicious brand under their 365-store brand name.

### Omega Swirl
This product is a revolution in omega-3 supplementation, especially for kids! This is the one fish oil supplement absolutely everyone is guaranteeed to love. You have to try it to believe it. For more information, visit www.Barleans.com.

### Panko Crumbs, Whole-Wheat
Look for Ian's Natural Foods (www .iansnaturalfoods.com).

### Soymilk
Silk (www.silksoymilk.com) is our favorite-tasting brand of soymilk. It's also widely available nationwide in supermarkets and natural foods stores. Look for Unsweetened Plain Silk.

### Sprouted Whole-Grain Breads, Tortillas, Buns, Pasta, etc
- Food for Life (www.foodforlife.com) makes a wide variety of delicious sprouted whole-grain products, including breads, tortillas, buns, pasta, cereal, and English muffins. This brand is available in natural foods stores. Look for the sprouted whole-grain breads in the frozen section of the supermarket (not in the bread aisle!)

- Alvarado Street Bakery (www.alvarado streetbakery.com) is another great brand to try.

### Tempeh

Lightlife (www.lightlife.com) makes a wide variety of delicious tempeh. These brands are available in many natural foods stores.

### Tofu

Nasoya (www.nasoya.com) seems to be the most widely available brand of tofu sold nationwide in both natural foods stores and mainstream groceries. You'll find tofu in the refrigerated section near the fresh foods or in the dairy case. Look for Nasoya extra firm, firm, soft, silken, and cubed varieties.

### Wheat Germ

Eating just 2 tablespoons of wheat germ a day is a great way to boost your fiber, vitamin E, folic acid, and overall nutrition. Try Kretschmers (www.kretschmer.com).

### Whole Grains and Whole Grain Flour

Whole grain flours are widely available in many mainstream supermarkets as well as natural foods stores. Look for the following brands:

- Arrowhead Mills (www.arrowhead mills.com)

- Bob's Red Mill (www.bobsredmill.com)

- Hodgson Mill (www.hodgsonmill.com)

- King Arthur Flour (www.kingarthur flour.com). This company makes the white whole-wheat flour we use in many of our recipes.

# metric conversion chart

### Liquid and Dry Measures

| U.S. | Canadian | Australian |
|---|---|---|
| ¼ teaspoon | 1 mL | 1 ml |
| ½ teaspoon | 2 mL | 2 ml |
| 1 teaspoon | 5 mL | 5 ml |
| 1 tablespoon | 15 mL | 20 ml |
| ¼ cup | 50 mL | 60 ml |
| ⅓ cup | 75 mL | 80 ml |
| ½ cup | 125 mL | 125 ml |
| ⅔ cup | 150 mL | 170 ml |
| ¾ cup | 175 mL | 190 ml |
| 1 cup | 250 mL | 250 ml |
| 1 quart | 1 liter | 1 litre |

### Temperature Conversion Chart

| Fahrenheit | Celsius |
|---|---|
| 250 | 120 |
| 275 | 140 |
| 300 | 150 |
| 325 | 160 |
| 350 | 180 |
| 375 | 190 |
| 400 | 200 |
| 425 | 220 |
| 450 | 230 |
| 475 | 240 |
| 500 | 260 |

# recipe index